Our Social
and Sexual
Revolution

Other books by John Stott:

Authentic Christianity
Authority of the Bible
Basic Christianity
The Contemporary Christian
The Cross of Christ
Human Rights and Human Wrongs
Understanding the Bible

Our Social and Sexual Revolution

MAJOR ISSUES FOR A NEW CENTURY

THIRD EDITION

JOHN STOTT

Baker Books
A Division of Baker Book House Co
Grand Rapids, Michigan 49516

Published by Baker Books
a division of Baker Book House Company
P.O. Box 6287, Grand Rapids, MI 49516-6287

First published as *Issues Facing Christians Today* in Great Britain in 1984 by Marshall Pickering

Second edition first published in 1990

This edition first published in 1990

This edition published in 1999 in two editions: *Our Social and Sexual Revolution* and *Human Rights and Human Wrongs*

Second printing, September 2002

Printed in the United States of America

ISBN 0-8010-6113-X

For current information about all releases from Baker Book House, visit our web site:
http://www.bakerbooks.com

Contents

Preface to the First Edition (1984)

One of the most notable features of the worldwide evangelical movement during the last ten to fifteen years has been the recovery of our temporarily mislaid social conscience. For approximately fifty years (c. 1920–70) evangelical Christians were preoccupied with the task of defending the historic biblical faith against the attacks of theological liberalism, and reacting against its "social gospel." But now we are convinced that God has given us social as well as evangelistic responsibilities in his world. Yet the half-century of neglect has put us far behind in this area. We have a long way to catch up.

This book is my own contribution to the catching up process. Its source may be traced to 1978–79, when Michael Baughen, now Bishop of Chester, but then Rector of All Souls Church, invited me to preach a series of occasional sermons under the title Issues Facing Britain Today. Several of these chapters began their life in the pulpit, and subsequently grew into lectures at the London Institute for Contemporary Christianity, whose raison d'être is to help people develop a Christian perspective on the complexities of the modern world.

I confess that several times in the course of writing I have been tempted to give up. I have felt now foolish and now presumptuous to attempt such an undertaking. For I am in no sense a specialist in moral theology or social ethics, and I have no particular expertise or experience in some of the fields into which I trespass. Moreover, each topic is complex, has attracted an extensive literature, only some of which I have been able to read, and is potentially divisive, even in a few cases explosive. Yet I have persevered, mainly because what I am venturing to offer the public is not a polished professional piece but the rough-hewn amateur work of an ordinary Christian who is struggling to think Christianly, that is, to apply the biblical revelation to the pressing issues of the day.

For this is my concern. I begin with a commitment to the Bible as "God's Word written," which is how it is described in the Anglican Articles and has been received by nearly all churches until comparatively recent times. Such is the basic presupposition of this book; it is not part of my present purpose to argue it. But we Christians have a second commitment, namely to the world in which God has placed us. And our two commitments often seem to be in conflict. Being a collection of documents which relate to particular and distant events, the Bible has an archaic feel. It seems incompatible with our western culture, with its space probes and microprocessors. Like every other Christian I feel myself caught in the painful tension between these two worlds. They are centuries apart. Yet I have sought to resist the temptation to withdraw from either world by capitulation to the other.

Some Christians, anxious above all to be faithful to the revelation of God without compromise, ignore the challenges of the modern world and live in the past. Others, anxious to respond to the world around them, trim and twist God's revelation in their search for relevance. I have struggled to avoid both traps. For the Christian is at liberty to surrender neither to antiquity nor to modernity. Instead, I have sought with integrity to submit to the revelation of yesterday within the realities of today. It is not easy to combine loyalty to the past with sensitivity to the present. Yet this is our Christian calling: to live under the Word in the world.

Many people have helped me develop my thinking. I thank the "apostolic succession" of my study assistants—Roy McCloughry, Tom Cooper, Mark Labberton, Steve Ingraham and Bob Wismer—who have compiled bibliographies, assembled groups for the discussion of sermon topics, gathered information and checked references. Bob Wismer has been specially helpful in the final stages, reading the manuscript twice and making valuable suggestions. So has Frances Whitehead, my secretary for twenty-eight years. She and Vivienne Curry typed the manuscript. Steve Andrews, my present study assistant, has been meticulous in proof correcting. I also thank friends who have read different chapters and given me the benefit of their comments—Oliver Barclay, Raymond Johnston, John Gladwin, Mark Stephens, Roy McCloughry, Myra Chave-Jones and my colleagues at the London Institute, Andrew Kirk (Associate Director) and Martyn Eden (Dean). I am particularly grateful to Jim Houston, founding Principal and now Chancellor of Regent College, Vancouver, whose vision of the need for Christians to have an integrated world view has stimulated both my own thinking and the founding of the London Institute.

J S
June 1984

Preface to the Second Edition (1990)

Six years have passed since the publication of *Issues Facing Christians Today*, and in this brief period the world has witnessed many changes. Détente between the superpowers has dawned, and disarmament has begun. Freedom and democracy, undreamed of only a year ago, have taken root in Eastern Europe and the Soviet Union, even while brutal repression has trampled on these tender plants in China. Old debates (like the nuclear threat) have moved on, while new debates (like the AIDS epidemic) have arisen.

Hence the need for a second and revised edition of this book. The statistics on armaments, human rights violations, other religions, unemployment, divorce and abortion have all been brought up to date. It has been necessary to read and reflect on newly published books on almost every issue. A number of these have been written by evangelical authors, which is an encouraging sign of our developing social conscience. Another sign of this is the merger of the London Institute for Contemporary Christianity with the Shaftesbury Project for Christian Involvement in Society in order to form "Christian Impact," and so combine research, education and thought with action. Yet other signs are the stronger commitment to social action explicit in the Manila Manifesto, which was adopted at the conclusion of the second "Lausanne" Congress on World Evangelization (1989), and the "Salt and Light" project sponsored by the British Evangelical Alliance.

This second edition of *Issues Facing Christians Today* also incorporates new material on many topics—on the rapid growth of the green movement and its warnings about ozone layer depletion and the greenhouse effect; on the Brundtland Report, "Our Common Future," and its concept of "sustainable development"; on the burdens of debt borne by many nuclear families in the West and—to a crippling degree—by Third World countries; on three important Christian documents recently published in South Africa; on further thinking by evangelical Christians about the role, ministry and leadership of women; on human fertilization and modern reproductive

9

technologies; on the theological, moral, pastoral and educational aspects of AIDS; and on the effectiveness of Christian social protest and witness.

I express my cordial thanks to Toby Howarth and Todd Shy, my former and present study assistants, for painstakingly rereading the whole book and making numerous suggestions; to Marty Eden, Elaine Storkey, Roy McCloughry, Maurice Hobbs, John Wyatt and Stephen Rand for perusing individual sections or chapters and proposing changes; and to Frances Whitehead for much retyping and some really skilful "scissor-and-paste" editing.

In conclusion, I feel the need to restate what I wrote in the preface to the first edition, namely that *Issues* represents the struggles of a person who lays no claim to infallibility, who is anxious to go on increasing his Christian integrity over against the pressures of a largely secular society, and who to that end is continuously seeking fresh light from Scripture.

J S
January 1990

Preface to the Third Edition (1999)

Issues Facing Christians Today was first published in 1984, and its second, updated edition appeared in 1990. Since then eight more years have passed, and a third, revised edition is already overdue. It is extraordinary that in the topic of every chapter the debate has moved on, and in some cases the situation has changed significantly.

With the collapse of Euro-Marxism, following the demolition of the Berlin Wall, much of the map of Europe has had to be redrawn. The end of the cold war has made possible some international disarmament treaties. The "Earth Summit" at Rio in 1992 both mirrored and stimulated growing public alarm over ozone layer depletion and global warming. New policies of development and proposals for debt cancellation have brought realistic hope to the poorest nations. The conciliatory leadership of President Mandela and the dismantling of apartheid shine brightly against the increase of racially motivated violence and the re-emergence of nationalism in Europe. Christians are also disturbed by the influences which undermine marriage and the family (especially cohabitation and same-sex partnerships) and which challenge the sanctity of human life (especially abortion and euthanasia).

Ten consultants, each a specialist in his own field, have been kind enough to read the chapter of their expertise and then to recommend changes to make, books to read and new issues to consider. I am most grateful for their criticisms and suggestions. They are (in alphabetical order) Sir Fred Catherwood, Martyn Eden, Dr. David Green, Gary Haugen, Sir John Houghton, Roy McCloughry, Dr. Alan Storkey, Pradip Sudra, Dr. Neil Summerton and Professor John Wyatt.

I reserve my special gratitude for John Yates, my current study assistant. Not only has he given himself the chore of reading the book's second edition several times over, made his own insightful suggestions, and updated the statistics, but he has also followed up our consultants' proposals, done some redrafting himself and advised me which books and articles I needed to read and ponder myself. I cannot speak too highly of his conscientious work.

J S
Autumn 1998

11

PART 1

Social
Issues

Work and Unemployment

Work occupies such a significant place in most people's lives that, if we are Christians, we must know how to think Christianly about it and about the trauma of unemployment. After all, the average worker still divides his or her day into three more or less equal periods—eight hours' sleep, eight hours' work and eight hours' leisure. So our work occupies a third of our day, indeed a half of our waking hours. We also acknowledge the importance of work by our habit of defining people in relation to it. Although convention teaches us to ask "how do you do?" the real question which interests us is "what do you do?"

Now please let me say it before you think it: a clergyman is the last person in the world to write about work. For, as everybody knows, he has not done an honest day's work in his life. As the old saying goes, he is "six days invisible and one day incomprehensible"! Some years ago I was traveling by train in South Wales when a rather drunk Communist miner entered my compartment. When he discovered that I was a pastor, he treated me to a lecture (in his sing-song Welsh accent) on work: "It's time you became productive, man; you're a parasite on the body politic."

So, then, with the possible exception of the clergy (and of course of the unemployed), we are all workers. In consequence, we need a philosophy of work which will determine our attitude to it.

Attitudes to Work

Some people are very negative towards their job and give the impression that, if possible, work is something to be avoided. This view has been well expressed in the following doggerel:

> I don't mind work
>> If I've nothing else to do;
>> I quite admit it's true
> That now and then I shirk
> Particularly boring kinds of work;
>> Don't you?
> But, on the whole,
>> I think it's fair to say
>> Provided I can do it my own way
>> And that I need not start on it today—
> I quite like work!

The same rather casual attitude to work was illustrated by the following message, which the head of a New York firm put on its notice board: "Some time between starting and quitting time, without infringing on lunch periods, coffee breaks, rest periods, storytelling, ticket selling, holiday planning, and the rehashing of yesterday's television programs, we ask that each employee try to find some time for a work break. This may seem radical, but it might aid steady employment and assure regular pay checks."

Other people tolerate their job as a necessary nuisance, a way of earning a living, and a tedious consequence of the Fall. I was astonished to read this latter concept in a serious book: "The orthodox view of work, which has been accepted by most managers and industrial psychologists, is a simple one, and fifty years of industrial psychology and more than a century of managerial practice have been founded upon it." What is it? It "accepts the Old Testament belief that physical labour is a curse imposed on man as a punishment for his sins, and that the sensible man labours solely in order to keep himself and his family alive or . . . to enable him to do the things he really likes."[1] The author evidently knows more about industry than Scripture. His concept of work is far from "the orthodox view" he claims it is. For according to Scripture work is a blessing not a curse, and it is the Creation not the Fall which has made us workers.

This second attitude to work, which regards it as either meaningless in itself or at best a necessary means to some quite different end (e.g., facilitating leisure pursuits), is the same in principle as the view held by some Christians that work is a useful sphere of witness. To be sure, the Christian should be a witness to Christ in every situation, but it is very inadequate to see the workplace as having no Christian significance in itself, but only as a well-stocked lake to fish in.

Yet another group of people have no particular understanding of their work. They have never stopped to think about it. They simply accept it. They are rather like H. L. Mencken, often referred to as "the sage of Baltimore," who once said: "I go on working for the same reason that a hen goes on laying eggs."[2] In other words, work is part of our human nature. We are compulsive workers, as hens are compulsive layers of eggs.

Those who are trying to develop a Christian mind on work, however, look first to Creation. The Fall turned some labor into drudgery (the ground was cursed, and cultivation became possible only by toil and sweat), but work itself is a consequence of our creation in God's image. God himself is represented in Genesis 1 as a worker. Day by day, or stage by stage, his creative plan unfolded. Moreover, when he saw what he had made, he pronounced it "good." He enjoyed perfect job satisfaction. His final act of creation, before resting on the seventh day, was to create human beings, and in doing so to make them workers too. He gave them some of his own dominion over the earth and told them to exercise their creative gifts in subduing it. So from the beginning men and women have been privileged stewards of God, commissioned to guard and develop the environment in his name.

Then in the second account of Creation, which concentrates on the human perspective, we read: "Now the LORD God had planted a garden. . . . The LORD God took the man and put him in the Garden of Eden to work it and take care of it" (Genesis 2:8, 15). Thus, God planted the garden and God created the man. Then he put the man he had made into the garden he had planted, and told him to cultivate and protect it. As he had put the earth in general into man's charge, now in particular he committed the garden to him. Later (Genesis 4:17–22) Adam's descendants are pictured as building cities, raising livestock, making and playing musical instruments, and forging tools of bronze and iron. It seems, in fact, to be the Middle Stone Age which is being described.

Here then is God the worker together with man the worker, who shares God's image and dominion. And (Christians will want to add) there is Jesus the worker, demonstrating at the carpenter's bench the dignity of manual labor. In the light of these revealed truths about God, Christ and human beings, what is the Christian understanding of work?

Self-Fulfillment

First, work is intended for the fulfillment of the worker. That is, an important part of our self-fulfillment as human beings is to be found, according to God's purpose, in our work. We can affirm this with confidence in view of the very first instruction which God addressed to man and woman: "Be fruitful and increase in number; fill the earth and subdue it" (Genesis 1:28). Here are three successive commands, each leading logically to the next. They could not subdue the earth without first filling it, and they could not fill it without first reproducing themselves. This original and composite commandment expresses, then, a basic aspect of our vocation as human beings.

Our dominion over nature is due to our likeness to God. Or, to express the same truth in different terms, our potential for creative work is an essential part of our Godlikeness. Our Creator has made us creative creatures. Dorothy Sayers was right, then, in her epigram: "Work is not primarily a thing one does to live, but the thing one lives to do."[3] Since the Creator has given us gifts, he intends them to be used. He wants us to be fulfilled, not frustrated.

Pope John Paul II is clear and outspoken about the fundamental place of work in human life. In his encyclical on "Human Work" entitled *Laborem Exercens* he writes: "Work is one of the characteristics that distinguish man from the rest of creatures, whose activity for sustaining their lives cannot be called work."[4] From the early chapters of Genesis, "the Church is convinced that work is a fundamental dimension of man's existence on earth."[5] For this reason, he continues, "human work is a key, probably the essential key, to the whole social question." If the latter is "making life more human," as the Second Vatican Council said it was, "then the key, namely human work, acquires fundamental and decisive importance."[6] So then, "work is a good thing for man," not only because through work he transforms nature to serve his needs, but because through it "he also achieves fulfilment as a human being, and indeed, in a sense, becomes 'more a human being.'"[7]

It would be an exaggeration, however, to affirm that work is actually "indispensable" to our humanness, for the climax of Genesis 1 is not the creation of man, male and female, to subdue the earth, but the institution of the Sabbath. We human beings are at our most human not so much when we work, as when we lay aside our work in order to worship. Thus the Sabbath "relativizes the works of mankind, the contents of the six working days. It protects mankind from total absorption by the task of subduing the earth, it anticipates the distortion which makes work the sum and purpose of human life, and it informs mankind that he will not fulfill his humanity in his relation to the work which he is transforming but only when he raises his eyes above, in the blessed, holy hour of communion with the Creator."[8] Here lies a fundamental difference between Marxism and Christianity. In the end a human being is not *homo faber* but *homo adorans*.

Nevertheless, we must say that if we are idle (instead of active) or destructive (instead of creative), we are denying a basic aspect of our humanity, contradicting God's purpose for our lives, and so forfeiting a part of our own fulfillment. This does not mean, of course, that a child, a hospital patient or a retired person is not a human being because he or she cannot work. Yet a child wants to grow up, and a sick person to get well, in order to be able to serve. Similarly, retired people are wise to seek an active retirement, in which they have opportunities for constructive service, even if it is unpaid. I shall come later to the particularly poignant plight of the unemployed. Pessimistic as the Preacher in Ecclesiastes was regarding the meaninglessness of life lived without God, and about "toilsome labor under the sun," he was able to be positive about our daily work: "A man can do nothing better than to eat and drink and find satisfaction in his work." Again, "there is nothing better for a man than to enjoy his work" (Ecclesiastes 2:24; 3:22).

The concept of self-fulfillment through work is certainly much more difficult in some countries and regions (where the choice of job is extremely limited), and in particular kinds of work. The mining of coal (or for that matter of copper, tin, gold and diamonds) involves dirt, discomfort and danger, and everything should be done by mine owners to reduce risks and unpleasantness. Then there is the tedium of the factory assembly line. E. F. Schumacher did not exaggerate when he wrote about monotonous work: "Mechanical, artificial, divorced from nature, utilizing only the smallest part of man's potential capacities, it sentences the great majority of workers to spending their working lives in a way which contains no worthy challenge, no stimulus to self-perfection, no chance of development, no element of Beauty, Truth or Goodness."[9] He drives home the anomaly of this by pointing out that "the modern world takes a lot of care that the worker's body should not accidentally or otherwise be damaged" and, if it is damaged, provides for his compensation. But what about "his soul and his spirit"? "If his work damages him, by reducing him to a robot—that is just too bad."[10] He then quotes Ananda Coomaraswamy, who says that "industry without art is brutality." Why? Because it damages the worker's soul and spirit.[11] Schumacher's solution is in the "small is beautiful" concept with which his name will always be associated.

Even in large factories attempts have been made to relieve monotony and increase responsibility by job-swapping or job rotation within a team. For example, in 1974 in southern Sweden, a Volvo car manufacturing plant became the first of its kind in the world to operate without a conveyor belt. Through management-union cooperation, flexible working schedules and hours were introduced along with the practice of teamwork. This has become the basis of all of Volvo's new factories and plants. At the newest one in Uddevalla this concept is at its height—teams work on stationary cars so that a sense of craftsmanship rather than tedium is nurtured. In the white-collar world as well, which has been the hardest hit by the revolution of information technology, operators may be mesmerized by their computer screen, especially if they are restricted to data entry, and so feel bored and alienated. They need to increase their human contacts. Indeed, we should support every attempt to "enrich" or "humanize" working conditions.

Other manual jobs, although not exactly tedious, are thought by some to be "menial" or "demeaning." Take refuse collection as an example. It can involve the handling of rubbish that is filthy or smelly or both. Yet it is, of course, a vital service to public health and hygiene, and as such should provide a measure of job satisfaction. I read in 1970 of Mr. Dennis Sibson, a dustman (or in the American tongue "garbage collector") from Middleton in Lancashire, who was awarded a Churchill traveling fellowship, which he used to study refuse collection and disposal on the European continent. He had previously been a clerk, a coalman, a window cleaner, a tool-setter and a decorator. But he said he found refuse work (he had had fourteen years of it) "most satisfying to himself and most useful to the public."[12]

The Service of Others and of God

Work is intended not only for the fulfillment of the worker, but also for the benefit of the community. Adam did not cultivate the Garden of Eden merely for his own enjoyment, but to feed and clothe his family. Throughout the Bible the productivity of the soil is related to the needs of society. Thus, God gave Israel a "land flowing with milk and honey," and at the same time issued instructions that the harvest was to be shared with the poor, the alien, the widow and the orphan. Similarly in the New Testament, the converted thief is told to stop stealing and to start working with his own hands, so that he "may have something to share with those in need" (Ephesians 4:28).

The knowledge that our work is beneficial and appreciated adds considerably to our sense of job satisfaction. I understand that Henri de Man's studies in Germany between the wars, and the Hawthorne experiments, which were conducted at the same time at the Chicago plant of the Western Electric Company, were the first pieces of scientific research into this now well-accepted fact. The Hawthorne studies in particular showed "that workers would increase their output even when the lights were dimmed to the strength of moonlight, if they thought that their labors were considered by other people to be important and significant."[13]

Certainly the Bible regards work as a community project, undertaken by the community for the community. All work needs to be seen as being, at least to some degree, public service. This principle throws light on the discussion about the purpose(s) of business. It is acknowledged by all that a successful business must: (1) make a profit; (2) provide adequate wages, good prospects and pleasant working conditions for the workforce; (3) invest in research and development; (4) declare a dividend for share-holders; (5) pay taxes to the government; and (6) serve the public. The point of controversy concerns the order in which these six purposes should be placed. Many business people insist that profit must head the list, since otherwise the firm will sink. And everybody agrees that profit is indispensable as an index of efficiency and a condition of survival. But Christians feel uncomfortable about giving priority to profit, lest it seem that the chief end of the company is self-service (although of course there is a distinction between retained profits and distributed profits). It appears more consistent with the Christian emphasis on "ministry" to give priority to the provision of whatever goods or services the company offers the public. We then of course have to add immediately that in order to serve the public, and so stay in business and/or expand in order to do so, the firm must not only pay its workforce and its taxes, but also make a profit, out of which it can plough something back for research and renewal of equipment, and pay a dividend. In other words, all six obligations of a business dovetail with one another. Some prefer to visualize them as the spokes of a wheel, in which priority is not given to any one purpose, rather than as the layers of a pyramid. Yet the Christian mind still wants to insist that service to the community should come first. After all, it is not only true that a firm cannot serve the public unless it makes a profit and so survives; it is also (and perhaps more) true that it cannot make a profit unless it serves the public acceptably.

More important even than the service of the community is the service of God, though the two cannot be separated. Christians believe that the third and highest function of work is that through it God should be glorified—that is, that his purpose should be revealed and fulfilled. E. F. Schumacher also gives three purposes of human work, as follows:

First, to provide necessary and useful goods and services.
    Second, to enable every one of us to use and thereby perfect our gifts, like good stewards.
    Third, to do so in service to, and in co-operation with others, so as to liberate ourselves from our inborn egocentricity.[14]

Now it appears that his first purpose is my second, and his second my first. It is when we come to the third that we differ. Schumacher sees life as a school, God as the schoolmaster, and work as one of the chief means by which our chronic self-centeredness is reduced, if not eradicated. "In the process of doing good work," he writes, "the ego of the worker disappears."[15] I do not wish to deny the wholesome ego-diminishing influences of work. But it seems to me that an even higher vision of work is to see it as being for the glory of God. How is this?

God has deliberately arranged life in such a way that he needs the cooperation of human beings for the fulfillment of his purposes. He did not create the planet earth to be productive on its own; human beings had to subdue and develop it. He did not plant a garden whose flowers would blossom and fruit ripen on their own; he appointed a gardener to cultivate the soil. We call this the "cultural mandate" which God gave to humankind. I like the story of the cockney gardener who was showing a clergyman the beauty of his garden, with its herbaceous borders in full and colorful bloom. Duly impressed, the clergyman broke out into spontaneous praise of God. The gardener was not very pleased, however, that God should get all the credit. "You should 'ave seen this 'ere garden," he said, "when Gawd 'ad it to 'isself!"[16] He was right. His theology was entirely correct. "Nature" is what God gives us; "culture" is what we do with it. Without a human cultivator, every garden or field quickly degenerates into a wilderness.

Usually we emphasize the indispensability of God's part. We sing at Thanksgiving or harvest:

> We plough the fields and scatter
> The good seed on the land,
> But it is fed and watered
> By God's almighty hand.

The opposite, however, would be equally true. We might sing instead:

> God plants the lovely garden
> And gives the fertile soil,
> But it is kept and nurtured
> By man's resourceful toil.

We should not be shy to declare this. It is not a proud statement; it is true. God does indeed provide soil, seed, sunshine and rain, but we have to do the ploughing, sowing and reaping. God provides the fruit trees, but we have to prune the trees and pick the fruit. As Luther once said in a lecture on Genesis 31:3, "For God will be working all things through you, he will be milking the cows through you and will be performing the most menial duties through you, and all duties, from the greatest to the least, will be pleasing to him." Of what use to us would be God's provision of an udder full of milk, if we were not there to extract it?

So there is cooperation, in which indeed we depend on God, but in which (we add reverently) he also depends on us. God is the Creator; man is the cultivator. Each needs the other. In God's good purpose, creation and cultivation, nature and nurture, raw materials and human craftsmanship go together.

This concept of divine-human collaboration is applicable to all honorable work. God has humbled himself and honored us by making himself dependent on our cooperation. Take the human baby, perhaps the most helpless of all God's creatures. Children are indeed a "gift of the Lord," although procreation is itself a form of cooperation. After the birth it is as if God drops the newborn child into the mother's arms and says, "Now you take over." He commits to human beings the upbringing of each child. In the early days the baby remains almost a part of the mother, so close are they to each other. And for years children depend on their parents and teachers.

Even in adult life, although we depend on God for life itself, we depend on each other for the necessities of life. These include not only the basic needs of physical life (food, clothing, shelter, warmth, safety and health care) but also everything which makes up the richness of human life (education, recreation, sport, travel, culture, music, literature and the arts), not to mention spiritual nurturing. So whatever our job—in one of the professions (teaching, medicine, the law, the social services, architecture or construction), in national or local politics or the civil service, in industry, commerce, farming or the media, in research, management, the services or the arts, or in the home—we need to see it as being cooperation with God, in serving the needs of human beings and so helping them fulfill his purpose and grow into human maturity.

In some jobs the cooperation is direct, and therefore easy to perceive. The farmer plants and sows; God gives the increase. Or take the case of medicine. The words of Ambroise Paré, the sixteenth-century French surgeon, sometimes described as "the founder of modern surgery," are inscribed on a wall of the École de Médecine in Paris: "I dressed the wound; God healed him." In other kinds of work the cooperation is indirect, in which case we need insight to grasp it. When asked whether his doctoral research in solid state physics was "useful," Robert Newport replied, "Well, it's not directly related to anything." But then he went on: "I hope that later my findings will link up with those of others and the results will be applied in industry." That is an example of what I mean.[17] And, although I have developed in a specifically Christian way this principle of looking beyond the immediate to the ultimate, it is surely applicable to very many jobs undertaken by non-Christians.

The story is told of a man (in the premechanization era) who, while taking a walk down a country lane, came across a stone quarry in which a number of men were working. He questioned several of them about what they were doing. The first replied irritably, "Can't you see? I'm hewing stone." The second answered without looking up, "I'm earning two hundred dollars a week." But when the same question was put to the third man, he stopped, put his pick down, stood up, stuck out his chest and said, "If you want to know what I'm doing, I'm building a cathedral." So it is a matter of how far we can see. The first man could not see beyond his pick, and the second beyond his Friday paycheck. But the third man looked beyond his tools and his wages to the ultimate end he was serving. He was cooperating with the architect. However small his particular contribution, he was helping to construct a building for the worship of God.

So *laborare est orare,* "work is worship," provided that we can see how our job contributes, in however small and indirect a way, to the forwarding of God's purpose for humankind. Then whatever we do can be done for the glory of God (1 Corinthians 10:31).

Some years ago I was given the opportunity by the Medical Officer of Health for the Port and City of London to see something of his responsibilities. We were shown round by Mr. T. L. Mackie, who at that time was the Port of London's Chief Health Inspector. His enthusiasm for his work was infectious, and in a letter he sent me the following week he divulged its origin. He wrote: "The work covers a rather comprehensive field of preventive medicine and environmental health control. To work for one's own ends, the pay packet, the 'perks,' security of tenure and eventual pension, is not enough for me. I like to think that I am responsible for a part of the greater human field pattern whereby we all subscribe of our best to the whole effort for human welfare according to our talents, and obey the will of our wonderful Creator. With this trend of thought and outlook, I go into action each day happily."

So divine-human cooperation in developing the resources of creation is a clear biblical motivation for work.

But Dr. Miroslav Volf, in his book *Work in the Spirit,* has challenged this view not as inaccurate but as inadequate. Careful in argument and lucid in style, he has developed a comprehensive theology of work. In essence he bids us look not so much back to the original creation as on to the new creation, whose fullness is yet to come. As there will be a fundamental continuity between our present body and our future resurrection body, so we are looking forward not to the destruction of the world, but to its transformation. It is this expectation which gives human work its significance, since "through it human beings contribute in their modest and broken way to God's new creation."[18]

Dr. Volf also rejects Luther's teaching on our different "vocations" in favor of Paul's teaching on our different "charisms" (*charismata,* "gifts of the Spirit"). These, he maintains, include daily mundane work, even that performed by non-Christians, for "all human work . . . is made possible by the operation of the Spirit of God in the working person."[19] I am left with some uneasy questions, however. Although indeed the Holy Spirit is at work in the world, and although the nations will bring their "splendor" into the New Jerusalem (Revelation 21:24, 26), does Paul's vision of the *charismata* really embrace the work of non-Christians? And can humans really cooperate with God in the eschatological transformation of the world? Is not the Kingdom of God, both in its present reality and in its future perfection, a gift of God, rather than a human achievement? Nevertheless, as we look to the future regeneration of the world, we are authorized to say that our present "labor in the Lord is not in vain" (1 Corinthians 15:58).

In the light of the three purposes for work which we have been considering, we are ready to attempt a definition:

Work is the expenditure of energy (manual or mental or both) in the service of others, which brings fulfillment to the worker, benefit to the community, and glory to God.

Fulfillment, service and worship (or cooperation with God's purpose) all intertwine, as indeed our duties to God, others and self nearly always do. Certainly self-fulfillment cannot be isolated from service. For job satisfaction is not primarily attained by a fair wage, decent conditions, security and a measure of participation in profits, important as these are. It arises from the job itself, and especially from that elusive thing, "significance." Moreover, the main component of significance in relation to our job is not even the combination of skill, effort and achievement, but the sense that through it we are contributing to the service of the community and of God himself. It is service which brings satisfaction, discovering ourselves in ministering to others. We need not only to develop this perspective on our own work, but, if we are employers or managers, to do our utmost to develop it in our workforce.

Some years ago I was shown around the Handicrafts Centre in Dacca, Bangladesh, which was operated by HEED (the Health, Education and Economic Development project). Here young people from refugee camps were being taught a skilled trade, carpet making or tapestry, weaving or straw art. What impressed me most was the degree of their concentration on what they were doing. They hardly noticed us and did not even look up as we walked by. They were absorbed in their craft. Their work had given them dignity, significance, a sense of self-worth through service.

The Trauma of Unemployment

When we have grasped how central a place work occupies in God's purpose for men and women, we see at once how serious an assault on our humanness unemployment is. Referring to the unemployed in the north of England during the Depression years, William Temple wrote: "The gravest and bitterest injury of their state is not the animal (physical) grievance of hunger or discomfort, nor even the mental grievance of vacuity and boredom; it is the spiritual grievance of being allowed no opportunity of contributing to the general life and welfare of the community."[20] It is a shocking experience to be declared "redundant," and still worse to have to think of oneself thus. Many people live in fear of it happening to them.

In 1963 the total number of unemployed in the United Kingdom (excluding school dropouts) was 500,000. By 1977 this had trebled to 1.5 million, and by 1982 that number doubled to 3 million (13 percent of the workforce), although the true figure may have been higher still, owing to the nonregistration of some unemployed people and the overmanning of some firms. From this shocking peak the figures fell to below 2 million in 1989 and in the 1990s have hovered roughly between 2 and 3 million people, between 6 percent and 11 percent of the workforce. Although unemployment in May 1997 was at a comparatively low figure of 6.9 percent, these numbers are still too high. In addition, certain groups are particularly hard hit, notably young people in their late teens and early twenties. The percentages are also higher than the average among ethnic (especially black) groups, disabled people, and unskilled workers in regions like Northern Ireland, South Wales and the big cities of Scotland and the north of England. There is also the growing problem of long-term unemployment, even intergenerational unemployment, handed down as a cruel birthright from parents to children.

On the European continent the figures vary considerably from country to country. Among European Union nations Spain retains the highest rate of unemployment at 20.9 percent and Luxembourg the lowest at 3.7 percent. Unemployment in the European Union remained steady at 10.8 percent throughout the first six months of 1997. This means that over 18 million people were out of work. Youth unemployment in Europe is twice that of adults, and the number of long-term unemployed has grown to account for over 50 percent of the currently unemployed. Elsewhere, in April 1997 unemployment was at 3.3 percent in Japan and 4.9 percent in the United States. In some developing nations the statistics are much higher.[21]

Moreover, the future is unpredictable, and the worldwide problem may well get worse. Although the deregulation and increasing globalization of markets have many advantages, they often make a negative impact on the labor market. Companies are able to search anywhere for cheap labor, which often means lost jobs in the industrialized world, while those who in turn receive new jobs in the developing world do not gain ample benefits from them. Most of the new jobs created in the 1990s have been part-time and, although meeting real needs, often do not bring in sufficient income for a family. By the year 2000 part-time workers will make up a third of the workforce in Britain.[22] Technology continues to race ahead, with many jobs previously performed by humans being efficiently completed by computers and robots. Hand in hand with globalization, new technologies lead to a constant flux in labor markets, with demands for increased minimum skills resulting in rapid obsolescence of both workers and training. There will be no sense in trying to resist these developments, however, like the nineteenth-century Luddites who went round smashing factory machines, beginning in 1811 with the newly installed knitting machines in the hosiery factories of Nottingham. We must learn to face these issues head on.

Unemployment is not a problem of statistics, however, but of people. In the Third World, where no wage-related unemployment benefit is available, it is often a question of actual survival, but in the West the suffering is more psychological than physical. It is a poignant personal and social tragedy. Industrial psychologists have likened unemployment to bereavement, the loss of one's job being in some respects similar to the loss of a relative or friend. They describe three stages of trauma. The first is shock. A young unemployed man in our congregation spoke of his "humiliation," and an unemployed woman of her "disbelief," since she had been given assurances that her job was safe. A restaurateur felt "immediately degraded" and said to himself, "I've become a statistic; I'm unemployed." On hearing that they have been sacked or laid off, some people are angry, others feel rejected and demeaned. Their self-image has suffered a bitter blow, particularly if they have dependents they cannot now provide for. Unemployment brings tension and conflict to their family life. At this stage, however, they are still optimistic about the future.

The second stage is depression and pessimism. Their savings are exhausted and their prospects look increasingly bleak. So they lapse into inertia. As one man summed it up, "I stagnate." Then the third stage is fatalism. After remaining unemployed for several months and being repeatedly disappointed in their applications for jobs, their struggle and hope decline, their spirit becomes bitter and broken, and they are thoroughly demoralized and dehumanized. In October 1996, 35 percent of Britain's unemployed had been out of work for over a year and 20 percent for over two years.[23]

Solutions and Palliatives

How should Christians react to the problems of unemployment? The ultimate solution belongs to the realm of macroeconomics. Everybody seems to be agreed that unemployment can be overcome only by more trade bringing more demand, bringing more jobs. But experts do not agree on how this growth can be secured. In Britain "making industry more competitive" is the cry from government, employers and unions. To this end some advocate a massive reflation of the economy by government investment and job creation. Others hope to stimulate a more dynamic economy in private (though government-encouraged) investment. Others accept E. F. Schumacher's "small is beautiful" dictum and believe we should turn from huge capital-intensive enterprises to modest labor-intensive projects. Yet others believe that new technologies will force this decentralization upon us anyway.

A significant Christian contribution to the macroeconomic debate was made in 1997 by the publication of *Unemployment and the Future of Work: An Enquiry for the Churches,* which had been conducted under the auspices of the Council of Churches for Britain and Ireland (CCBI). It is outspokenly Christian in its understanding of the necessity and dignity of work, and of unemployment as "a social evil of the greatest magnitude,"[24] incompatible with both love and justice. Its authors recommend a combination of policies which over a period of years could achieve the goal of full employment. A chapter is devoted to each of the following eight proposals: (1) tax reform to create many more jobs in the private sector; (2) much more employment in the public sector, financed by higher taxation; (3) a fresh start for the long-term unemployed; (4) a national minimum wage; (5) better conditions of work and fairer pay bargaining; (6) reform of the social security benefit system, in order to reduce reliance on means-testing; (7) priority in the education system to be given to basic skills for all young people; and (8) a national employment forum, at which such policies are debated by all interested parties.[25]

We turn now from long-term to short-term remedies, or from solutions to palliatives. Successive governments have done much in their regional policies, training and retraining schemes, and job creation programs.

Now the new Labour government has publicized its ambitious "Welfare to Work" plan. Its "New Deal for 18–24-year-olds" entices private-sector employers with a weekly rebate for up to six months in return for employing them, while offering them either subsidized employment equal to benefit plus a fixed amount, or full-time study, or a job with the environmental task force. New Labour's program also offers to all 16- and 17-year-olds access to full-time or part-time education or training; to employers who hire the long-term unemployed tax rebates; and to single parents with young children a "proactive Employment Service."

In addition to such government involvement, there is still room for voluntary initiatives. More than two hundred Local Enterprise Trusts now exist. These have been formed by leading companies like ICI, Pilkingtons and Marks and Spencer, often with the cooperation of the local authority, to offer expert advice on facilities and finance to those wishing to establish new businesses. "There are one and one-third million small businesses in

Britain," wrote George Goyder in 1987, "employing some five million work-ers. In West Germany there are half as many again, in Japan five times, and in the USA ten times as many. We need to double the number of small busi-nesses in Britain. We could employ another two to three million people in this way."[26]

Various proposals are also being made not so much to increase demand for labor as to decrease supply. The principle behind them is to redistrib-ute the same amount of work, by spreading it over more people. One arrangement being canvassed is "job-splitting" or "job-pairing," by which the same job is shared between two people, who work either a "week on-week off" or a "morning-afternoon" rhythm, giving them more freedom, although also of course less pay. Other people are urging the reduction of the weekly total of hours worked, the strict curtailment of overtime, the banning of "black economy" jobs, the extension of annual leave, the pro-vision of more sabbaticals and earlier voluntary retirement.

Has the Christian Church any specific contribution to make?

The Role of the Church

I have been encouraged by David Bleakley's two books *In Place of Work . . . The Sufficient Society: A Study of Technology from the Point of View of Peo-ple* and *Work: The Shadow and the Substance, a Reappraisal of Life and Labour.* They contain much food for thought and much stimulus to action. David Bleakley believes that in the present transition period the Church should have a key role. In the Industrial Revolution it missed its opportunity, and ever since, the working masses of Britain have been alienated from it. This must not happen again. The Church could keep Britain united during the dangerous period of industrial transformation. And, since the unemployed (the chief casualties) have no union to represent them or plead their cause, the Church could be the voice of the voiceless. It is well placed to do so. "Straddling as it does the whole spectrum of the community, it can be a unique lobby, articulating the Christian social demand and encouraging its people to discover and apply . . . such demands through national and local church initiatives."[27]

Let me spell out at least three ways in which the Church can and should be helping.[28]

First, many of us need to change our attitudes towards the unemployed and persuade the public to do the same. Those who have been schooled in the values of the so-called "Protestant Work Ethic" (industry, honesty, resourcefulness, thrift, etc.) tend to despise those who are losers in the strug-gle to survive, as if it were their fault. No doubt there are a few work-shy people who do not want a job and prefer to sponge on the community. But they must constitute a tiny minority. The great majority of unemployed people want to work, but cannot find a job. They are victims of the recession and of the new technology. There is need therefore for more Christian sympathy towards them and more pastoral care. We have to repent of looking down on the unemployed, and of ever imagining that the words "workless" and "worthless" might be synonyms. I was chagrined to hear of a man in our church who, after being unemployed for two years, stayed away from public worship because he was scared of being asked what he was doing and, on the discovery that he was out of work, of being made to feel a failure. But at least within the Christian community no stigma should be attached to unemployment. Paul's dictum "If a man will not work, he shall not eat" (2 Thessalonians 3:10) was addressed to voluntary not involuntary unemployment, to the lazy not the "redundant." So we need to welcome and support the unemployed in the local church; otherwise our pious talk about "the Body of Christ" becomes a sick joke.

Secondly, the Church can take its own initiatives. For several decades now an increasing number of local congregations have come to realize that the buildings they inherited from the past are both too large for their needs and unsuitable for their responsibilities. Many have therefore developed imaginative plants to preserve (and usually remodel) an area for worship, and convert the rest for other purposes, especially for appropriate service to the local community. Then, in order to indicate its new multipurpose character, some have dropped the traditional word "church" and renamed their building (or complex), a "Christian Center." Some such centers accommodate a children's play group or nursery school, a club for "moms and toddlers," a luncheon club and podiatry service for old people, an open youth group, a coffee bar, etc. They are also beginning to be used to serve the unemployed.

CAWTU (Church in Action with the Unemployed), though no longer functioning, was helpful in emphasizing three areas in which local churches can take the initiative.[29] The first is "Pastoral Care (coping with being out of work)." Why not open a "drop-in center" or "resource center" on church premises, where unemployed people can find companionship, information, a library, refreshments and recreation? Secondly, "Work Experience (a better chance to get jobs)." Why not sponsor a local initiative which offers training to young people, or provides long-term unemployed people with temporary work which benefits the community? See the examples below for ideas. Thirdly, "Job Creation (new jobs and permanent work)." This might involve creating a new job at the church (in administration or maintenance), or starting a neighborhood cooperative (for odd jobs), or launching a new business (joining with others to set it up).

Here are some examples of local Christian initiatives, which are mostly taken from a wider selection in *Unemployment and the Future of Work* (pp. 182–85).

The Peckham Evangelical Churches Action Network (PECAN) was set up in 1988 in response to long-term unemployment on the local housing estates. PECAN now supports thirty Christian staff and eighteen volunteers who are involved in training over one thousand local unemployed people every year. They take a uniquely proactive approach to recruitment, going door-to-door in the area, and so making personal visits to over thirty thousand homes a year. They have an over 70 percent success rate in getting the unemployed into jobs or further vocational training courses. PECAN's success has inspired similar initiatives such as the Hackney Employment Link Project (HELP), which also helps the unemployed back into work and has experienced rapid growth in recent years.

Emmaus communities in Cambridge, Coventry, Greenwich, Dover, Belfast and elsewhere are designed to be self-supporting residences for the unemployed homeless. Those who come to live in an Emmaus community agree to work a forty-hour week and to sign off benefits. They are in turn given housing, training, work and weekly wages. Since 1991 Emmaus has responded to the needs of over five hundred homeless people and has a goal of establishing twenty-five communities in Britain by the year 2000.

New Life Electrics in London (a Quaker project) trains and employs the previously unemployed in the repair and reconditioning of household electrical items. Not only does it provide work for those who need it, but it also performs a valuable service to the community where the replacement of cookers and other appliances is not a viable alternative.

The London Churches' Employment Development Unit is an ecumenical group which gives advice to churches on how to set up and manage projects for the unemployed. Over twenty different projects were active in 1993, with nearly fifteen hundred people being helped.

As an outgrowth of the Jubilee Centre in Cambridge, the Relationships Foundation is fighting unemployment through local initiatives (City Life). In Teesside a program is seeking to nurture better relationships between the long-term unemployed and the nonprofit sector, between residents in affluent and poorer areas, and among local businesses. By setting up channels of communication the initiative is helping people to connect and understand one another and is getting the unemployed back into work.

In 1996 the Evangelical Alliance and Tearfund joined forces to launch UK Action, a wide-ranging project which helps support local evangelical initiatives in understanding and fighting poverty. For example, the Toxteth Tabernacle Baptist Church, with help from UK Action, is running a skills training center for teenagers who are truant, expelled from school or excluded. The center is building bridges to the community by providing valuable training for the young and unemployed. UK Action serves as both a catalyst and a consultancy; it stimulates and coordinates church initiatives in community service and job training. It has so far funded over twenty-five projects, and is considering many more.

In South Wales, St. John's Church, Penydarren, Merthyr Tydfil, developed a large and flourishing program. Canon Bill Morgan (the Vicar) and his church council decided to demolish two of their buildings, sell the land, buy and modernize a factory, and convert their church's crypt into an operations center for their project, which they were running in conjunction with the Manpower Services Commission. They formed two companies, the St. John's Industry Company, which gives a two-year workshop training to unemployed older teenagers, and the St. John's Community Programme Agency, which enables unemployed adults to spend a year in voluntary building, social service, conservation work and urban ministry. By 1988 their workforce had grown to 1,300 people with an annual budget of £6 million.

The third way in which the Church can help is by a determined effort to make, publicize and act on the distinction between "work" and "employment." For although all employment is work (we are not paid for doing nothing), not all work is employment (we can work without being paid for it). What demoralizes people is not so much lack of employment (not being in a paid job) as lack of work (not using their energies in creative service). Conversely, what gives people a sense of self-respect is significant work. Adam was not paid for cultivating the Garden of Eden. The housewife who works at home and students who work at their books are not usually paid (though some of them are agitating to be paid!). I know that the paycheck is important, and that those receiving unemployment benefits tend to feel like parasites (quite falsely, since they have themselves contributed to the National Insurance Scheme). Nevertheless, work significance is more important than wage or salary in giving us a sense of self-worth. To employ people to dig holes and fill them up again brings pay without significance; to work creatively but voluntarily brings significance without pay. Of the unemployed people I have known personally, several have spent time in study, one who had a camera used the opportunity to improve his photographic techniques in the hope that later he would be able to make Christian audiovisuals, while a young woman spent many hours visiting and supporting some alcoholic friends who lived in the apartment below her.

The current social revolution will not leave any of us untouched. If the average working week is reduced (which is what the Trades Union Congress are pressing for), how shall we spend our extra free time? Should the Church not be both suggesting and offering some constructive alternatives to television and video? For creative leisure, though unpaid, is a form of work. The possibilities are numerous: "do-it-yourself" repairs, redecorations and improvements at home; servicing the car, motorbike or bicycle;

self-education through evening classes, correspondence courses or Open University; cultivating the garden or allotment, growing your own vegetables, keeping pigs or chickens; working with wood or metal; dressmaking, knitting and embroidery; making music; painting, pottery and sculpting; reading and writing; and where possible doing these things together, spending more time with family and friends.

Then there is the whole sphere of community service, either through the local church or a voluntary organization or on one's own initiative: visiting the sick, the elderly or prison inmates; redecorating an old person's home; working with mentally or physically handicapped people; baby-sitting; picking up other people's children from school; teaching children with learning disabilities, or ethnic families for whom English is a second language, to read and write; helping in the local hospital, school, club or church.

Some readers will doubtless dismiss all this as a typical middle-class reaction, quite impractical for working-class unemployed people in towns. And to some extent this is true. I am not so stupid as to recommend people who live in an inner-city apartment to keep pigs! But in principle I still appeal to the great biblical truths on which we have been reflecting. Humankind by creation is creative; we cannot discover ourselves without serving God and our neighbor; we must have an outlet for our creative energies. So, if the unemployed have no facilities for the range of activities I have mentioned and they are not available elsewhere in the community, should not the church provide them? Is it impossible for the church to make available a workshop (and tools), a garage or studio, in which people can both learn and practice new skills? And could not most local churches develop a much broader program of service to the local community? Increasing numbers of unemployed, semiemployed and retired people will need to be encouraged to use their leisure time creatively. As a result of automation, as Marshall McLuhan wrote in 1964, "we are suddenly threatened with a liberation that taxes our inner resources of self-employment and imaginative participation in society."[30]

Conclusion

The conclusion of this chapter in the second edition of *Issues* (1990) was entitled "A More Radical View." It quoted the pessimistic forecasts of some futurologists in the eighties, who tried to visualize the nature and place of work in the twenty-first century. For example, the International Labour Organisation estimated that in order to achieve worldwide full employment, a billion new jobs would have to be created. This led its Director-General to comment that full employment of the conventional kind would never return. For population growth, the new technologies, the fear of inflation and global trade competition would combine to make the recovery of full employment an impossible dream.

This certainly looks like being the case in Europe. John Palmer, in his book *Trading Places,* has a chapter entitled "The End of the Old Industrial Order." In it he documents how the European steel, coal, shipbuilding and textile industries all collapsed before the expanding productivity of Brazil, South Korea, Taiwan and Japan, and how nothing has arisen in Europe to compensate for the huge layoffs involved.[31]

The same basic pessimism lay behind two books which were both published in 1985, the first by a Christian and the second not. They look courageously into a future without full employment and plead for fresh thinking. Michael Moynagh in *Making Unemployment Work* urges us to move from a "work ethic" (which makes work the basis of worth) to a "life ethic" (which sees worth as preceding work in the sense of employment, and therefore as independent of it).[32] James Robertson in *Future Work* goes further. He develops three possible scenarios of the future, whose key words are respectively "employment," "leisure," and "ownwork."[33] The last two scenarios are contrasting visions of a post-industrial society. He calls them "HE" and "SHE," "HE" standing for "Hyper-Expansionist" and "SHE" for "Sane, Humane and Ecological." "HE" will acquiesce in an unhealthy polarization between "a minority of highly skilled and highly responsible people" who will run everything, while "the rest of us will be living lives of leisure."[34] "SHE," by contrast, will be "sane" (people taking control of their own life and work), "humane" (nobody exploiting or being exploited) and "ecological" (everybody living in harmony with their environment). James Robertson's word for this self-organized activity is "ownwork." It embraces "a wide range of flexible options for work and useful activity, including part-time employment, self-employment, irregular and casual employment, cooperative and community work, voluntary work, do-it-yourself activities, and productive leisure as well as full-time employment."[35]

Michael Moynagh and James Robertson both realize that a society which places equal value on paid work and voluntary service, on "employment" and "ownwork," will need a new financial base. They propose that, in place of the present complex system of social security, the government would pay everybody a "social wage" (Michael Moynagh) or "Guaranteed Basic Income" (James Robertson). This would be adequate for subsistence, untaxed and unconditional, although for many it would be supplemented by earned income, which would be taxable. So wealth creation would continue as at present. Critics of these proposals, while acknowledging that they would diminish the two-class nature of society, abolish poverty, render the black economy otiose, give everybody a greater freedom of choice and increase the level of voluntary service, nevertheless regard them as somewhat utopian.

Can it be right, however, for Christians, who believe work to be an indispensable element in God's original purpose for human beings, to acquiesce in the problem of large-scale unemployment, and even declare it insoluble? I think not. The books I have read which have been published in the nineties breathe a spirit of optimism. In North-South economic inequality, for example, not only has substantial progress been made in the alleviation of poverty but, given a generous influx of capital (comparable to the Marshall Plan after World War II), we are assured that it can be abolished.

The same is true of the problem of unemployment. The tone of the CCBI report *Unemployment and the Future of Work* is splendidly optimistic throughout. It refuses to accept the inevitability of mass unemployment, and insists that an explicit, realistic, national goal should be "enough good work for everyone,"[36] understanding "good work" as referring to jobs of real value, with fair pay and decent conditions. Whereas the Director-General of the ILO declared full employment to be "an impossible dream," the authors of the CCBI report contradict him: "We have heard nothing to convince us that decent paid work for all is an impossible dream."[37] Unemployment can be solved only by creating more jobs, and more jobs can be created only by greater investment in both the public and private sectors.

So what stands in the way? Sir Fred Catherwood, from his long and wide experience of industry and politics, writes in *Jobs and Justice, Homes and Hope* with refreshing outspokenness: "Unrestrained greed is well on its way to destroying employment. It is greed which keeps taxes low and interest rates high, crippling the industrial recovery which we need to restore full employment."[38] He has a later chapter entitled "Naked Greed," in which he tells us that the selfishness which puts personal profit above social concern is now called "the new reality."[39] Political parties looking for votes cannot afford to ignore it.

The CCBI report is equally outspoken. But instead of analyzing greed, it issues a positive call for sacrifice. "It becomes a question of priorities: job creation as against low taxation. Sacrifice is necessary in seeking the common good. We do not think that the deep running sores of unemployment and poverty can be healed without some sacrifice on the part of those of us who are better off."[40] These stirring words echo the challenge which David Sheppard, until 1997 Bishop of Liverpool, has often addressed to "comfortable Britain."

Is such a call realistic? Yes, it is. To be sure, we believe in original sin, namely that our human nature has an inherited twist of self-centeredness. In consequence, greed is natural to us, while altruism and sacrifice are unnatural. Nevertheless, we also know that human beings have higher and better instincts, to which it is possible to appeal, especially if it is evident to them that individual unselfishness can benefit the community. In the end, the problem of unemployment is neither economic nor political, but moral and spiritual. Christians should blaze a trail, since sacrifice, not greed, should characterize those who seek to follow Jesus Christ.

The Christian understanding of work as self-fulfillment through the service of God and neighbor should have several wholesome consequences. We shall value our own work more highly; see to it that those we may employ are able to do the same; feel deeply for the unemployed and try to ensure that though out of employment they are not out of work. In summary, all of us should expect to remain workers all our lives, so that even after we have retired, we may spend whatever energy we have left in some form of service.[41]

2

Industrial Relations

Right attitudes to work are essential to our enjoyment of it; right relationships at work are equally important. Management and labor may be highly motivated, and yet at the same time deeply dissatisfied because they are at loggerheads with one another.

Britain has had a bad record of industrial relations. The low point was the winter of 1978–79, which was described at the time as a state of "industrial civil war." The Trades Union Congress had agreed with the government to a policy of wage restraint, but had added a warning that this could not be sustained for more than three years. They proved right. There were strikes by bakers, refuse collectors, truck drivers and railway workers, hospital workers and ambulance drivers, journalists, teachers and social workers. The number of working days lost through industrial action in 1978 is said to have been 9,306,000. The situation greatly improved in the 1980s, however, and the nineties have been comparatively strike-free.

Industrial peace is of concern to all thoughtful people, but especially to Christians. For we are in the business of right relationships. John V. Taylor, formerly Bishop of Winchester, has justly called God's Kingdom "the kingdom of right relationships."[1] Reconciliation is at the top of the Christian agenda, because it lies at the heart of the gospel. Sin disrupts relationships; salvation rebuilds them. Jesus came on a mission of reconciliation. He is the supreme peacemaker; he tells his followers to be peacemakers too.

Moreover, relationships at work are particularly important because God means work, as we have seen, to be a cooperative enterprise, in which we collaborate with him and others for the common good. Britain and her allies experienced this solidarity during World War II when united against a common evil, but that unity soon fell apart afterwards, and even the valiant efforts of government, management and unions to cooperate in the sixties and seventies did not altogether restore it.

The Biblical Principle of Mutuality

As in the other topics of this book, my task is not to presume to recommend policies (which is the calling of those involved in government, employment and unions, and for which I have no expertise), but rather to try to clarify biblical principles, so that we can think straight and take whatever action is appropriate to our responsibility.

I invite you therefore to reflect on the situation in Israel after King Solomon died. I recognize that an industry or business is not a kingdom, and that any analogy between them is bound to be only partial. Yet there are some significant parallels. The early united monarchy (under Saul, David and Solomon) had not been uniformly absolutist. At times there had been a reasonable degree of consultation, as when David "conferred with" his officers, and then with the whole assembly, about bringing the ark to Jerusalem. He did not wish to make a unilateral decision, but to take action only "if it seems good to you and if it is the will of the LORD our God." Then after consultation, we are told, "The whole assembly agreed to do this, because it seemed right to all the people" (1 Chronicles 13:1–4).

David's son and successor Solomon, however, despite all his wisdom and greatness, was a despot. His ambitious building program was completed only by the use of forced labor. Industrial relations (if I may use this term) were at an all-time low. So when he died, the people described his oppressive regime as a "heavy yoke" and appealed to his son Rehoboam to lighten it. When Rehoboam consulted his father's elder statesmen, they advised him, "If . . . you will be a servant to these people and serve them . . . they will always be your servants" (1 Kings 12:7). This splendid principle was rejected by Rehoboam, and in consequence the kingdom split into two. But it remains the essential basis of every constitutional monarchy (the motto of the Prince of Wales has since the fourteenth century been *Ich dien*, "I serve") and indeed of every democratic institution, in at least two ways.

First, it embodies the principle of mutual service: "If you will serve them, they will serve you." Jesus himself went beyond a prudential arrangement (we serve in order to be served) and affirmed that true leadership must be interpreted in terms of service ("Whoever wants to become great among you must be your servant"). Later Paul stated it ("Each of you should look not only to your own interests, but also to the interests of others"), and went on to illustrate it from the incarnation and death of Jesus (Mark 10:43; Philippians 2:4, 5–8).

Secondly, it is mutual service based on mutual respect. One might say it is service based on justice, and not on expediency alone. To be sure, expediency enters into it ("you serve them and they will serve you"), but the principle's real foundation is justice, namely that the other party is a group of human beings with human rights, created in God's image as we have been, and therefore deserving our respect, as we deserve theirs. To oppress the poor is to insult their Maker; to serve them is to honor him (see Proverbs 14:31; 17:5; 22:2). It was this truth which lay behind the many detailed social instructions of the Old Testament—for example, the commandment to pay servants their wages the same day, to care for the deaf and the blind, to have compassion on the widow and the orphan, to leave the gleanings of the harvest to the poor and the alien and to administer justice impartially in the courts. And the same principle also lay behind the New Testament instructions to masters and servants to respect each other. For they served the same Lord and were responsible to the same Judge.

Turning from biblical principle to contemporary reality, the contrast is stark. Wherever there is tension in industrial relations, let alone collision, the fault is seldom if ever limited to one side. Our basic self-centeredness skews our vision, so that we see everything from our own perspective. We seek our own interests rather than the other's. It is a situation of conflict born of suspicion and rivalry, instead of a situation of mutual service born of respect and trust. Such a state of affairs, one need hardly say, is wholly incompatible with the mind and spirit of Jesus Christ, and in his name we should set ourselves resolutely against it. But how? How can mutual suspicion be replaced by mutual service, and competition by cooperation?

This is all the more necessary today, because recently a new enemy has appeared and is undermining good relationships between directors, shareholders, managers and workers. This is the corporate shareholder. Because the main shareholders in large companies are nowadays often not individual investors but invisible and impersonal owners like huge investment trusts, insurance and pension funds, whom Sir Fred Catherwood calls "absentee landlords,"[2] their priority concern is to receive unreasonably high short-term dividends. Will Hutton has described this development and its consequences in a chapter entitled "Tomorrow's Money Today."[3] In order to satisfy its shareholders' forceful demands, the company is tempted to adopt short-sighted policies, for example trimming their workforce too severely and reducing investment in research and development, which threatens the long-term health and growth of the enterprise. If, on the other hand, the company's directors resist these temptations, they run the risk either of losing their shareholders or of falling victim to a "hostile takeover," so-called because the predator's motive is often sheer greed and not the good of the company. The fear of a possible takeover then causes a general sense of instability, particularly of job insecurity, throughout the company from top to bottom. Everybody is under unwelcome pressure: directors to cut corners, managers to serve their own future instead of the firm's, and workers to cling to their job lest they be replaced by others on an insecure short-term contract. In such a situation of uncertainty and anxiety, a preoccupation with healthy relationships would seem to be largely an irrelevance.

Yet relationships of mutual respect can have a transforming influence on the company. This is well illustrated in the experience of the American industrialist Wayne Alderson. For four generations the Aldersons had been coal miners. During his boyhood Wayne's father would come home from the pit saying, "If only they'd value me as much as they value the mule" (it was easier to replace a miner than a well-trained mule), while his three brothers who had jobs in the local steel works would say, "If only they would value us as much as they value the machines." Thus the importance of human value was instilled into him in his formative years and was later to flower in his "Value of the Person" concept. In the early 1970s Wayne Alderson became Vice President of Operations in the Pittron Corporation, which had a steel foundry in Glassport, Pennsylvania, near Pittsburgh. The firm was struggling to survive after a disastrous eighty-four-day strike, which left an aftermath of implacable bitterness and recrimination between management and men. Mr. Alderson conceived a plan for better production, quality, relationships and morale which he called "Operation Turnaround." Determined to end the old management style of confrontation, he called for cooperation instead, walked daily through the foundry, greeted the men by name, asked them about their work and home, visited them when they were sick, in fact treated them like human beings. At the request of a few of them he then started a small Bible study, which grew into a brief "chapel" service in a storage room underneath a furnace. As a result of the mutual confidence which he developed with the men, absenteeism and labor grievances virtually disappeared, while productivity and profits rose substantially. The old sterile days of confrontation were over. People called it "the Miracle of Pittron." After nearly two years Pittron was sold and Wayne Alderson lost his job. He started an itinerant ministry as speaker, consultant and peacemaker, to spread his "Value of the Person" vision. Its three key ingredients, he says, are love (a positive "I'm for you" attitude), dignity (people count) and respect (appreciation instead of criticism). He goes on: "Christ is at the center of the Value of the Person approach. But even an atheist can accept the worth of the person."[4]

Similarly, "I am committed," wrote Kenneth N. Hansen, formerly Chairman of the Board of Service Master Industries Inc., "to using work to help people develop, rather than to using people to accomplish the work as the end."

Once there is a desire for mutual respect and mutual service, there will be at least three consequences.

Abolish Discrimination

The first consequence is that discrimination will be abolished—both the realities and the symbols, which together perpetuate an unwholesome "them-us" confrontation.

For example, has there ever been a justification for paying workers by the hour and the week, and higher grades an annual salary? Or for insisting that wage earners clock in, while salaried staff do not have to? Or for restricting workers to the works' canteen, while providing the rest with a posh "staff restaurant"? In recent years many companies have put an end to such offensive distinctions, but many have not. "We know there are 'untouchables' on other continents," commented Jock Gilmour, a shop steward in the car industry; "what we haven't recognized is that our own industrialized society can have its untouchables too." I know, of course, that my three examples are trivial in themselves, but they are status symbols which appear deliberately to give self-respect to some and deny it to others.

I also understand that many of the old discriminatory practices of ten or twenty years ago have already been abolished, not least through the influence of the Japanese, who insist on the same conditions for everybody. Nevertheless, bad habits die slowly, and continuing vigilance is needed. Besides, behind the symbols of discrimination there lies the reality of social injustice, namely the excessive disparity between the high paid and the low paid.

Total egalitarianism should not be the Christian goal, for God himself has not made us identical in either our natural or spiritual endowments. What the Christian should oppose is the inequality of privilege, and what we should seek to ensure is that all differentials are due to merit, not privilege. In fact, it is a healthy and confidence-building arrangement when discrimination is both open and limited to pay, and does not extend to hidden perquisites for senior management (e.g., private health care, "top hat" pension schemes and free theatre tickets).

Human beings have a built-in sense of fair play, so that in all industrial relations arguments there are appeals to "fairness," and complaints of "unfair practices." This concept is the central focus of the book *Social Values and Industrial Relations,* subtitled *A Study of Fairness and Inequality.*[5] Already in 1881 Engels had described the expression "a fair day's wage for a fair day's work" as "the old time-honoured watchword of British industrial relations."[6]

The income policies, which operated in Britain in the sixties and seventies, paid careful attention to wage differentials, and the traditional distinction between "skilled" and "unskilled" workers seems to be universally accepted. It should therefore be possible to go further and develop some kind of graduated pay scale, such as was introduced into the Netherlands in the post-war years. It would take into consideration not only skill but such additional factors as length of training, mental and manual effort, risk and responsibility, efficiency and achievement, experience and length of service, together with working conditions (e.g., dirt, discomfort, danger and tedium). The mood of today is against outside interference, but not against a domestic arrangement, worked out by management and labor together, and covering the whole range of employees.

Meanwhile, there is manifest injustice in the status quo. More than five million employees in Britain are paid less than £4 an hour, and one million of these as little as £2.50. The national minimum wage, to which the new (1997) Labour government is committed, will take care of this. But what about the ridiculously high salary increases which some top directors regularly vote themselves? The Greenbury Committee was set up in 1995 in response to public anger over these, and the Cadbury Committee (set up in 1991) had examined the financial aspects of corporate governance in general. The recommendations of both committees were broadly supported by the TUC, except for two criticisms. First, the codes of practice they produced were voluntary, lacking any enforcement procedure. Secondly, primacy was given to the interest of shareholders, whereas all staff are "stakeholders." So what could be done? In 1996, in the colorful language of John Monks, General Secretary of the Trades Union Congress, "fat cat greed should be curbed by involving employee representatives on the remuneration committees which set top directors' pay. This would bring a sense of reality to their decisions."[7] He also stated the principle succinctly: "All staff in a company contribute to its performance, and while roles clearly differ, interdependence is at the heart of all good working relationships."[8]

I confess that I have admired the Scott Bader Commonwealth, ever since I first read about it in E. F. Schumacher's *Small Is Beautiful* (1973) and subsequently corresponded with Mr. Ernest Bader. Mr. Bader is a Quaker, who came to England from Switzerland before World War I. The company he founded is a leading producer of plastics, and in 1951 he converted it into a "Commonwealth" in which "there are no owners or employees" because they are "all co-owners and co-employees." In 1979 E. F. Schumacher (who was a director) wrote:

> We have settled the maximum spread between the highest paid and the lowest paid; that is, before tax. It may shock many people [egalitarians, he must mean] that, in spite of a lot of goodwill from all concerned, that spread is still one to seven. There is no pressure from the community that it should be narrowed, because it is understood that this spread is necessary. But of course this includes everybody, the lowest paid juvenile compared with the highest paid senior employee.

The scale is reviewed and fixed by "a sort of parliament of workers."[9]

There must be differentials. But unwarranted discrimination in pay, conditions or promotion, "unwarranted" because based on privilege not merit, must be abjured. It is incompatible with social justice and with the Christian ideal of mutual respect.

Increase Participation

It seems to be increasingly recognized that the workers in any enterprise, on whose skill and labor its success largely depends, should have a share in both decision making and profits. Although some directors and managers resist this, and naturally feel threatened by it, the principle accords with natural justice. I want to concentrate on the concept of decision making, since the Christian mind discerns in it a basic component of humanness.

However we define the "Godlikeness" of humankind, it will surely include the capacity to make choices and decisions. Adam in the Genesis story is certainly regarded, and therefore treated, by God as a morally responsible person. True, the first command addressed to him was identical with that addressed to the living creatures of the sea, namely "be fruitful and increase in number" (Genesis 1:22, 28), and the injunction to the fish did not denote that they had freedom of choice. Yet what animals do by instinct, humans do by free decision. The divine mandate to subdue the earth clearly implies responsibility, and a higher degree still is implicit in the words, "You are free to eat from any tree in the garden; but you must not eat from the tree of the knowledge of good and evil" (2:16–17). Here side by side are a liberal permission and a single prohibition. It was assumed that Adam was able both to distinguish between "You may" and "You may not," and to choose between them. Moreover God held him responsible for his choice.

Christian tradition has always taught this biblical truth, that moral freedom is an essential ingredient in the dignity of human personhood. "For the supreme mark of a person," wrote William Temple, "is that he orders his life by his own deliberate choice."[10] In consequence, he added, "society must be so arranged as to give to every citizen the maximum opportunity for making deliberate choices and the best possible training for the use of that opportunity. In other words, one of our first considerations will be the widest possible extension of personal responsibility; it is the responsible exercise of deliberate choice which most fully expresses personality and best deserves the great name of freedom."[11] Intuitively people know this. They want to be treated as adults with freedom to decide things for themselves; they know that if decision making is taken away from them, their humanness will be demeaned. They will be reduced either to a child instead of an adult, or to a robot instead of a person.

The essential difference between a "community" and an "institution" is that in the former members retain their freedom to choose, while in the latter it is to some degree taken away from them. Erving Goffman's interesting book *Asylums* is, strictly spreaking, an investigation into "the social situation of mental patients and other inmates."[12] But he begins with some general observations. What he calls a "total institution" is a place of residence or work where people "lead an enclosed, formally administered round of life."[13] This includes hospitals, orphanages, old people's homes, prisons, army barracks, boarding schools, monasteries and (I would have thought, although they are nonresidential) many factories. In such places, the day's activities are "tightly scheduled" and "imposed from above by a system of explicit formal rulings and a body of officials."[14] The key factor is the bureaucratic control, and the existence of a "basic split between a large managed group, conveniently called 'inmates,' and a small supervisory staff."[15] "Characteristically, the inmate is excluded from knowledge of the decisions taken regarding his fate."[16] Therefore in "total institutions" an inmate ceases to be "a person with adult self-determination, autonomy and freedom of action."[17]

So important is this principle, if Christians are to help create genuine community life and to protest against the dehumanizing effects of institutional life, that I will give several examples and then come back to our topic of industrial relations. Before looking at the factory from this perspective, we will look at the school or college, the hospital and the prison.

Christians distinguish sharply between education and indoctrination. Indoctrination is the process by which the leader imposes his or her viewpoint on the malleable mind of the child. In true education, however, the teacher acts as a catalyst to develop the child's ability to learn by observation and reasoning. The former is oppressive, the latter genuinely liberating. To be sure, the teacher cannot and should not adopt a position of complete neutrality, for children need guidance as they grow in discernment. Yet the crucial question is which mind is given pride of place—the teacher's mind as it instructs the children's minds, or the children's minds as they learn how to use them, in order to make their own value judgments and moral decisions. This process of self-education in interaction with teachers should be even more evident in universities and colleges, and also in churches where the preacher should never treat his congregation as nothing more than an absorbent sponge.[18] The students' demands of the 1960s also seemed substantially right, namely that, since it is their education which is at stake, they should have a say in academic questions such as those of curriculum and examinations, and an opportunity to evaluate their teachers' performance. School children and college students, as their age and maturity increase, should be given growing opportunities to make their own decisions.

Prison is very different, of course, because inmates have had their freedom taken from them, following a fair trial, by the judicial authority of a court. It cannot be right to treat prisoners as if they were free citizens. Nevertheless, they should not be treated as if they were slaves or robots either. They are still adult human beings, still persons who bear God's image, even while being punished for their offenses. I was struck by Chuck Colson's comments on this in one of the contributions he made to the 1979 London Lectures in Contemporary Christianity. Reflecting on his experience of incarceration, following his involvement in the Watergate cover-up, he said: "You make absolutely no decisions for yourself. The time of your meals, your work assignments—everything is decided for you. You have an overwhelming sensation of helplessness. Your individual identity is destroyed."[19]

Turning now to the medical field, there is a constant danger that the doctor-patient relationship, already unnatural because of the awe in which doctors are held, will degenerate further beyond paternalism to control. Patients remain persons, and when decisions have to be made affecting their health and even their life, they should be left free to make them. Although it is obviously difficult for doctors to explain to their patients complex medical conditions and procedures in nontechnical language, they are under obligation to do their best to do so; otherwise the notion of "informed consent" to treatment, surgery or research would be meaningless. According to the Nuremberg Code of 1946–49, "the voluntary consent of the human subject is absolutely essential." This means not only that there shall be no duress, but that he "should have sufficient knowledge and comprehension of the elements of the subject matter involved as to enable him to make an understanding and enlightened decision."[20] Similarly the 1964 Helsinki Declaration on human experimentation (drawn up by the World Medical Association) included the clause that "clinical research on a human being cannot be undertaken without his free consent after he has been fully informed."[21]

Yet patients often feel that they are being bypassed, and even manipulated, because they are kept in the dark about their condition and treatment and are consequently powerless. Solzhenitsyn gives us a moving example of this in Oleg Kostoglotov, the chief character he created in his book *Cancer Ward*.[22] Like Solzhenitsyn himself, Oleg had been in a concentration camp before he entered the cancer ward. Indeed, throughout the book Solzhenitsyn seems to be drawing a subtle parallel between prison and hospital, especially in the fact that neither prisoners nor patients are allowed to make any decisions for themselves. Oleg has a sturdy independence of mind and spirit, however. "Everything that's gone wrong in my life," he says, "has been because I was too devoted to democracy. I tried to spread democracy in the army, that is, I answered my superiors back."[23] Ludmila Afanasyevna Dontsova, who is in charge of the radiotherapy department, reacts strongly

45

against what she regards as his uncooperative attitude. "You will go home when I consider it necessary to interrupt your treatment," she says with great emphasis. "Ludmila Afanasyevna!" responds Oleg in exasperation. "Can't we get away from this tone of voice? You sound like a grown-up talking to a child. Why not talk as an adult to an adult? . . . You see, you start from a completely false position. No sooner does a patient come to you than you begin to do all his thinking for him. . . . And once again I become like a grain of sand, just like I was in the camp. Once again nothing depends on me."[24] Then later, writing to his friends and describing the ward's barred windows, bunk beds, terrified inmates, one-by-one processing, as if he were in prison, Oleg goes on: "By some right . . . they [the doctors] have decided, without my consent and on my behalf, on a most terrible form of therapy—hormone therapy."[25]

I return at last to industry and to industrial relations. I realize that western hospitals are not like those in the Soviet Union during Stalin's oppressive regime, and that in any case there are differences between factories on the one hand and schools, colleges, prisons and hospitals on the other. Nevertheless, I have been anxious to show that decision making is a basic right of human beings, an essential component of our human dignity.

The cry for industrial democracy, in order to facilitate a greater participation of workers in their own enterprise, does not make factories a special case, but is the expression within industry of the universal cry for the humanization of society. We now take political democracy for granted, and are grateful to those who struggled long to secure universal suffrage, so that ordinary citizens might share in governing their country and in making the laws they are then required to obey. Is not the propriety of industrial democracy equally self-evident? Already more than fifty years ago William Temple wrote: "The cause of freedom will not be established till political freedom is fulfilled in economic freedom."[26] He looked back with feelings of horror to the oppressive beginnings of the Industrial Revolution: "The pioneers showed little respect for the personality of those who earned their living by working in factories and mills. They were often called 'hands,' and a hand is by nature a 'living tool,' which is the classical definition of a slave."[27] Indeed, in a historic letter to the *Leeds Mercury* in 1830, Richard Oastler, a Christian landowner in Yorkshire, had the courage to draw this very analogy, three years before Wilberforce and his friends had secured the abolition of slavery in the British colonies. "Thousands of our fellow creatures and fellow subjects, both male and female, are at this moment existing in a state of slavery more horrid than the victims of that hellish system of colonial slavery." He went on to refer particularly to little children from seven to fourteen years of age, who were working thirteen hours a day in the factories, with only a half-hour break.[28]

We have come a long way in 170 years, thank God. And yet we still have some way to go. William Temple continued: "The worst horrors of the early factories have been abolished, but . . . the 'workers' usually have no voice in the control of the industry whose requirements determine so large a part of their lives."[29] He stated the principle in these clear terms: "Every citizen should have a voice in the conduct of the business or industry which is carried on by means of his labour."[30]

At the heart of many industrial disputes (so I understand from my reading) is the question of rules and rule -making—not just what the rules require or forbid, but who makes the rules and why. Management is often dictatorial in making or changing rules, regarding this as "managerial prerogative." Workers, on the other hand, usually go by what they call "C and P" (Custom and Practice), the unwritten but established conventions of the place. The Donovan Report emphasized the tension between these two systems, the "formal" (official agreements) and the "informal" (unwritten procedures), and expressed its dislike of this situation.[31] It is the difference between regulations and traditions, and so between two different kinds of authority, power wielded from above and common sense or custom from below.

Moreover, each side sees the need to legitimize its rules. This necessity is the particular emphasis of the book *Ideology and Shop-Floor Industrial Relations* (1981).[32] It discusses the process of legitimization in industrial relations, the arguments which each side uses to justify or challenge rules, and the ideology, worldview or value system which lies behind this process. Industrial relations are broader than rules and rule making, however. The whole policy and program of the company are concerned. It has to be admitted that in many companies the workers lack self-respect because they lack responsibility. They feel oppressed and powerless. The "them and us" mentality is enforced because other people make all the decisions (remote, faceless people), while their role is exclusively to react, and indeed to obey. The analogy with slavery, though very inexact, is yet instructive at this point. Christians opposed slavery because human beings are dehumanized by being owned by someone else. Christians now should oppose all forms of labor in which human beings are used by someone else. True, the evil is much smaller, because the work is undertaken voluntarily and is regulated by a contract. Yet it is a contract which diminishes humanness if it involves the relinquishing of personal responsibility and the undertaking to obey without consultation.

Christians will agree that at the very least there should be a procedure of consultation, and, more important, that this should not be a piece of window dressing but a genuine discussion early in the planning process which is reflected in the final decision. After all, production is a team process, in which the workers' contribution is indispensable; should not decision making be a team process too, in which the workers' contribution is equally indispensable? Self-interest undoubtedly lies at the root of each side's viewpoint.

Managers tend to begin their thinking with profit, on which the company's survival depends; whereas workers tend to begin with rising costs and therefore wages, on which their personal survival depends. Their different starting points are understandable. But in discussion each side comes to understand the other's legitimate concerns, and then to see that the two, far from being incompatible, are in fact interdependent.

Once the principle of worker-participation has been conceded, there can be a legitimate difference of opinion about the best ways and means to ensure it. The obligation to inform employees about the business is already imposed on firms by Company Law; the question is how much to consult them. A variety of structures have been advocated and tried, ranging from thorough consultation at all levels to the election of worker-directors.[33]

In response to a European Commission directive about employee-directors, the British Institute of Management during the chairmanship of Sir Fred Catherwood proposed in 1974 that every company should have a "works council" elected by all the employees. Two of its members would then be chosen (by agreement between council and board) to sit on the board of directors.[34]

Next, the Labour government appointed the Bullock Committee on Industrial Democracy. Its majority report (1977) recommended a positive partnership between management and labor, both in developing a corporate strategy for the company and in making and implementing decisions. They expressed themselves in favor of the company having employee-directors. But the minority led by Clive Jenkins insisted that the workers could be represented only by their unions and not by elected nonunionized employees. So there was a deadlock.

In May 1978 the Labour government issued a White Paper on Industrial Democracy, which accepted the principle of participation. If this government had had the opportunity to produce legislation on this basis, they would have (1) obliged employers in companies of more than five hundred employees to discuss with representatives of the workforce all major proposals affecting them, including plans for investment, merger, expansion and contraction; (2) encouraged companies to develop a two-tier board structure (a policy board and a management board) and to arrange for employees to be represented on the policy board; and (3) given a statutory right to employees in firms of more than two thousand to be represented on the policy board alongside the shareholders' representatives. A minority report disagreed, on the grounds of lack of evidence and size of risk.

Reactions to these proposals were mixed, though on the whole they were more hostile than friendly. The Confederation of British Industry, representing the employers, said they thought that the Bullock Committee had been given biased terms of reference and that they were more concerned to give workers control of the company than participation in it. The unions were negative because they believed board representation and collective bargaining to be fundamentally incompatible. Historically, it has been by collective bargaining that the trade unions have undermined the undisputed power of the employers and indeed secured some power of their own over wages and conditions of work. In other words, both sides understandably wanted to preserve their present power, even if this meant a continuing degree of confrontation.

Now the focus of attention has shifted to Europe. In 1989 the European Union's "Social Charter" (formerly the "Charter on the Fundamental Social Rights of Workers") was signed by all the member states, except Britain. It called for significant changes, but lacked the power of enforcement.

So in 1991 the "Social Chapter" of the Maastricht Treaty gave the charter a legal basis. Britain under John Major opted out, but the new (1997) Labour government is committed to opting in. The "Social Chapter" empowers the European Community to issue "directives" for the implementation of its policies. Thus, the Working Time Directive (1996) provides for a maximum working week of forty-eight hours, at least eleven consecutive hours' rest each day, one day's rest in seven, three weeks' paid leave a year, rising to four in 1999, and some other health and safety measures. Still more germane to our topic, the Works Council Directive (1996) requires the creation of works councils in companies which employ (a) more than one thousand people in one member state and (b) more than two hundred people in two. This deliberately includes multinationals. By January 1997, in spite of the British opt-out, the UK already had more than one thousand seats on nearly two hundred European works councils.[35]

I doubt if any Christian would disagree with the way Robin Woods, at that time Bishop of Worcester and Chairman of the Church of England's Board for Social Responsibility, summed the situation up in a letter to *The Times:* "It is consistent with Christian vision that society should develop in such a way that each person can exercise his God-given ability to make choices, to take responsibility, and to share in shaping his own environment. We believe that employees have a stake in their company which is at least as significant as that of the shareholders."[36]

The second kind of participation is profit sharing. Another clear biblical principle seems to be involved, namely that "the worker deserves his wages" (1 Timothy 5:18). Presumably then there should be some correlation between work and wage. If a company prospers, shared power (responsibility) should bring shared profit. If shareholders benefit from profit, so should workers, whether in bonuses of company stock or deferred benefits (e.g., pensions). The "pact" between the British Liberal and Labour parties at the end of the 1970s introduced the idea of tax incentives for firms which developed profit-sharing schemes.

The world pioneer in this area appears to have been Karl Zeiss of Jena, Germany, who in 1896 transferred the ownership of his firm to the workforce, while in the United States it was Sears, Roebuck, who in 1916 decided to use 10 percent of the firm's annual pretax profits to enable employees to buy its shares in the open market. In Britain, however, the credit for being first in the profit-sharing field seems to belong to the John Lewis Partnership in Oxford Street, London. John Lewis was twenty-eight years old when he opened a small drapery shop there in 1864. By the turn of the century his son Spedan had become troubled in conscience that he, his father and his brother as shareholders were jointly drawing from the business substantially more than all their employees put together. So he determined to devise a more equitable division of the rewards of industry, and in 1920 the first distribution of "Partnership Benefit" was made, representing an extra seven weeks of pay. Spedan Lewis later made two irrevocable settlements in trust for the benefit of the workers. From 1928 to 1970 the "Partnership Bonus" (as it is now called) was made in the form of stock, but since 1970 it has been wholly in cash. The company's policy is stated thus: "After paying preference dividends and interest, and providing for amenities, pensions and proper reserves, the remainder of the profits in any year is distributed to the members of the Partnership in proportion to their pay. In this way the profits are shared among all who work in the business." The percentage of the total profits applied to the Bonus rose from 12 percent in 1967 to 20 percent in 1980, and has been even higher since.

Such an arrangement was innovative in the twenties. Today similar profit-sharing arrangements or profit-linked share plans are multiplying in Britain and continental Europe. The "Wider Share Ownership Council" was established in 1958 to promote such projects.[37] Also, during the eighties, many large American corporations adopted "employee stock-ownership plans" (ESOPs), encouraged by tax incentives to do so. Cynics said that their real purpose was to gain the support of employee stockholders in resisting unwelcome takeover bids. But ESOPs also increase the stake which employees have in the company's future, encourage them (and through them their assistants) to work harder, and so boost its productivity and profits.

Both aspects of participation (decision making and profit sharing) appeal to the Christian mind on the ground not only of expediency (increased industrial peace and productivity) but also of justice (workers have a right to share in power and profits).

Emphasize Cooperation

The fundamental concept of mutual respect and mutual service, whose implications for industry we are exploring, should lead not only to the abolition of discrimination, but also to the increase of participation and so of cooperation.

Trade unions developed in the nineteenth century (with the active involvement of many Christians) to protect workers against exploitative bosses. Since workers had no rights under British Company Law at that time, they were forced to organize themselves from outside. Over the years they have secured great gains for labor, both in wages and in conditions. They were therefore absolutely necessary; without their sense of collective responsibility and their persistent struggles labor would probably still be exploited today.

Since the end of the 1970s, however, the unions have been steadily losing power in Britain. Various reasons have been given for this: (1) when manual workers are replaced by robots or computers, the skilled technicians who operate them are less unionized and less prone to strike action; (2) the rise of transnational corporations has made collective bargaining more difficult; (3) so has the spread of flextime, especially for women workers; (4) some unions have forfeited public sympathy by taking up a stance which is more political than industrial, by making unreasonable wage demands which further depress the economy, by strike action which causes inconvenience and even suffering to the innocent public and by violence in the picket lines. The Conservative government took advantage of these factors by introducing what became the Trade Unions Act 1984. Many people will agree that union power needed to be better controlled. At the same time, organized labor must have adequate mechanisms for the redress of injustices, and justice is by no means always on the side of the bosses. Many trade unionists work hard and long to find solutions to conflict in the face of incompetent or intransigent managers, and that patient work often goes unacknowledged.

The tragedy is, however, that the first loyalty of the workers tends to be given to their union rather than their firm, and that confrontation is still built into the very structures of industry. Why should we assume that this structural confrontation is inevitable and therefore everlasting? Why must the language of "winning" and "losing," whenever there is an industrial dispute, be perpetuated? Why should we not dream of, and work towards, the day when better structures will be developed which express cooperation? The Labour government's White Paper "Industrial Democracy," to which I have already referred, defined the goal as "a positive partnership between management and workers, rather than defensive co-existence." When management and labor are locked in confrontation, the public also suffers; when they cooperate in the service of the public, their relations to each other improve. But such a partnership is possible only if management and labor feel secure in their jobs, as we considered earlier. Insecurity grows when shareholders have no commitment to the company and behave like "absen-

51

tee landlords," for in such a situation the company is very vulnerable to a takeover. Security grows, however, when (as in continental Europe) shareholders become involved in and supportive of the companies they own.

I would like to give you an example of how the atmosphere and attitudes of a whole company can change, which illustrates some of the principles we have been considering.

Towards the end of the 1960s Gerald Snider, an American businessman, worked for a multinational company, whose identity it is not necessary to divulge. He found himself Vice President and General Manager of a group of European companies. He was in fact Acting President, since the ultimate responsibility for them was his.

He told me the story of one particular company which, when he assumed responsibility for it, was in extremely bad shape. The factory's product was inferior in design and quality. The plant was dirty, the machinery out-of-date and the environment bad. Although wages were competitive, the workers took little interest in their work and were suspicious of management, even hostile. Absenteeism was rampant. As many as 20 percent of the workforce did not show up on Mondays. In consequence, to make up for absenteeism, the plant was seriously overstaffed. Indeed, one of Gerald Snider's first acts was to declare four hundred of the eighteen hundred workers redundant. It was an extremely unpleasant task, but the only alternative would have been to close the plant down.

As he thought about the whole situation, it became clear to him that the fundamental cause of the factory's malaise was the bad relationships between the workers and their supervisors. To be sure, each employee maintained the required contact with those above and below him. But it was more a ritual than a relationship. The factory was organized by directives which descended from on high through five levels—from managing director through plant manager, personnel manager, supervisor and foreman to the production workers. There was no consultation and no intelligent, willing cooperation. Indeed, there were no genuine relationships at all.

Gerald Snider saw that, if the factory was to survive, it was necessary not only for the quality of its product to be acceptable to the marketplace, but for the employees at every level both to understand the company's objectives and to cooperate in order to achieve them. So he decided to take an unheard-of step. He would call the entire workforce together, in order to take them into his confidence and explain the situation to them. Immediately the most strenuous objections were raised. "It isn't done," he was told. "You fellows in the United States may get away with it, but in our country we don't do things that way." A whole week of discussion followed, in which managers and supervisors (who felt threatened by what they thought would be the undermining of their authority) advanced every contrary argument they could think of. But the General Manager was adamant.

So one day at 11:45 A.M., for a quarter of an hour of the company's time, everybody assembled in the factory's auditorium. Mr. Snider outlined the serious situation which had arisen on account of the poor quality of the product and the poor performance of the workforce. Indeed, of all the companies for which he was responsible in Europe, theirs showed the lowest production and the highest absenteeism. He then propounded his program for survival. On the one hand, the company was prepared to invest millions of pounds in modernizing equipment and tools, and in improving the work environment. On the other, he asked for their wholehearted cooperation. Absenteeism would have to stop. There could be no more Saturday work at double or treble time; what had to be done must be done during the working week.

Above all, he added, he was anxious to improve relationships and simplify communication between all levels. He was even now giving them a direct account of the factory's problems, goals and needs. He wanted them to have equally direct access to management and to him personally. For he was convinced that if mutual understanding could grow, mutual responsibility would grow with it. So, when the plant opened at seven o'clock the following morning, he would be there and available to them.

To his surprise, and to the personnel department's astonishment (since they had prophesied that the men would not accept a direct approach from the General Manager), his speech was greeted with loud applause. And when he walked through the factory early the following morning, already the old sullenness had gone. Men smiled as he passed. Some also made suggestions, especially the foremen, who occupy a key position between management and labor. A daily meeting between them began, which resulted in a number of useful suggestions. Another important decision was to close the two dining rooms previously reserved for executives and supervisors, so that everybody would eat in the same restaurant, sharing the same conditions and the same food and having the same opportunity to meet, know and trust one another.

Gradually, too, the General Manager's other promises were fulfilled. Modern equipment was installed. The factory was redecorated. The washrooms were cleaned. The new procedures for open communication continued to be fostered. So as the management's good faith became evident, the workers' good faith increased. Production went up significantly. Absenteeism was reduced from over 20 percent to under 5 percent. The quality of the product improved. The crisis was over.

Gerald Snider was brought up in a Christian home and has remained a practicing Christian. Although he modestly disclaims any self-conscious application of Christian principles to his business life, and although he did not put forward his proposals for the survival of his factory as a specifically "Christian" solution to the problem, nevertheless his actions reflected the teaching of the Bible. On the one hand, he was convinced of the dignity of work in God's intention ("If you can't enjoy your work, you shouldn't be there," he said to me). On the other, he recognized the value of human beings as God's supreme creation in his own likeness. In the production process, therefore, workers must not be treated as "objects," who receive directives from the top without explanation or consultation, but rather as "subjects," who are given the chance to understand their contribution to the whole enterprise, and who participate in it with a good will.

Cooperation cannot be engineered by itself; it is a by-product of a common vision and goal. This fact is increasingly recognized by those who pursue that elusive thing called "good management." The main emphasis of Thomas J. Peters and Robert H. Waterman in their best-selling book *In Search of Excellence* is the necessity, if a company is to succeed, of "shared values," which unite and motivate the entire workforce. After investigating the management techniques of America's sixty-two best-run companies, they developed the "7-S McKinsey Framework," which they present as an alliterative "managerial molecule." The six outer satellites are Strategy, Structure, Systems, Style, Staff and Skills, but the nucleus at the center, round which all these revolve, is Shared values, alternatively described as "superordinated goals."[38] One of the most vital of these is respect for people, both employees and customers. "Treating people—not money, machines or minds—as the natural resource" is of paramount importance.[39]

Japanese management has largely been built on this kind of American foundation. Why, then, is Japanese industry often more productive than American industry? What is the secret of the economic prowess of the Japanese? Richard Tanner Pascale and Anthony G. Athos set out to answer these questions in their book *The Art of Japanese Management.* In particular they investigated the Matsushita Electric Company. They found that this large corporation was using all the American principles of management (Japanese people joke that "BA" stands for "Been to America"!). But they also found something else. Matsushita has not only composed an "employees' creed" (which includes a reference to "the combined efforts and cooperation of each member of our Company") and seven "spiritual values" (one of which is "harmony and cooperation"), but has actually set these to music. "Matsushita was the first company in Japan to have a song and a code of values. 'It seems silly to Westerners,' says an executive, 'but every morning at 8:00 A.M., all across Japan, there are 87,000 people reciting the code of values and singing together. It's like we are all a community.'"[40]

Mr. Pascale and Mr. Athos recognize that this emphasis on cooperation has a strongly cultural origin. The Americans prize "independence," but the Japanese "interdependence." Of a person who has difficulties in relating to others, Americans say, "He hasn't found himself"; the Japanese, "He doesn't belong."[41] So all members of the workforce belong to a "work group" of about ten people, in which harmony is developed and to which loyalty is expected. It is not suggested that this kind of cultural arrangement can be transferred as is from Japan to Europe or America. Nevertheless, the contrast between the competitive individualism of the West and the productive cooperation of the East, which Richard Pascale and Anthony Athos describe, is surely significant. Company morale arising from shared values is easier to develop in small businesses; if huge corporations are to experience it, they may need to break into smaller autonomous units.

The shared values of a company will inevitably include a recognition of its multiple responsibilities. In his trailblazing books *The Future of Private Enterprise* (1951) and *The Responsible Company* (1961), George Goyder considered the alternatives of "a form of private enterprise based on the profit motive" and "a form of public enterprise called nationalization," and proposed "a third and better way through the creation of responsible industrial companies, neither wholly private nor wholly public."[42] His concern was to make companies accountable not only to their shareholders (which was at that time their only obligation according to Company Law in Britain), but also to their workers, their consumers and the community at large. Goyder went on to make proposals as to how this could be done legally, in particular by adding to the company's "Memorandum of Association" a clause which would define its general purposes. In order to bring private industry under social control without depriving it of freedom, he further suggested that every firm, in addition to an annual financial audit, should establish a triennial "social audit" relating to pricing policies (affecting consumers), labor relations (affecting employees) and local interests (affecting the community). "The social audit," he wrote, "is the natural result of business accepting its full responsibility."[43] Such a firm, being halfway between a private and a public company, might well be called "a Participating Company."[44]

In 1987 George Goyder produced a further book entitled *The Just Enterprise*, in which he emphasizes the social responsibilities of the company and defines it not just as "an instrument for maximizing profit in the interest of shareholders" but as "a wealth-creating organism in the service of the consumers, employees and the community as well as the shareholders."[45] It is this balance which makes an enterprise "responsible" or "just." In fact, "the creation of a sense of partnership in industry and commerce is the most urgent task facing us in domestic politics."[46] To this end what is needed, he writes, is (1) a general purposes clause relating specially to the company's duties to the customer, (2) an understanding that the directors are trustees, responsible to forward the interests of the company as a whole according to its defined purposes, (3) the opportunity for employees to become shareholders, (4) the transformation of the Annual General Meeting into a genuinely public democratic forum, in which "freely chosen representatives of the workers, consumers and the community" are allowed "not only to ask questions but to speak about corporate policy and comment on the chairman's statement,"[47] and (5) the "social audit" which must be an "independent appraisal of the company's social performance."[48]

It seems clear, then, that every company should define its goals and assign a priority order to them. In 1975 the Confederation of British Industry approved a report of its Company Affairs Committee entitled "The Responsibility of the British Public Company." Its paragraph 22 reads: "While law establishes the minimum standard of conduct with which a company must comply . . . a company like a person must be recognized as having functions, duties and moral obligations that go beyond the pursuit of profit and the specific requirements of legislation." So several organizations, and some individual companies, have issued a "Code of Practice" which summarizes their ideals and goals. For example, a thorough "Code of Business Ethics" has been produced by CABE, the Christian Association of Business Executives.[49]

Of course every firm must make a profit, but its priority concern should be the public whom the company (management, shareholders and workers together) exists to serve. Just as the first responsibility of hospital workers is their patients, of teachers their pupils, and of lawyers and social workers their clients, so the first responsibility of every business and industry is their customers—not just because the survival of the enterprise depends on pleasing the public, but because service to the public is its raison d'être. "Put most simply, a company exists to produce goods and services for its customers. . . . In a free society the consumer is king, and business exists to satisfy his needs."[50] In addition, the company itself is best served when management, labor and shareholders are united in serving the public. "If you serve them, they will serve you."

If the followers of Jesus Christ cannot develop relationships of respect and trust, across social barriers, we can hardly blame the world for failing. But improved relationships need not be limited to the Church. We should work expectantly for greater respect and cooperation in every segment of human society. We should not acquiesce in industrial conflict or be pessimistic about resolving it. For all human beings, though fallen and self-centered, have an inborn sense of dignity and justice. So better relations are possible.

3

The Multiracial
Dream

On 28 August 1963 Martin Luther King Jr., who was committed equally to nondiscrimination and to nonviolence, in other words to justice and peace, led a march of 250,000 people, three-quarters of whom were black and one-quarter white, to Washington, D.C. And there he shared his dream of a multiracial America:

> I have a dream that one day on the red hills of Georgia the sons of former slaves and the sons of former slave owners will be able to sit down together at the table of brotherhood.
>
> I have a dream that one day even the state of Mississippi, a state sweltering with the heat of injustice . . . and oppression, will be transformed into an oasis of freedom and justice.
>
> I have a dream that one day in Alabama, with its vicious racists . . . little black boys and black girls will be able to join hands with little white boys and white girls as sisters and brothers. . . .
>
> With this faith we will be able to transform the jangling discords of our nation into a beautiful symphony of brotherhood.
>
> With this faith we will be able to work together, to stand up for freedom together, knowing that we will be free one day . . . [1]

A third of a century has passed since then, and still the fulfillment lingers. Yet it is right for Christians to dream this dream. For God has given us in Scripture a vision of the redeemed as "a great multitude that no one could count, from every nation, tribe, people and language, standing before the throne" (Revelation 7:9). That dream, we know, will come true. Meanwhile, inspired by it, we should seek at least an approximation of it on earth, namely a society characterized by racial justice (no discrimination) and racial harmony (no conflict). Perhaps even the word "multiracial" is not specific enough, and "interracial" would be better, since the former South African Nationalist government used to describe its vision of separate "homelands" as "multiracial development," and that is not at all how the word should be used. A helpful definition of racial integration was given by Roy Jenkins when he was Home Secretary: "I define integration," he said, "not as a flattening process of assimilation, but as equal opportunity, accompanied by cultural diversity, in an atmosphere of mutual tolerance."[2]

Before considering some biblical teaching about race, I think we need to look at some examples of "racism," both historical and contemporary, and be aware of the false foundations on which it is built.

Slavery and the American Racial Problem

It is not possible to jump straight to the contemporary problem of race in Europe and America and ignore the evils of slavery and of the slave trade out of which it has largely sprung. Although slavery was abolished in the British colonies 165 years ago, no sensitive white Briton can meet a West African or West Indian without seeing them as probable descendants of slaves, or visit their countries without remembering the appalling traffic in human beings in which our country engaged for at least two hundred years. Similarly, no sensitive American can confront the race issue in the United States today without looking back beyond the Civil War to the cruelty and degradation of life on the plantations.

It is generally accepted that "the slave has three defining characteristics: his person is the property of another man, his will is subject to his owner's authority, and his labour or services are obtained through coercion."[3] Being regarded as nothing but movable and disposable property, slaves were normally deprived of elementary human rights, e.g., the right to marry or to own or bequeath possessions or to witness in a court of law. Although slavery of different kinds and degrees was universal in the ancient world, it is inexcusable that the professedly Christian nations of Europe (Spain and Portugal, Holland, France and Britain) should have used this inhuman practice to meet the labor needs of their New World colonies. Worse still, practicing Christians developed an elaborate defense of slavery on the grounds of social and economic necessity (there was no other source of labor in the colonies to provide raw materials for the Industrial Revolution in Europe), racial superiority (Negroes deserved no better treatment), biblical permission (Scripture regulates but nowhere condemns slavery), humanitarian benefit (the trade transferred slaves from African savagery to American civilization), and even missionary opportunity (African infidels would be introduced to Christianity in the New World). The blatant rationalizations of slave owners make one blush with embarrassment today.

The inherent evil of slavery (which in principle is the evil of racism also) is that it affronts, indeed denies, the Godlike dignity of human beings. Being the property of their owners, slaves were advertised for sale alongside horses and cattle, mules and pigs, corn and plantation tools. Having first been captured, chained and branded in West Africa, they were then shipped across the Atlantic in such overcrowded and unhygienic conditions that about half of them died during the passage. Then on arrival they were auctioned, forced to work, often separated from wife and children, if recalcitrant flogged, if escaped pursued by bloodhounds, and if caught killed.

Some writers argued that the reason why they were property is that they were animals. In his *The History of Jamaica* (1774) Edward Long developed the outrageous argument that in the Creator's "series or progression from a lump of dirt to a perfect man" African Negroes are inferior to human beings. "When we reflect on . . . their dissimilarity to the rest of mankind, must we not conclude that they are a different species of the same genus?"[4] The French author J. H. Guenebault went even further in his *Natural History of the Negro Race* (1837). Having given his opinion of the physical form and mental inferiority of Negroes, he wrote: "It is then impossible to deny that they form not only a race, but truly a species, distinct from all other races of men known on the globe." They belong to "the ape genus," he declared, and placed them somewhere between orangutans and white human beings.[5]

A third inferiority theory, popularized by Ulrich B. Phillips in his *American Negro Slavery* (1918), is that Negroes were neither property nor animals but children. He was evidently fond of his slaves in a paternalistic way, but could not take them seriously as adults. Stanley M. Elkins in his book *Slavery* (1959) examines the familiar image of the plantation slave as "Sambo." He was "docile but irresponsible, loyal but lazy, humble but chronically given to lying and stealing. . . . his relationship with his master was one of utter dependence and childlike attachment: it was indeed the childlike quality that was the very key to his being."[6] The Sambo stereotype was of "the perpetual child incapable of maturity."[7] Professor Elkins goes on to develop the thesis that Negro "infantilism" was due neither to race, nor to culture, nor even to slavery in general, but to the absolutist structure of the North American plantation system. He draws a striking analogy between the victims of North American slavery and those of Nazi concentration camps. For the latter (if they survived) were "reduced to complete and childish dependence upon their masters," namely the SS guards.[8] Thus, the same mechanism operated in Negro plantation and Nazi concentration camp, since both were hideous forms of slavery, and the victims of both were sub-jugated into infantilism.[9]

The horror of eighteenth-century slavery, then, was that it regarded adult men and women as tools, animals or children. In consequence, they were thought to have an inborn inferiority. Christian opponents of slav-ery found it necessary, therefore, to demonstrate that Negro slaves were human beings who were in no way inferior to others. So Wilson Armis-tead, a Quaker businessman from Leeds, subtitled his book *A Tribute for the Negro* (1848) in the following words: "A vindication of the moral, intel-lectual and religious capabilities of the coloured portion of mankind, with particular reference to the African race." He dedicated it to three Negroes and "many other noble examples of elevated humanity in the negro . . . beautifully designated 'the image of God cut in Ebony.'" His intention, he wrote, was to demonstrate "from facts and testimonies that the white and the dark coloured races of man are alike the children of one Heavenly Father and in all respects equally endowed by him," and to prove "that the negro is indubitably and fully entitled to equal claims with the rest of mankind."[10]

This brief excursus into slavery is far from being irrelevant. For racists, even if they concede the humanness of black people, nevertheless also hold that they have an inborn inferiority. They may defend their position as a so-called "scientific theory of race" or merely cherish "vague notions about a unilinear evolution from monkey to man" which encourage them to believe that such "races" are "lower" in the "scale" of evolution than is the group to which they belong; "that there is a hierarchy of 'races.'"[11] It was to demolish this illusion that Dr. Ashley Montagu wrote his defin-itive book *Man's Most Dangerous Myth: The Fallacy of Race.* Of course he agrees, as a physical anthropologist, that humankind may be divided into four "major groups" (Caucasoid, Mongoloid, Negroid and Australoid) and into many smaller "ethnic groups" (by nationality, language, culture, etc.). But he insists that these groups are arbitrary, overlapping and fluid; that they merely describe populations whose distinctions are due partly to cultural development (as a result of geographical separation) and partly to "temporary mixtures of genetic materials common to all mankind";[12] and that the differences are definitely not due to "inborn physical and mental traits" which are ineradicable.[13] Indeed, that concept of "race" is a superstition, "the witchcraft of our time,"[14] and a stratagem invented to justify discrimination.

Columbus Salley and Ronald Behm begin their book *What Color Is Your God?*[15] with three historical chapters tracing the development of the racial problem in America. The first ("Christianity and Slavery") takes us up to the Civil War (1863). The second ("Christianity and Segregation") runs from 1863 to 1914. This is the period following the Civil War, in which "Black

Codes" were formulated to give blacks some permissions, but to keep them weak and inferior. The Ku Klux Klan was formed, with shameful support from white racist Christians. White churches were segregated and silent, while black churches were conformist and otherworldly. The third period runs from 1914 to about 1980 ("Christianity and Ghettoization"). It began with the mass migration of blacks to the cities of the north and west, and the consequent "Great White Exodus" from the same cities. "Institutional racism" restricted blacks to certain areas and certain roles, and gave them inferior education, housing and employment. There were riots and lynchings. Again in this period, as in the previous ones, the Church was largely mute and ineffective. In the 1960s, however, the search for black identity and power led to the more organized Civil Rights movement, and so to the legislation which ended segregation and discrimination. Even this was only a beginning, however. In 1968 the National Advisory Commission on Civil Disorders, which had been appointed by President Lyndon B. Johnson, reported (the "Kerner Report"). Here is its conclusion: "Our nation is moving toward two societies, one black, one white—separate and unequal." Further, "segregation and poverty have created in the racial ghetto a destructive environment totally unknown to most white Americans. . . . White institutions created it, white institutions maintain it, and white society condones it." "Racism is American society's most exposed weakness," wrote Ashley Montagu. "It is America's greatest domestic failure, and the worst of its international handicaps."[16]

The 1990s opened with the bold experiment called "Affirmative Action," by which federal law required appropriate representation of black and ethnic minorities in education, employment and other situations. Since it appears to discriminate between Americans solely on racial grounds, however, it is judged by many to be unconstitutional and is being dismantled in some states in favor of a "color-blind" approach.

Two highly publicized trials in the early nineties involved African Americans, namely Rodney King (whose brutal beating by Los Angeles police was captured by a video camera) and O. J. Simpson (who was accused of murdering his ex-wife). The outcome was an almost complete polarization of the American public by color.

It is extremely regrettable that the Nation of Islam, now led by Louis Farrakhan, is both expressing and fomenting black nationalism. Yet we may be thankful that an increasing number of evangelical Christians are acknowledging racism as a sin and repenting of it. One of the seven promises undertaken by the Promise Keepers, in their huge rallies of men from all ethnic backgrounds, is to reach beyond racial barriers in order to demonstrate their unity in Christ.

German Anti-Semitism and South African Apartheid

Anti-Semitism in Germany and apartheid in South Africa seem at first sight so different from one another as to be entirely unsuitable for comparison. There is an obvious difference between Jews and blacks, for example, and in the laws relating to them. In particular, the unspeakable outrage of the "Holocaust" has had no parallel in South Africa. Nevertheless, although it will shock some readers to learn this, the theory of "race" on which both systems were built is almost identical. So is the sense which many Germans and South Africans have expressed that they are "destined to rule" and must at all costs preserve their racial "purity."

In *Mein Kampf*, published eight years before he came to power, Hitler had already extolled the splendor of the Aryan race.

> Every manifestation of human culture, every product of art, science and technical skill, which we see before our eyes today, is almost exclusively the product of the Aryan creative power. . . . it was the Aryan alone who founded a superior type of humanity. . . . he is the Prometheus of mankind, from whose shining brow the divine spark of genius has at all times flashed forth. . . .[17]

Borrowing his ideas from Wagner's dream of Germanic greatness, Nietzsche's notion of a "daring ruler race" and Darwin's concept of the ruthless struggle needed for survival, Hitler developed both his illusions of Aryan destiny and his insane phobia of the Jews, who, he declared, were economically, politically, culturally, religiously and morally destroying civilization.[18] The insulting and irrational language he used of them is unrepeatable. He dared even to claim that in dealing with them he would be acting on behalf of the Almighty Creator.[19] In this he was able to quote Christian scholars who had developed a "Creation Theology" to justify racism. Paul Althaus, for example, recognizing marriage, family, race and Volk as God's order of creation, wrote: "We champion the cause of the preservation of the purity of the Volk and of our Race."[20] Hitler himself knew, it seems, that this racial theory of Aryan Herrenvolk ("master race") had no scientific basis. In private he conceded this. Yet he continued to use it because he needed it as a politician: "With the conception of race, National Socialism will carry its revolution abroad and recast the world."[21]

The origins of the Afrikaners' sense of divine destiny are bound up with their history. When the Dutch first arrived at the Cape of Good Hope (1652), they saw themselves as the heirs and bearers of European Christian civilization. And when their Great Trek began in 1835, and they traveled in ox wagons north and east to escape from British rule, their conviction of a special destiny increased. They saw a parallel between themselves and the Old Testament people of God. Their trek was a new exodus, a divine deliverance from alien oppression, and on their arduous journey they were tested like Israel in the wilderness. The hostile black nations they had to overcome were their equivalent to the Amalekites and the Philistines. After the Battle of Blood River, in which they defeated the Zulus, they entered into a solemn covenant with God, and henceforth thought of the Transvaal and the Orange Free State as the promised land to which God had brought them. This sacralization of their early history imprinted itself on the Afrikaner consciousness. They thought of themselves as a chosen people, an elect nation. "Afrikanerdom is not the work of men," said Dr. D. F. Malan, the Nationalist leader who became Prime Minister in 1948, "but the creation of God."[22] Thus, Afrikaners believed that they had a Messianic vocation, that they were born to rule and that God had called them to preserve Christian civilization in Africa.

Added to their history (which gave them this sense of destiny) is their theology (which gave them their theory of race). It was this combination of history and theology which undergirded their determination to ensure their distinct survival by means of apartheid. For, said the Dutch Reformed Church (until 1989, see below), "the Scriptures . . . teach and uphold the ethnic diversity of the human race" and regard it as a "positive proposition" to be preserved. Consequently, "a political system based on the autogenous or separate development of various population groups can be justified from the Bible."[23] The way this view of separate development was presented was often evenhanded, for an equal concern was expressed that all racial groups would be preserved intact. Nevertheless, the impression was clearly given that the Nationalist government's primary concern was the preservation of white Afrikanerdom, and moreover in a position of superiority. Certainly Dr. Verwoerd was frank enough to say to Parliament in 1963: "Keeping South Africa white can mean only one thing, namely white domination; not leadership, not guidance, but 'control' supremacy."

The parallel between German National Socialists and South African Nationalists, then, which some will doubtless find offensive, really cannot be refuted (it is not an accident that a number of South African political leaders studied at German universities in the thirties). It lies in the resolve at all costs to maintain "racial purity," and to legislate for it by prohibiting mixed marriages. In *Mein Kampf* Hitler wrote that miscegenation was to be opposed with the utmost vigor, in order to preserve the purity of Aryan stock. Intermarriage, he declared, invariably causes physical and mental degeneration. It "is a sin against the will of the Eternal Creator."[24] In South Africa the Prohibition of Mixed Marriages Act became law in 1949. It made marriage between "Europeans and non-Europeans" (i.e., between "whites" and "nonwhites") illegal, while an Act of 1968 extended this law to include South African male citizens domiciled outside the country. Professor Dupreez tried to give this legislation a theological basis. "Is it God's will," he asked, implying that it is not, "that all the nations he has created in such rich diversity should now be equalized and assimilated, through inter-marriage, to a uniform and mixed race?"[25]

In response to this Nazi and South African fear of "bastardization," two points need to be made. First, there is no such thing as pure racial stock. We are all of us mongrels. "Not one of the major human groups is unmixed, nor is any one of its ethnic groups pure; all are, indeed, much mixed and of exceed-ingly complex descent."[26] "Pure British blood," for example, is a figment of the imagination. At the very least we are a mixture of Jute, Celt, Goth, Saxon, Roman and Norman. And there is certainly a small percentage (6 percent) of black blood in Afrikaners. Secondly, as Ashley Montagu puts it,

> one of the most strongly entrenched popular superstitions is the belief that interbreeding or crossing between "races" . . . results in inferior offspring. . . . The commonly employed stereotype has it that the half-caste inherits all the bad and none of the good qualities of the parental stocks. . . . There is not a particle of truth in any of these statements. . . . The truth seems to be that, far from being deleterious to the resulting offspring and the generations follow-ing them, interbreeding between different ethnic groups is from the biologi-cal and every other standpoint highly advantageous to mankind. . . . It is through the agency of interbreeding that nature in the form of man's genetic system shows its creative power.[27]

Christians will dislike both Dr. Montagu's personification of "nature" and his references to "interbreeding" (a word more appropriate to animals than humans), but these expressions in no way affect the point he is mak-ing. He goes on to quote Lord Bryce in 1902 that "all the great peoples of the world are the result of a mixing of races,"[28] and then gives numerous examples, like crosses between Tahitian women and the English mutineers from the *Bounty*, between Australian aboriginals and whites, between American Indians and Europeans, between black and white Americans, the ethnic mixture in Hawaii, and so on.[29]

Change in South Africa

During the second half of the eighties in South Africa a number of Chris-tian statements were issued and a number of events took place which, although expressive of different viewpoints, gave ground for hope that the whole apartheid structure would be completely destroyed.

In September 1985 Michael Cassidy and nearly four hundred other Chris-tian leaders from a variety of races and denominations launched the National Initiative for Reconciliation. Describing the Church as "a community of hope," its statement affirmed the sovereignty of God, called for humility, repentance, prayer and fasting before the Cross, espoused non-violence even at the cost of suffering and urged President Botha to end the State of Emergency, release detainees and begin talks with representative leaders with a view to eliminating discrimination.

A few weeks later a group of about 150 black theologians issued the Kairos Document. Passionate in concern and shrill in tone, it sought to relate liberation theology to the *kairos*, the contemporary South African crisis, and outlined the three options. The first it called the "State Theology" of the Afrikaner churches, which justified the racist status quo by an appeal to Romans 13, the need for "law and order" and the threat of communism. This theology, it declared, "is not only heretical, it is blasphemous." Secondly, there was the "Church Theology" of the English-speaking churches which, though cautiously critical of apartheid, sought reconciliation without repentance, and peace without justice. This too was rejected. The third option (which was ardently commended) was a "Prophetic Theology." Claiming to return to the Bible and its prophetic tradition, it identified the nationalist government as "the oppressor" and declared it guilty of such tyranny that it had forfeited its legitimacy. The right stance to adopt towards such a regime, therefore, was not negotiation but confrontation. The document ended with a "challenge to action" through the Church's solidarity with the oppressed, and through campaigns and protests, civil disobedience and participation in the armed struggle for liberation.

In July 1986 130 black "Concerned Evangelicals" published their hard-hitting Evangelical Witness in South Africa. Consciously interacting with the Kairos Document, although not specifically addressing it, they wrote a courageous, outspoken essay in evangelical self-criticism. For here were black evangelicals deliberately identifying with their white fellow-evangelicals in order to condemn the whole evangelical constituency for its Greek dualism (being concerned for people's "spiritual," as opposed to their "material," welfare), its western capitalistic conservatism, its pursuit of reconciliation without repentance, its misuse of Romans 13 to defend the status quo, the patronizing attitude of whites (even many missionaries) to blacks, ulterior motives in evangelism (especially to secure the subservience of black converts to an unjust regime) and gospel preaching which was silent about the brutalities of the apartheid system. Alongside these criticisms, "Evangelical Witness" called for true repentance. That is, it made a radical and comprehensive demand for change.

Then in October 1986 the Dutch Reformed Church issued "Church and Society," which was a "Testimony" approved by its synod. It was a thorough exposition of "Basic Scriptural Principles" and "Practical Implications," in the course of which the following astonishing statements were made: "Racism is a grievous sin which no person or church may defend or practise. . . . As a moral aberration, it deprives a human being of his dignity, his obligations and his rights. It must be rejected and opposed in all its manifestations" (para. 112). Again, "apartheid . . . a forced separation and division of peoples, cannot be considered a biblical imperative. The attempt to justify such a prescription as derived from the Bible must be recognized as an error and be denounced" (para. 305), for it "contravenes the very essence of neighbourly love and righteousness, and inevitably the human dignity of all involved" (para. 306). This was an extraordinary about-face for a church which previously had supported and defended apartheid.

It seems to be of great significance that in 1985 and 1986 these four Christian documents, in spite of the distinction between so-called "state," "church" and "prophetic" theologies, should all have condemned apartheid as an indefensible system and have committed themselves to its abolition. Their united witness and protest must have had a significant influence on the government.

During this same period some important events, in the state rather than the Church, also took place. In 1986 the hated Pass Laws, which for forty years had required nonwhites to carry their pass books and which had decreed where they might live and work, were abolished. Then in March 1989 a distinguished judicial commission, appointed by the government and chaired by Mr. Justice Olivier, called in its report (1) for the total dismantling of apartheid, (2) for the repeal of two of its main legal pillars, the Group Areas Act (which forbade residential integration) and the Population Registration Act (which made classification by race compulsory), both passed in 1950, and (3) for a universal franchise which would inevitably lead to black majority rule. The same year Mr. F. W. de Klerk replaced Mr. P. W. Botha as President and immediately signaled the direction in which he intended to move by releasing some long-imprisoned leaders of the African National Congress (though not at first intending to release its acknowledged senior leader, Nelson Mandela), and by turning a blind eye to the ANC marches and rallies which followed. Meanwhile, the whole world, outraged by the continuance of apartheid and what Michael Cassidy called "its dehumanizing awfulness,"[30] was waiting, hoping, praying and agitating for the multiracial society which must one day take its place.

During the 1990s, with almost bewildering speed, the structures of apartheid were dismantled and a democratic South Africa was born. In 1990 Nelson Mandela was released from prison after twenty-six years, talks began between the Nationalist Party and the African National Congress, the state of emergency was lifted and the ANC agreed to cease their armed struggle. At the same time violence continued, much of it between the ANC and the Zulu "Inkatha" movement, fueled by white police.

In 1991 Nelson Mandela was elected ANC president without opposition, and a significant turning point was reached when official multiparty talks began at the Convention for a Democratic South Africa (CODESA). In 1992 the National Party's referendum resulted in a 69 percent vote for a continuation of the reform process initiated by President F. W. de Klerk. But CODESA reached a stalemate, and serious Inkatha violence led to strike action by the ANC. By the end of the year, however, official negotiations had resumed, culminating in plans for a five-year power-sharing "Government of National Unity." It was fitting that the 1993 Nobel Peace Prize was awarded jointly to Nelson Mandela and F. W. de Klerk. The general election of 27 April 1994 won the ANC 252 of Parliament's 400 seats, brought Nelson Mandela to the presidency and paved the way for a new constitution.

The Truth and Reconciliation Commission was brought into being in 1995, with Archbishop Desmond Tutu as its chairman. It has been a remarkable initiative inspired by Christian principles and based on the final clause of the Interim Constitution which reads:

> This Constitution provides a historic bridge between the past of a deeply divided society characterised by strife, conflict, untold suffering and injustice, and a future founded on the recognition of human rights, democracy, peaceful co-existence and development opportunities for all South Africans, irrespective of colour, race, class, belief or sex.

The Commission rightly brackets "truth" and "reconciliation," since its primary brief has been to investigate, discover and publish the truth about human rights violations, as the only basis on which the perpetrators could be forgiven and their victims (or their relatives) could receive both limited reparation and the restoration of honor and dignity. Reconciliation is offered to those (1) who have offended against human rights between 1960 and 1995, (2) whose offense was politically motivated, (3) who make a full disclosure of all the relevant facts and (4) who apply for amnesty.

British Attitudes and Tensions

There is no need to deny that British colonial rule brought some positive good to the countries colonized, not so much in material terms (e.g., roads and railways), as in education, health care and standards of public justice. Yet these benefits have tended to be eclipsed by the offensive attitude of superiority implicit in "the British Raj mentality." Sometimes, I regret to say, this was expressed in racial terms ominously reminiscent of the German and South African outlook we have just considered. Cecil Rhodes, for example, spoke of "the predominance of the Anglo-Saxon race" and of the need to preserve it. And successive British Secretaries of State for the

Colonies talked similarly, even using the language of "destiny," although fortunately such an illusion was never embodied in official policy.

Racial pride remained, however. Consequently, as Margery Perham demonstrated in her 1961 Reith Lectures *The Colonial Reckoning*, Africans felt themselves to be "humiliated rather than oppressed," and the East African cry for *uhuru* (freedom) was not primarily for political independence but for personal dignity.[31] Similarly, to Jomo Kenyatta the quest for the independence of Kenya was "not just a question of Africans ruling themselves, though that was the first thing," but also "an end to the colour bar, to the racist slang of the settler clubs, to the white man's patronizing attitudes of half a century and more."[32] At a political rally at Wundanyi in January 1962 Kenyatta said about his attitude to Europeans: "I am not against anyone. I am only against *ubwana*, the boss mentality."[33]

This British boss mentality was perhaps even more obvious in India. Paul Scott has brought it to life in his "Raj Quartet" novels on the decline and fall of British India, perhaps specially in the first, *The Jewel in the Crown*. Its hero is Hari Kumar (whose name is anglicized as "Harry Coomer"), who was sent for a while to a public school in Britain and on his return home experienced a painful tension between his English and Indian identities. The British élite looked through him. He felt he had become invisible to white people, for "in India an Indian and an Englishman could never meet on equal terms."[34] It would be hard to resist Arnold Toynbee's verdict that "the English Protestant rulers of India . . . distinguished themselves from all other contemporary Western rulers over non-Western peoples by the rigidity with which they held aloof from their subjects."[35]

The British colonial record is a necessary background to understanding the last forty years of racial tensions in Britain. It may be dated from 1958, when racial conflict flared up in Notting Hill, London, and in Nottingham, and may be considered under the headings of immigration, race relations and institutional racism.

Immigration

It was the British Nationality Act of 1948 which defined a British citizen as anybody who had been born in Britain or in a British colony, and which gave citizens freedom of entry and settlement. From then onwards, however, British immigration law has become steadily more restrictive and racially motivated. The Commonwealth Immigrants Act of 1962 removed the automatic right to enter and settle, although the Act of 1968 gave it to some East African Asians during the Kenyan government's program of Africanization. The Immigration Act of 1971 went further and introduced a distinction between "patrials" (with at least one grandparent who had been born in the UK) and "non-patrials," giving the former the right of entry but denying it to the latter even if they had lived in Britain for years. Of course every country has the right and duty to limit the number of immigrants it can welcome. What made many Christians ashamed about this legislation, however, was first that it reduced some former citizens to the status of aliens and secondly that it was weighted against colored immigrants (e.g., no restriction was placed on immigrants from the Republic of Ireland). The churches protested vigorously against this concealed racism, which is what released cabinet papers have shown it to be. At the same time, we were very thankful that in 1972 Ugandan Asians evicted by Idi Amin were granted a free entry into Britain.

The British Nationality Act of 1981, however, traveled further down the road of restriction. It formally abolished the *jus soli* ("law of the soil"), which for hundreds of years had granted British citizenship to all those born on British territory. In its place the Act established three distinct citizenship categories. "British citizenship" was granted only to those whose parents were British or "settled" (with unrestricted stay). The other two categories were "British Dependent Territory citizens" and "British Overseas citizens," who would be mostly colored people and would have no right of abode. Despite lobbying by the churches, this Act failed to express the true, multiracial, character of British society.[36]

These thirty-five years of restrictive immigration law have caused acute suffering to many innocent people. For example, the abolition of the *jus soli* means that an appreciable number of families, whose children were born in the UK and have been brought up here for even ten to fifteen years, no longer have the right of abode and have had to face the trauma of deportation. The booklet "Breaking up the Family" (Churches Commission for Racial Justice) provides several case studies. The number of deportations reached a peak of five thousand in 1993.

Another special case is that of asylum seekers. Church leaders fought hard against the 1996 Asylum and Immigration Bill during its passage through Parliament. They secured some amendments, but in substance it remains unchanged and is harsh towards innocent people whose only fault is that they are seeking asylum. Many have even been held in detention (i.e., prison) without trial.

The CCRJ paper "The Churches, Immigration Law and Sanctuary" (1995) recommends amnesty as a compassionate alternative to deportation, and supports those churches which—as a last resort—offer sanctuary to people threatened with deportation, provided that (1) there is "a well-founded fear of persecution" or (2) there is "a serious threat to family life" or (3) there would be "a basic denial of justice and compassion."

New Labour's 1997 election manifesto promised to streamline appeals by visitors denied a visa, and to make their "immigration and asylum procedures far more fair and efficient." Jack Straw, Home Secretary, has also promised to recognize a new offense of "racial harassment." We now wait hopefully for these promises to be redeemed.[37]

Race Relations

The sixties and seventies, in which the British government's immigration policy was developed, were also the period of race relations law. Indeed, Christian observers see a fundamental incompatibility between them, in that the Immigration Acts were racially discriminatory, while the Race Relations Acts aimed at promoting racial harmony. Yet this reflected the inconsistencies of British society in which the voices of both fanaticism and moderation could be heard. On the one hand, racial tension was fomented by Enoch Powell's speeches and by the National Front. On the other, there was a widespread desire for interracial respect and peace. Enoch Powell was MP for Wolverhampton South West, near Birmingham. He spoke of the "madness" of allowing such a large inflow of colored immigrants, of "watching the nation heaping up its own funeral pyre," of "seeing the River Tiber foaming with much blood" and of Britons "becoming strangers in their own country."

In 1967 the National Front was formed out of a coalition of extreme right-wing movements. Its declared policy was to halt immigration, promote the repatriation of colored immigrants, support white Rhodesia and fight communism. Its leaders (Colin Jordan, John Tyndall and Martin Webster) had all been involved in Nazi activities and been ardent admirers of Hitler. Here are some representative statements which these three leaders have made. Colin Jordan said in 1959, "I loathe the Blacks—we're fighting a war to clear them out of Britain."[38] John Tyndall (chairman of the National Front until 1974) wrote a pamphlet in 1966 entitled "Six Principles of British Nationalism," whose fourth was concerned with the preservation of the British "race": "We therefore oppose racial integration and stand for racial separateness."[39] And Martin Webster wrote in 1975 that "racialism is the only scientific and logical basis for nationalism. . . . we seek to preserve the identity of the British nation. . . . If the British people are destroyed by racial interbreeding, then the British nation will cease to exist."[40] It is not difficult to detect in these intemperate utterances the same myth of racial purity and racial superiority which found expression in Nazi policy and in the doctrine of apartheid. I am heartily ashamed to have to record that this myth is held by anyone in Britain, even though the National Front is only a tiny minority.

The British National Party, founded in 1982, is larger, however, and even put up more than fifty candidates for the 1997 General Election. Although it avoids the insolent racial rhetoric of the National Front, its manifesto calls

for a ban on the immigration of nonwhites, and for the repatriation or reset-
tlement of nonwhites already here, until Britain becomes "a white country" again.

But the mood of the country as a whole was much more accurately mirrored in the laws governing race relations. The 1968 Race Relations Act created the Race Relations Board, whose brief was both to investigate complaints of racial discrimination and to promote racial integration. Then the
1976 Race Relations Act created the Commission for Racial Equality, which
was given some teeth to enforce the law; made it unlawful to discriminate
on the basis of race in such areas as employment and education; made
"incitement to racial hatred" a criminal offense; gave local authorities the
responsibility to eliminate discrimination and to promote equal opportunity and racial harmony; and permitted "positive action" in favor of ethnic
minorities, e.g., in training schemes.

Granted the existence of these two contradictory moods (the one inflam-
matory and the other conciliatory), it is hardly surprising that they came
into collision. Already in 1976 and 1979 there were clashes in Southall (West
London) fueled by the National Front. And more serious street riots broke
out between 1980 and 1983 in Bristol, Brixton (South London), Toxteth (Liverpool), Manchester, Nottingham, Leeds and other cities. Local social workers attributed the violence to widespread bitterness over the racially prej-
udiced British Nationality Act (1981) and over the decay and deprivation
of the inner city, involving disadvantage to blacks in housing, education
and employment.

Lord Scarman was commissioned by the Home Secretary to investigate
and report. He concluded that these communal disturbances were not pre-
meditated, but spontaneous, and that "there was a strong racial element in
the disorders." In short, "the riots were essentially an outburst of anger and
resentment by young black people against the police."[41] This statement iden-
tifies two main problems, the first social and racial and the second the behavior of the police. As to the former, Lord Scarman concluded: "'Institutional
racism' does not exist in Britain; but racial disadvantage and its nasty associate, racial discrimination, have not yet been eliminated. They poison minds
and attitudes: they are, and so long as they remain will continue to be, a
potent factor of unrest."[42] He recommended temporary reverse discrimination—that is, discrimination in favor of ethnic minorities—in order to
redress this balance.

Institutional Racism

There was general appreciation for the Scarman Report on account of its
candor and lack of bias. Lord Scarman had approached the Brixton situa-

tion without prejudice or presuppositions and had listened carefully to all opinions. This did not prevent people, however, from disagreeing (even incredulously) with his statement that there was no "institutional racism" in Britain. Our reaction will of course depend on our definition, but "institutional racism" is normally taken to denote a racial discrimination which goes beyond personal attitudes and is embedded in social structures. This certainly exists in Britain. Two examples will suffice.

The first concerns the police and the whole criminal justice system. Lord Scarman himself alluded to this. He conceded that "a major cause of the hostility of young blacks towards the police was loss of confidence by significant sections, though not all, of the . . . public in the police."[43] Whether justified or not, criticisms of racial prejudice and harassment were frequently leveled at them. Criticism is directed not only at the personal racist attitudes of some police officers and at the widespread abuse of their stop-and-search powers, but also at the injustices which black people believe to be ingrained in the system. David Haslam writes: "Once black people are arrested and charged, it becomes increasingly difficult for them to demonstrate their innocence. Many say it feels as if it is for them to prove their innocence rather than for the police to prove their guilt."[44]

Here are further aspects of institutional racism in the justice system which are extremely disturbing. (1) Far too few police officers come from ethnic minorities—less than 3 percent of the Metropolitan Police, for example. There are also too few black judges and magistrates. (2) The Police Complaints Authority is not the entirely independent body it claims to be. Its members are appointed by the Home Secretary, and it is a case of police investigating police. Lord Scarman picked this up. He recommended greater police accountability and the introduction of a genuinely independent element into the police complaints procedure. (3) There have been too many unexplained deaths in police custody and too many miscarriages of justice. (4) In too many major assaults on, and even murders of, black people the perpetrators have not yet been apprehended several years later. Some are notorious cases of murder like those of Stephen Lawrence, Quddus Ali and Muktar Ahmed.

Unemployment is the second area in which racism is institutional as well as personal. In his 1977 book *Racial Disadvantage in Britain,* David J. Smith stated that in employment "there is still very substantial racial discrimination against Asians and West Indians," and that this was "mostly based on colour prejudice."[45] In the 1980s Bishop David Sheppard reported the same thing: "Rates of unemployment for black people are generally more than double those for all workers of the same age group."[46] The same disproportion has continued into the 1990s, and has even deteriorated. *Labour Market Trends* (June 1996) reported that white unemployment was 9.5 percent for men and 6.5 percent for women, whereas the corresponding figures for people from ethnic minorities were 20 percent for men and 17 percent for women—"a vast and shocking difference."[47] Worse still is the unemployment rate among blacks under 25: it is nearly three times higher than among whites. John Monks, General Secretary of the Trades Union Congress, was not exaggerating when he called the level of racial discrimination in the jobs market "intolerable."[48] The Churches' Commission for Racial Justice is rightly encouraging companies to adopt the so-called "Wood-Sheppard Principles on Race Equality in Employment." Named after Bishop Wilfred Wood of Croydon, the Church of England's first black bishop, and Bishop David Sheppard, formerly Bishop of Liverpool, these principles call for "positive action" to redress the current inequalities.[49]

In sum, racism can be both personal and institutional. It also has two origins. One is a pseudo-scientific myth, and the other is pure prejudice. The myth, which is foundational to Hitler's anti-Semitism, South Africa's apartheid and Britain's National Front, was defined by UNESCO in 1967 as a "false claim that there is a scientific basis for arranging groups hierarchically in terms of psychological and cultural characteristics that are immutable and innate." The popular prejudice is not based on any particular theory, but is a psychological reaction to people of other ethnic groups arising usually from resentment, fear or pride.

What is needed is an equally powerful conviction that racism is an affront to the unique dignity of human beings. Nothing I have read has helped me to understand better the damage which racism does to people than *The Autobiography of Malcolm X*. His red-hot anger was due in part to "the world's most monstrous crime" of slavery, in part to the black American's economic dependence on white America, but above all to the humiliation caused by the white man's "malignant superiority complex."[50] The problem, he writes, is not "civil rights" but "human rights":

Human rights! Respect as human beings! That's what the American black masses want. That's the true problem. The black masses want not to be shrunk from as though they are plague ridden. They want not to be walled up in slums, in the ghettoes, like animals. They want to live in an open, free society where they can walk with their heads up, like men and women.[51]

In his well-researched and passionate book *Race for the Millennium: A Challenge to Church and Society*, David Haslam has a chapter entitled "The Necessity of Struggle." In it he outlines "three stages through which white people need to go before true reconciliation can occur." The first is "listening to black people," the second "repenting of white sin," and the third "responding in committed, sacrificial action to the inequalities and injustices to which black people are subject."[52] Only then, he writes, does "the opportunity for reconciliation" arise.[53]

73

There are encouraging signs that we who belong to the Church's evangelical community are at last waking up to our racial responsibilities. Evangelical Christians for Racial Justice was founded in 1972 and over the years has maintained a conscientious witness. Its "Christian Manifesto on Race" is based on six principles: (1) the human race is one race; (2) the human race is diverse; (3) the human race is fallen; (4) Christ died for all and is Lord of all; (5) the Christian Church is a new humanity in Christ; (6) God's people should seek justice for all.

Moreover, in preparation for the National Assembly of Evangelicals which met in Bournemouth in November 1996, an Evangelical Alliance consultation survey revealed that 62 percent of member churches and 70 percent of member societies agreed that "addressing racial injustice in the UK should be a higher priority for the evangelical churches than at present." The Bournemouth Declaration also acknowledged our shared responsibility "to oppose all forms of racism in church and society."

Biblical Foundations for Multiracialism

We turn from the realities of racial mythology, prejudice and tension in the contemporary world to the biblical vision of a multiracial society. It was thoroughly developed by the apostle Paul in his famous sermon to the Athenian philosophers (Acts 17:22–31). Ancient Athens was a center of ethnic, cultural and religious pluralism. From the fifth century B.C. it had been the foremost Greek city-state, and when it was incorporated into the Roman Empire, it became one of the leading cosmopolitan cities in the world. As for religions, it is easy to understand Paul's comment that the Athenians were "very religious," for according to a Roman satirist, it was "easier to find a god there than a man." The city was crammed with innumerable temples, shrines, altars, images and statues.

What then was Paul's attitude to this multiracial, multicultural and multireligious situation? He made four affirmations.

First, he proclaimed the unity of the human race, or *the God of Creation*. God is the Creator and Lord of the world and everything in it, he said. He gives to all human beings their life and breath and everything else. From one man he made every nation of men, that they should inhabit the whole earth, so that human beings would seek and find him, though he is not far from any of us. For "in him we live and move and have our being" and "we are his offspring." From this portrayal of the living God as Creator, Sustainer and Father of all humankind, the apostle deduces the folly and evil of idolatry. But he could equally well have deduced from it the folly and evil of racism. For if he is the God of all human beings, this will affect our attitude to them as well as to him.

Although in terms of an intimate personal relationship God is the Father of those he adopts into his family by his sheer grace, and our brothers and sisters are fellow members of his family, nevertheless in more general terms God is the Father of all humankind, since all are his "offspring" by creation, and every human being is our brother or sister. Being equally created by him and like him, we are equal in his sight in worth and dignity, and therefore have an equal right to respect and justice. Paul also traces our human origin to Adam, the "one man" from whom God made us all. This is confirmed by the known homogeneity of the human race, which is asserted even by scholars who have no belief in Adam. Here is the statement of Ashley Montagu, the physical anthropologist: "Concerning the origin of the living varieties of man we can say little more than that there are many reasons for believing that a single stock gave rise to all of them. All varieties of man belong to the same species and have the same remote ancestry. This is a conclusion to which all the relevant evidence of comparative anatomy, palæontology, serology and genetics points."[54] As for human blood, apart from the four blood groups and the Rh factor (which are present in all ethnic groups), "the blood of all human beings is in every respect the same."[55]

This human unity is not destroyed by interbreeding. We should totally reject the fears of miscegenation entertained by Afrikaners and Hitler's biological myth which is being revived by the National Front. In 1964 John Tyndall launched the "Greater Britain Movement," whose official program said: "For the protection of British blood, racial laws will be enacted forbidding marriage between Britons and non-Aryans. . . . A pure, strong, healthy British race will be regarded as the principal guarantee of Britain's future."[56] But there is no such substance as "British blood."

Secondly, Paul proclaimed the diversity of ethnic cultures, or *the God of History*. The living God not only made every nation from one man, that they should inhabit the earth, but also "determined the times set for them and the exact places where they should live" (Acts 17:26; cf. Deuteronomy 32:8). Thus, the times and the places of the nations are in the hand of God. We may not use this fact to justify the conquest and annexation of foreign territory, although even these historical developments are not beyond God's sovereign control. Probably Paul is alluding to the primeval command to multiply and fill the earth, for such dispersal under God's blessing inevitably resulted in the development of distinctive cultures, quite apart from the later confusing of languages and the scattering under his judgment at Babel.

Now culture is the complement of nature. What is "natural" is God-given and inherited; what is "cultural" is man-made and learned. Culture is an amalgam of beliefs, values, customs and institutions developed by each society and transmitted to the next generation. Human cultures are ambiguous because human beings are ambiguous. "Because man is God's creature, some of his culture is rich in beauty and goodness. Because he is fallen, all of it is tainted with sin and some of it is demonic."[57]

Scripture celebrates the colorful mosaic of human cultures. It even declares that the New Jerusalem will be enriched by them, since "the kings of the earth will bring their splendor into it," and "the glory and honor of the nations will be brought into it" (Revelation 21:24, 26). If they will enrich human life and community in the end, they can begin to do so now. Paul was a product of three cultures. By descent and upbringing a "Hebrew of the Hebrews," he also possessed Roman citizenship and had absorbed Greek language and concepts. We too can enhance our human life by learning other languages and experiencing other cultures. We need to ensure, therefore, that a multiracial society is not a monocultural society. We must simultaneously assert both the unity of the human race and the diversity of ethnic cultures.

The South African Nationalist Party made much of this diversity. South Africa, they argued, had never been a single nation, but a kaleidoscope of distinct racial groups, each with its own national and cultural identity. What was needed, therefore, they deduced, was not a single integrated state (the "melting pot" model), but "multinational development" or "separate freedoms"—that is, apartheid—each racial group preserving and advancing its own uniqueness. "We do not want intermingling of racial groups in South Africa," wrote Professor Dr. J. C. G. Klotze. "It is in accordance with Scripture that the ideal situation would be for each people to inhabit its own country (Acts 17:26)."[58] Apart from the question of whether "nations" and "racial groups" are the same thing, and whether Acts 17:26 includes the latter, the South African apartheid policy seems to have depended on two other errors. First, the assumption was that distinct cultures could be preserved only if racial groups were segregated from each other. But this is patently untrue, as we know in Britain where the Irish, Welsh, Scots and English intermingle, while their cultural distinctives also survive. Not only is it unnecessary to keep apart in order to preserve our own cultures, but it is impossible to do so if we are to enjoy each other's, as God surely means us to do. Secondly, the assumption underlying the policy to segregate racial groups in order to preserve them was that to integrate them would inevitably mean to destroy them. But integration is not the same as assimilation, and does not necessarily lead to it. On the contrary, although intermarriage should be fully permissible, natural affinities and cultural tensions are likely to keep the number of mixed marriages comparatively small.

Thirdly, Paul proclaimed the finality of Jesus Christ, or *the God of Revelation.* He concluded his sermon with God's call to universal repentance because of the coming universal judgment, for which God had both fixed the day and appointed the judge (verses 30–31). Paul refused to acquiesce in the religious pluralism of Athens or applaud it as a living museum of religious faiths. Instead, the city's idolatry provoked him (verse 16)—probably to jealousy for the honor of the living and true God. So he called on the city's people to turn in repentance from their idols to God.

We learn, then, that a respectful acceptance of the diversity of cultures does not imply an equal acceptance of the diversity of religions. The richness of each particular culture should be appreciated, but not the idolatry which may lie at its heart. For we cannot tolerate any rivals to Jesus Christ, believing as we do that God has spoken fully and finally through him, and that he is the only Savior, who died and rose again and will one day come to be the world's Judge.

Fourthly, Paul proclaimed the glory of the Christian Church, or *the God of Redemption*. It is clearer in some of the apostle's letters than it is in Luke's record of this sermon that Jesus died and rose to create a new and reconciled community, his Church. Thus the flow of history is being reversed. The Old Testament is the story of human scattering, of nations spreading abroad, falling apart, fighting. But the New Testament is the story of the divine ingathering of nations into a single international society. It is hinted at here in verse 34, in which we are told that a few men believed, one of whom was named Dionysius, and a woman named Damaris, and a number of others. So here was the nucleus of the new community, in which men and women of all ages, and of all racial, cultural and social origins, find their oneness in Christ.

Since God has made all nations and determines their times and places, it is clearly right for each of us to be conscious of our nationality and grateful for it. But since God has also brought us into his new society, he is thereby calling us into a new internationalism. Every Christian knows this tension, and nobody more keenly than Paul who was at the same time a patriotic Jew and the apostle to the Gentiles. Christian "internationalism" does not mean that our membership of Christ and his Church obliterates our nationality, any more than it does our masculinity or femininity. It means rather that, while our racial, national, social and sexual distinctions remain, they no longer divide us. They have been transcended in the unity of the family of God (Galatians 3:28). Raymond Johnston was right to say that "a proper understanding of nationhood calls attention to the human need for roots, a security and an identity mediated by the community, on the basis of which each individual knows that he 'belongs.'"[59] Yet it needs to be added that in Christ we have found even deeper roots, and an even stronger security and identity, for through him God has called us into a new and wider unity.

The Church must therefore exhibit its multiracial, multinational and multicultural nature. There has been considerable debate in recent years whether a local church could or should ever be culturally homogeneous. A consultation on this issue concluded that no church should ever acquiesce in such a condition:

> All of us are agreed that in many situations a homogeneous unit church can be a legitimate and authentic church. Yet we are also agreed that it can never be complete in itself. Indeed, if it remains in isolation, it cannot reflect the universality and diversity of the Body of Christ. Nor can it grow to maturity. Therefore every homogeneous unit church must take active steps to broaden its fellowship in order to demonstrate visibly the unity and the variety of Christ's Church.[60]

The Statement goes on to suggest how this might be done.

Only a true theology, the biblical revelation of God, can deliver us from racial pride and prejudice. Because he is the God of Creation, we affirm the unity of the human race. Because he is the God of History, we affirm the diversity of ethnic cultures. Because he is the God of Revelation, we affirm the finality of Jesus Christ. And because he is the God of Redemption, we affirm the glory of the Christian Church. Whatever policies for racial integration may be developed, we should try to ensure that they will reflect these doctrines. Because of the unity of humankind, we demand equal rights and equal respect for racial minorities. Because of the diversity of ethnic groups, we renounce cultural imperialism and seek to preserve all those riches of culture which are compatible with Christ's lordship. Because of the finality of Christ, we affirm that religious freedom includes the right to propagate the gospel. Because of the glory of the Church, we must seek to rid ourselves of any lingering racism and strive to make it a model of harmony between races, in which the multiracial dream comes true.

4

Poverty, Wealth and Simplicity

Wealth increasing for evermore, and its beneficiaries, rich in hire-purchase, stupefied with the telly and with sex, comprehensively educated, told by Professor Hoyle how the world began and by Bertrand Russell where it will end; venturing forth on the broad highways, three lanes a side . . . blood spattering the tarmac as an extra thrill; heaven lying about them in the supermarket, the rainbow ending in the nearest bingo hall, leisure burgeoning out in multitudinous shining aerials rising like dreaming spires into the sky . . . many mansions, mansions of light and chromium, climbing ever upwards. This kingdom, surely, can only be for posterity an unending source of wry derision—always assuming there is to be any posterity. The backdrop, after all, is the mushroom cloud; as the Gadarene herd frisk and frolic, they draw ever nearer to the cliff's precipitous edge.[1]

Thus, Malcolm Muggeridge satirizes the affluence of the West, its materialism, superficiality and selfishness. It is bad enough in itself and seems to be on the increase. When contrasted with the *barriadas* and *favelas* of Latin America, and the ghettoes, slums and shantytowns of other parts of the world, it becomes inexcusable. Not that the contrast between wealth and poverty corresponds neatly with the North-South divide. For the OPEC countries are rich, and so are some East Asian communities.

Moreover, poverty has not been eliminated from North America or Europe. In the United States in 1995 there were 36.4 million people living below the poverty line, or 13.8 percent of the population.[2] In Britain in 1995 there were still 9.7 million people, adults and children, living on incomes at or below the level of supplementary benefit, which is the state's definition of the boundary between poverty and subsistence.[3] And more than twice that number live in relative poverty. Hence the launching in Britain in July 1982 of "Church Action on Poverty." And three years later Britain was shocked by the carefully researched findings of *Faith in the City*, the report of the Archbishop of Canterbury's Commission on Urban Priority Areas. "Chapter after chapter of our Report," its conclusion begins, "tells the same story: that a growing number of people are excluded by poverty or powerlessness from sharing in the common life of our nation. A substantial minority—perhaps as many as one person in every four or five across the nation, and a much higher proportion in the UPAs—are forced to live on the margins of poverty or below the threshold of an acceptable standard of living."[4]

The truth is that a grave disparity between wealth and poverty is to be found not only between nations, but within most nations as well. As the Latin American Roman Catholic bishops put it at Puebla in 1979: "The cruel contrast between luxurious wealth and extreme poverty, which is so visible throughout our continent and which is further aggravated by the corruption that often invades public and professional life, shows the great extent to which our nations are dominated by the idol of wealth."[5]

Three Approaches to Poverty

How should Christians approach the harsh fact of poverty in the contemporary world?

First, we could approach the problem rationally, with cool statistical detachment. Indeed, this is where we must begin. There are almost six billion inhabitants of planet earth, a quarter of whom remain in severe poverty. The 1997 Human Development Report, while enthusiastically recognizing that "progress in reducing poverty over the 20th century is remarkable and unprecedented," also notes that "the advances have been uneven and marred by setbacks—and poverty remains pervasive." Indeed, "an estimated 1.3 billion people survive on less than the equivalent of $1 a day. . . . Nearly a billion people are illiterate. . . . Some 840 million go hungry or face food insecurity."[6]

One subject which brings this home to us is that of the provision of clean, safe water. In the West it is piped into our homes and instantly available to us at the turn of a tap. None of us would dream of regarding this as a luxury. We take it for granted. In the developing world only 68 percent of the population have access to safe drinking water, while in the least developed countries this percentage drops to 38.[7] Almost two billion people in the Third World are without access to proper sanitation facilities so that "waterborne diseases . . . and a wide array of serious or fatal diarrheal illnesses are responsible for more than 35 percent of the deaths of young children in Africa, Asia and Latin America."[8] That is why the United Nations declared the 1980s the International Drinking Water Supply and Sanitation Decade. Although wide-scale improvements were made during the decade and have continued since, the needs continue to be great.

Meanwhile, whereas one-fifth of the world's population lack the basic necessities for survival, rather more than another one-fifth live in affluence and consume about four-fifths of the world's income. In 1988 the "total disbursements" from these wealthy nations to the Third World "amounted to $92 billion" (less than 10 percent of worldwide spending on armaments), "but this was more than offset by the total debt service of $142 billion, resulting in a net negative transfer of some $50 billion" from the Third World to the developed countries.[9] More recently "annual losses to developing countries from unequal access to trade, labour and finance have been estimated at $500 billion, 10 times what they receive in foreign aid."[10] The gross disparity between wealth and poverty constitutes a social injustice with which the Christian conscience cannot come to terms.

Secondly, we could approach the phenomenon of poverty emotionally, with the hot-blooded indignation aroused by the sights, sounds and smells of human need. When I recently visited Calcutta airport, the sun had already set. Over the whole city hung a pall of malodorous smoke from the burning of cowdung on a myriad fires. Outside the airport an emaciated woman clutching an emaciated baby stretched out an emaciated hand for baksheesh. A man, whose legs had both been amputated above the knee, dragged himself along the pavement with his hands. I later learned that over a quarter of a million homeless people sleep on the streets at night, and during the day hang their blanket—often their only possession—on some convenient railing. My most poignant experience was to see men and women scavenging in the city garbage dumps like dogs. For extreme poverty is demeaning; it reduces human beings to the level of animals. To be sure, Christians should be provoked by the idolatry of a Hindu city, as Paul was by the idols in Athens, and moved to evangelism. But, like Jesus when he saw the hungry crowds, we should also be moved with compassion to feed them (compare Acts 17:16–17 with, e.g., Mark 8:1–3).

It is not only the absolute poverty of Third World slums which should arouse our emotions, however, but also the relative (though real) poverty of the decayed and deprived inner city areas of the West, which the affluent seldom if ever see. This was the emphasis which David Sheppard, Bishop of Liverpool until 1997, made in his Richard Dimbleby Lecture broadcast in 1984. He urged "Comfortable Britain" to stand in the shoes of the "Other Britain." He spoke with deep feeling of youth and long-term unemployment, neglected housing, poor opportunities in schooling and the sense of alienation, even desertion. He felt indignant, indeed angry, because poverty "imprisons the spirit," spawns "sick human relationships" and wastes God-given talent. He then described four "keys" which could begin to unlock the prison.[11]

The third way, which should stimulate both our reason and our emotion simultaneously, is to approach the problem of poverty biblically. As we turn again to that Book in which God has revealed himself and his will, we ask: how according to Scripture should we think about wealth and poverty? Is God on the side of the poor? Should we be? What does the Scripture say? Moreover, as we ask these questions, we have to resolve to listen attentively to God's Word, and not manipulate it. We have no liberty either to avoid its uncomfortable challenge, in order to retain our prejudices, or to acquiesce uncritically in the latest popular interpretations.

Psalm 113 seems a good place to begin. It is an invitation to Yahweh's servants, indeed to all people "from the rising of the sun to the place where it sets," to praise his name, since he "is exalted over all the nations, his glory above the heavens." It continues:

> Who is like the LORD our God,
>   the One who sits enthroned on high,
> who stoops down to look
>   on the heavens and the earth?
> He raises the poor from the dust
>   and lifts the needy from the ash heap;
> he seats them with princes,
>   with the princes of their people.
> He settles the barren woman in her home
>   as a happy mother of children.

verses 5–9

The psalmist is affirming something distinctive—indeed unique—about Yahweh, which enables him to ask the rhetorical question, "Who is like the LORD our God?" It is not just that he reigns on high, exalted above both the nations and the sky; nor only that from these lofty heights he condescends to look far below to the heavens and the earth; nor even that on the distant earth he regards with compassion the depths of human misery, the poor discarded on the scrapheaps of life and trampled in the dust by their oppressors. It is more than all these things. It is that he actually exalts the wretched of the earth; he lifts them from the depths to the heights; "He raises the poor from the dust and . . . seats them with princes." For example, he takes pity on the barren woman (whose childlessness was regarded as a disgrace) and makes her a joyful mother. That is the kind of God he is. No other god is like him. For it is not primarily the wealthy and the famous with whom he delights to fraternize. What is characteristic of him is to champion the poor, to rescue them from their misery, and to transform paupers into princes.

This affirmation is many times repeated and exemplified in Scripture, usually with its corollary that the God who lifts up the humble also puts down the proud. This was the essence of Hannah's song when after years of childlessness her son, Samuel, was born:

> He raises the poor from the dust
>> and lifts the needy from the ash heap;
> he seats them with princes
>> and has them inherit a throne of honor.

1 Samuel 2:8

This too was the theme of the Magnificat, which the Virgin Mary sang after learning that she (and not some famous, noble or wealthy woman) had been chosen to be the mother of God's Messiah. God had looked upon her lowly state, she said; the Mighty One had done great things for her, for which she gave him thanks and praise:

> He has performed mighty deeds with his arm;
>> he has scattered those who are proud in their inmost thoughts.
> He has brought down rulers from their thrones
>> but has lifted up the humble.
> He has filled the hungry with good things
>> but has sent the rich away empty.

Luke 1:51–52

In Psalm 113, and in the experiences of Hannah and Mary, the same stark contrast is painted, although the vocabulary varies. The proud are abased and the humble exalted; the rich are impoverished and the poor enriched; the well-fed are sent away empty, and the hungry filled with good things; powerful rulers are toppled from their thrones, while the powerless and the oppressed are caused to reign like princes. "Who is like the LORD our God?" His thoughts and ways are not ours. He is a topsy-turvy God. He turns the standards and values of the world upside down.

Jesus himself is the greatest example of this. One of his favorite epigrams seems to have been that "everyone who exalts himself will be humbled, and he who humbles himself will be exalted" (e.g., Luke 18:14). He did not only enunciate this principle, however; he personally exhibited it. Having emptied himself of his glory, he humbled himself to serve, and his obedience took him even to the depths of the cross. "Therefore God exalted him to the highest place . . ." (Philippians 2:5–11).

It is this principle, which pledges the reversal of human fortunes, which alone can bring hope to the poor. But who are the "poor" whom God is said to "raise"? And what does he do when he "raises" them? These words demand definition.

Who Are the Poor? The Paradox of Poverty

A number of studies of the biblical material have been made and published.[12] They focus on the Old Testament, in which a cluster of words for poverty, deriving from six main Hebrew roots, occur more than two hundred times. These may be classified in a variety of ways, but the principal division seems to be threefold. First, and economically speaking, there are the indigent poor, who are deprived of the basic necessities of life. Secondly, and sociologically speaking, there are the powerless poor, who are oppressed victims of human injustice. Thirdly, and spiritually speaking, there are the humble poor, who acknowledge their helplessness and look to God alone for salvation. In each case God is represented as coming to them and making their cause his own, in keeping with his characteristic that "he raises the poor from the dust."

The first group, the indigent poor, are economically deprived. They may lack food or clothing or shelter, or all three. Sometimes, as the biblical authors recognize, their poverty may be due to their own sin, whether laziness, extravagance or gluttony. The Book of Proverbs has much to say about this. The sluggard is exhorted to study the ways of the ant, in order to learn wisdom. For ants gather and store food during the summer, while sluggards stay in bed: "A little sleep, a little slumber, a little folding of the hands to rest—and poverty will come on you like a bandit and scarcity like an armed man" (Proverbs 6:10; see vv. 6–11; cf. 24:30–34; similarly, "lazy hands make a man poor, but diligent hands bring wealth" [10:4; cf. 19:15; 20:13; 28:19]). Closely linked to laziness, as causing poverty, are greed and drunkenness: "drunkards and gluttons become poor, and drowsiness clothes them in rags" (Proverbs 23:20–21; cf. 21:17). Not only did these particular sins bring individual poverty, however. National poverty also was due to sin. For during the theocracy, when God ruled over his people in Israel, he promised to bless their obedience with fruitfulness of field and orchard and to curse their disobedience with barrenness (see e.g., Leviticus 26; Deuteronomy 8 and 28; Isaiah 1:19–23; 5:8–25 for national blessings and curses).

Generally speaking, however, the Old Testament writers saw poverty as an involuntary social evil to be abolished, not tolerated, and represented the poor (who included widows, orphans and aliens) as people to be succored, not blamed. They are regarded not as sinners but as "the sinned against"—an expression popularized at the 1980 Melbourne Conference by Raymond Fung, a Baptist minister who had spent eleven years serving factory workers in Hong Kong.[13]

In the Law, God's people were commanded not to harden their hearts or close their hands against their poor brother or sister, but to be generous in maintaining those who could not maintain themselves, by taking them into their home and feeding them without charge. Their regular tithes were also to be used to support the Levites, the aliens, the orphans and the widows (Deuteronomy 15:7–11; Leviticus 25:35–43; Deuteronomy 14:29; 26:12). If an Israelite lent money to somebody in need, he was not to charge interest on it. If he took a pledge to secure his loan, he was not to go into the house to fetch it, but to stand respectfully outside and wait for it to be brought out to him. If he took as pledge his neighbor's cloak, he was to return it before sunset because the poor person would need it as a blanket to sleep in (Exodus 22:25; Leviticus 25:36–37; Deuteronomy 24:10–11; Exodus 22:26–27; Deuteronomy 24:12). In particular, the support and the relief of the poor were the obligations of the extended family towards its own members.

Employers were to pay their workers' wages promptly, the same day that they were earned. Farmers were not to reap their fields "to the very edges," nor to go back to pick up a dropped or forgotten sheaf, nor to gather the gleanings after harvesting, nor to strip their vineyard bare, nor to gather fallen grapes, nor to go over the branches of their olive trees a second time. For the borders, the gleanings and the fallen fruit were all to be left for the poor, the alien, the widow and the orphan. They too must be allowed to share in the harvest celebrations. Every third year, a tenth of the agricultural produce was to be given to the poor. Every seventh year fields were to lie fallow and vineyards and olive groves to be unharvested, for the benefit of the poor who could help themselves to the fruit (Leviticus 19:13; Deuteronomy 24:14–15; Leviticus 19:9–10; 23:22; Deuteronomy 16:9–12; 24:19–22; 14:28–29; 26:12–15; Exodus 23:10–11; Leviticus 25:1–7).

The Old Testament Wisdom Literature confirmed this teaching. One of the characteristics of a righteous man is that he cares about "justice for the poor"; he "is generous and lends freely," and "has scattered abroad his gifts to the poor"; whereas "if a man shuts his ears to the cry of the poor, he too will cry out and not be answered" (Proverbs 29:7; Psalm 112:1–9; Proverbs 21:13; cf. 14:20–21; 19:7; 31:20; Job 31:16–23; Ezekiel 16:49). The wise teachers of Israel also grounded these duties on doctrine, namely that behind the poor, Yahweh himself was standing, their Creator and Lord, so that people's attitude to him would be reflected in their attitudes to them. On the one hand, "He who mocks the poor shows contempt for their Maker"; on the other, "He who is kind to the poor lends to the LORD" (Proverbs 17:5; 19:17).

Jesus himself inherited this rich Old Testament legacy of care for the poor and put it into practice. He made friends with the needy and fed the hungry. He told his disciples to sell their possessions and give alms to the poor, and when they gave a party, to remember to invite the poor, the crippled, the lame and the blind, who would probably be in no position to invite them back. He also promised that in feeding the hungry, clothing the naked, welcoming the homeless and visiting the sick, they would thereby be ministering to him (Luke 12:33; 14:12–14; Matthew 25:35–40).

The second group, the powerless poor, are socially or politically oppressed. It was clearly recognized in the Old Testament that poverty does not normally just happen. Although sometimes it was due to personal sin or national disobedience, and to God's judgment on them, it was usually due to the sins of others, that is, to a situation of social injustice, which easily deteriorated because the poor were not in a position to change it. We do not understand the Old Testament teaching on this subject unless we see how frequently poverty and powerlessness were bracketed. At the same time, although the poor often had no human helper, they knew that God was their champion. For "he stands at the right hand of the needy one." Again, "I know that the LORD secures justice for the poor and upholds the cause of the needy" (Psalm 109:31; 140:12).

Moses' law laid emphasis on the need for impartial justice in the courts, in particular for the poor and powerless. "Do not deny justice to your poor people in their lawsuits. . . . Do not accept a bribe, for a bribe blinds those who see and twists the words of the righteous." "Do not pervert justice; do not show partiality to the poor or favoritism to the great, but judge your neighbor fairly." "Do not deprive the alien or the fatherless of justice." Moreover, the reason repeatedly given was that they themselves had been oppressed in Egypt, and the Lord had liberated them (Exodus 23:6, 8; Leviticus 19:15; Deuteronomy 24:17; 27:19; 15:15).

The Wisdom Books were as explicit as the Law Books in demanding justice for the helpless. In Psalm 82 the judges were instructed to "defend the cause of the weak and fatherless" and "maintain the rights of the poor and oppressed." In Proverbs 31 King Lemuel was exhorted by his mother to "speak up for those who cannot speak for themselves, for the rights of all who are destitute," to "speak up and judge fairly" and "defend the rights of the poor and needy" (Psalm 82:1–3; Proverbs 31:8–9; cf. Job 29:11–17; Proverbs 22:22–23; 29:7, 14).

It is well-known that the prophets were even more outspoken. They not only urged the people and their leaders to "seek justice, encourage the oppressed, defend the cause of the fatherless, plead the case of the widow," and conversely forbade them to "oppress the widow or the fatherless, the alien or the poor," but were fierce in their condemnation of all injustice. Elijah rebuked King Ahab for murdering Naboth and stealing his vineyard. Amos fulminated against the rulers of Israel because in return for bribes they trampled on the heads of the poor, crushed the needy, and denied justice to the oppressed, instead of letting "justice roll on like a river, and righteousness like a never-failing stream." Jeremiah denounced King Jehoiakim for using forced labor to build his luxurious palace. Other examples could be given. The national life of Israel and Judah was constantly tarnished by the exploitation of the poor. And James in the New Testament, sounding just like an Old Testament prophet, also inveighs against the rich. It is not their wealth in itself which he condemns, nor even primarily their self-indulgent luxury, but in particular their fraudulent withholding of wages from their workforce and their violent oppression of the innocent. (See Isaiah 1:17; Zechariah 7:8–11; 1 Kings 21; Amos 2:6–7; 4:1–3; 5:11–15; 8:4–6; 5:24; Jeremiah 22:13–17. Other examples of the prophetic stress on justice are Isaiah 3:13–15; 5:7–10; 10:1–2; Jeremiah 5:28–29; Ezekiel 18:10–13; James 5:1–5.)

In contrast to this dark tradition of the prophets' diatribe against injustice, their predictions of the Messiah's righteous reign shine the more brightly: "with righteousness he will judge the needy, with justice he will give decisions for the poor of the earth" (Isaiah 11:4; see vv. 1–5).

It is abundantly clear from this evidence that the biblical writers saw the poor not only as destitute people, whose condition must be relieved, but as the victims of social injustice, whose cause must be championed. The biblical perspective is not "the survival of the fittest" but "the protection of the weakest." Since God himself speaks up for them and comes to their aid, his people must also be the voice of the voiceless and the defender of the defenseless.

The third group, the humble poor, are spiritually meek and dependent on God. Since God succors the destitute and defends the powerless, these truths inevitably affect their attitude to him. They look to him for mercy. Oppressed by human beings, and helpless to liberate themselves, they put their trust in God. It is in this way that "the poor" came to be synonymous with "the pious," and their social condition became a symbol of their spiritual dependence. Zephaniah describes them as "the meek and the humble, who trust in the name of the LORD," and Isaiah calls them the "humble and contrite in spirit" who tremble at God's Word (Zephaniah 2:3; 3:12; Isaiah 66:2; cf. 49:13).

It is particularly in the Psalms, however, that the otherwise rather blurred portrait of the humble poor comes into sharp focus. For the psalter is the hymnbook of the helpless (see e.g., Psalms 22, 25, 37, 40, 69, 74, 149). It is here that we listen to their expressions of dependence upon God, and to God's promises to come to their aid. They are "the lonely and afflicted" who cry to him to be gracious to them; they commit their way to the Lord, are quiet before him, and wait patiently for him to act. They are given the assurance that "the poor will eat and be satisfied," that "the meek will inherit the land," and that "he crowns the humble with salvation" (Psalm 25:16; 37:5, 7; 40:1; 22:26; 37:11; 149:4).

More striking even than these references to the poor and meek as a group, however, are the individual testimonies to Yahweh's salvation. There is Psalm 34, for example: "This poor man called, and the LORD heard him; he saved him out of all his troubles." As a result, he determines to "boast in the LORD" and is confident that others who are "afflicted" like him will hear and rejoice with him, and will in their turn call upon Yahweh. For, he goes on to affirm, "The LORD is close to the brokenhearted and saves those who are crushed in spirit" (vv. 1–6, 15–18). Another example occurs in Psalm 86. The psalmist describes himself as savagely assaulted by arrogant, godless and ruthless men. His only hope is in God. "Hear, O LORD, and answer me," he cries, "for I am poor and needy. Guard my life, for I am devoted to you. You are my God; save your servant who trusts in you." And he goes on to express his confidence that God will rescue him, because he is "a compassionate and gracious God, slow to anger, abounding in love and faithfulness" (Psalm 86:1–4, 14–17).

All this biblical teaching enables us to affirm that God succors the indigent poor, champions the powerless poor and exalts the humble poor. In each case "he raises the poor from the dust," whether it be the dust of penury or of oppression or of helplessness.

Good News for the Poor

At the risk of oversimplification, however, it will be helpful (especially if we are to grasp what the Christian attitude to poverty should be) if we reduce these three categories to two, namely the material poverty of the destitute and powerless, and the spiritual poverty of the humble and meek. God concerns himself with both. In both cases "he raises the poor from the dust," but the way he does it is different. For the first kind of poverty is a social evil which God opposes, while the second is a spiritual virtue which he approves. Moreover, there is only one human community in which the two are combined, namely the Kingdom community, the new and redeemed society in which God rules through Christ by his Spirit.

This is clear from the Old Testament expectation of the Kingdom of God. God promised the coming of his ideal King, who would both judge the poor with justice and give the blessing of his rule to the humble and lowly. We meet such people in the first two chapters of Luke's Gospel. Zechariah and Elizabeth, Joseph and Mary, Simeon and Anna were humble, poor believers. They were looking and waiting for the Kingdom of God, in which God would throw down the mighty from their thrones and exalt the humble and meek.

Clearer still was the fulfillment through Jesus Christ. Who are the "poor" he spoke about, those to whom he had been anointed to preach the good news of the Kingdom and to whom the Kingdom would be given (Luke 4:18–19; Matthew 11:5; cf. Luke 7:22; Matthew 5:3; cf. Luke 6:20)? They surely cannot be either just the materially poor (for Christ's salvation is not limited to the proletariat) or just the spiritually poor (for this overlooks his ministry to the needy). He must have been referring to both in combination. The "poor" are those to whom the Kingdom comes as great good news, partly because it is a free and unmerited gift of salvation to sinners, and partly because it promises a new society characterized by freedom and justice.

The Church should exemplify both these truths. On the one hand it consists of the spiritually poor, the "poor in spirit," who acknowledge their bankruptcy before God. They have no righteousness to offer, no merit to plead, no power to save themselves. They know that the only way to enter God's Kingdom is to humble themselves like little children and receive it as a gift. So they come as beggars, with nothing in their hands, and on their lips the publican's prayer, "God be merciful to me, a sinner." To such Jesus says: "Blessed are the poor in spirit, for theirs is the kingdom of heaven." By contrast, the rich or self-satisfied, who imagine they have something to offer, are sent away empty.

On the other hand, the Church must proclaim the good news of the Kingdom to the materially poor, welcome them into the fellowship, and share in their struggles. Indeed, the special concern for the poor shown by the biblical authors, and more particularly by Jesus himself, has led some contemporary thinkers to speak of God's "bias" in their favor. Bishop David Sheppard's 1983 book was entitled *Bias to the Poor*. "I believe that there is a divine bias to the disadvantaged," he writes, "and that the church needs to be much more faithful in reflecting it."[14] He concludes his analysis of deprivation in Liverpool with these words:

> If we can put ourselves in the shoes of the poor and disadvantaged, we may see how matters appear to their consciousness. . . . They are to do with the righteousness of God which has a persistent tendency to favour those at a disadvantage. They are to do with God taking flesh in the person of Jesus, living out his life in a special relation to the poor.[15]

I confess that I am uncomfortable with the word *bias*, since its commonest meaning is "prejudice," and I do not think God is "biased" in that sense. Less misleading is the language of the Latin American bishops. At their Second General Conference at Medellín in 1970 they spoke of a "preference for, and solidarity with, the poor." At their Third General Conference ten years later at Puebla in Mexico, they affirmed "the need for conversion on the part of the whole church to a preferential option for the poor."[16] It is because of Jesus' ministry to the poor that "the poor merit preferential attention."[17] "Preferential" does not mean "exclusive," however, for the next chapter of the conference's report is entitled "A Preferential Option for Young People." Nevertheless, the option for the poor is "demanded by the scandalous reality of economic imbalances in Latin America."[18]

The 1980 Melbourne Conference quoted the Puebla conclusions, and then echoed them in asserting that "God has a preference for the poor."[19] It seems to me, however, that better than the vocabulary of personal "bias" or "preference" is the language of mission priority. Because of God's own care for the poor, and because of their exploitation by the unscrupulous and their neglect by the Church, they should now receive a "positive" or "reverse" discrimination. The Church should concentrate its mission where the need is greatest, and move from the center out "towards the periphery,"[20] to the "sinned against," in other words to the poor and the oppressed.

Moreover, the Church should not tolerate material poverty in its own fellowship. When Jesus said, "The poor you will always have with you" (Mark 14:7), he was not acquiescing in the permanence of poverty. He was echoing the Old Testament statement "there will always be poor people in the land" (Deuteronomy 15:11). Yet this was intended not as an excuse for complacency but as an incentive to generosity, as a result of which "there should be no poor among you" (v. 4). If there is one community in the world in which justice is secured for the oppressed, the poor are freed from the indignities of poverty and physical need is abolished by the voluntary sharing of resources, that community is the new society of Jesus the Messiah. It happened in Jerusalem after Pentecost, when "there were no needy persons among them," as Luke is at pains to show, and it can (and should) happen again today. How can we allow our own brothers and sisters in God's family to suffer want?

The Church, then, as the community which is called to exemplify the ideals of the Kingdom of God, should bear witness to the biblical paradox of poverty, by opposing one kind and encouraging the other. We should set ourselves both to eradicate the evil of material poverty and to cultivate the good of spiritual poverty. We should hate injustice and love humility. It is in these two complementary ways that the gospel may be said to be "good news for the poor," and God may be described as on their side.

Not that our Christian concern should be confined to those poor who are church members. Although we have a special responsibility to "the family of believers" (or, in older versions of the Bible, "the household of faith"), we are also required to "do good to all people" (Galatians 6:10). How will this express itself to the poor? Certainly in terms of personal philanthropy, as we seek to help needy individuals and families in our neighborhood and further afield. But we cannot allow our duty to stop there. For the Bible itself indicates, as we have seen, that most poverty is the fault rather of society than of the poor themselves. We therefore have a social as well as a personal responsibility towards them, and this will begin with a painful appraisal of the causes of poverty. I call it "painful" because the tendency of the affluent is to blame the poor, or to find some other scapegoat, whereas the problem may lie in the very structure of society in which we ourselves (willy-nilly) are implicated.

This is the thesis of Robert Holman's carefully researched, well written and overtly Christian book *Poverty: Explanations of Social Deprivation.*[21] He rejects as incomplete three common scapegoat explanations—"individual" (genetic, economic or psychological inadequacies in the poor themselves), "cultural" ("the transmission of poverty from one generation to the next"[22]), and "the deficient agent" (the inefficiency of teachers, social workers and bureaucrats). Instead, he traces the cause of most poverty (at least in Britain) to the stratified structure of society itself, in which resources (especially income, wealth and power) are unequally divided. "Poverty exists," he writes, "in order to support or uphold these social divisions."[23] It is tolerated, even justified, because it (and therefore its affluent opposite) is made to appear merited, and because it provides a useful pool of workers who have no choice but to undertake the most unattractive occupations.

Bob Holman's approach is sociological. In consequence, he avoids the polarized economic debate between those who blame poverty on capitalism, on the ground that it is inherently covetous and therefore exploits the poor, and those who blame socialism, on the ground that it perpetuates the dependency of the poor and undermines the enterprise of wealth creators. Neither position has a monopoly of truth. Christians should oppose in both systems what they perceive to be incompatible with biblical faith. Faith places an equal emphasis on creativity and compassion and refuses to foster either at the expense of the other.

Three Options for Rich Christians

Conscientious Christians have further questions to ask. It is one thing to discern what our attitude to the poor should be; it is another to define our attitude to poverty itself. Involuntary material poverty is a scandal, as we have seen; but what about voluntary poverty? And what is an authentically Christian attitude to money and property? What should rich Christians do?

In the context of western affluence there are three options before us. The first is to become poor, the second to stay rich, and the third to cultivate generosity, simplicity and contentment.

First, should we become poor? Paul wrote: "For you know the grace of our Lord Jesus Christ, that though he was rich, yet for your sakes he became poor, so that you through his poverty might become rich" (2 Corinthians

91

8:9). This voluntary self-impoverishment of Jesus was the theological ground on which the apostle based his appeal to the Christians of Greece to contribute to the relief of the Christians of Judea. Did he intend them to divest themselves of all their possessions for the sake of their Jewish brothers and sisters? Does he mean us to do the same? At first sight it seems so, and arguments have been advanced for this from the example, teaching and early Church of Jesus.

The Example of Jesus

Renouncing the wealth of heaven, Jesus was certainly born into a poor home. When Joseph and Mary came to the Temple to present their child to the Lord, they availed themselves of the law's provision for poor people and brought as their sacrifice a pair of doves instead of a lamb and a dove. During his public ministry as an itinerant preacher Jesus had no home and few possessions. To an applicant for discipleship he once said: "Foxes have holes and birds of the air have nests, but the Son of Man has no place to lay his head." He taught from a borrowed boat, rode into Jerusalem on a borrowed donkey, spent his last evening in a borrowed room and was buried in a borrowed tomb. He and his apostles shared a common purse and depended for their support on a group of women who sometimes accompanied them (Luke 2:2–24; cf. Leviticus 12:6–8; Luke 9:57–58; Mark 4:1; 11:1–11; 14:12–16; 15:42–47; John 12:6; Luke 8:1–3). The poverty of Jesus seems to be beyond question.

Yet he was a carpenter by trade, which means that he belonged to the craftsman class. Professor Martin Hengel writes:

> Jesus himself did not come from the proletariat of day-labourers and landless tenants, but from the middle class of Galilee, the skilled workers. Like his father, he was an artisan, a *tekton*, a Greek word which means mason, carpenter, cartwright and joiner all rolled into one. . . . As far as we can tell, the disciples whom he called to follow him came from a similar social milieu.[24]

Moreover, the women who supported him evidently "cared for his needs" adequately (Mark 15:41). So he was not destitute.

The Teaching of Jesus

To would-be followers Jesus said: "Any of you who does not give up everything he has cannot be my disciple." The twelve apostles did this literally. Simon and Andrew "left their nets and followed him"; James and John "left their father Zebedee in the boat with the hired men and followed him"; and Levi-Matthew "got up and followed him," abandoning his tax-collector's booth and work. Similarly, Jesus told the rich young ruler to sell all his possessions, give the proceeds to the poor and then follow him. It was this which prompted Peter to blurt out: "We have left everything to follow you!" (Luke 14:33; Mark 1:16–20; 2:13–14; 10:21, 28).

Does Jesus then expect all his followers to give up everything in order to follow him? The apostles did it. And the rich young man was challenged to do it. But is it a universal rule? In reply, we must be careful not to whittle down the radical summons of Jesus by a little prudential exegesis. He did say that we should store our treasure in heaven not on earth; that we must put devotion to God's rule and righteousness above material things; that we must beware of covetousness; and that it is impossible to serve God and money simultaneously (Matthew 6:19–21; cf. Luke 12:33–34; Matthew 6:33; Luke 12:15; Matthew 6:24). But he did not tell all his followers to get rid of all their possessions. Joseph of Arimathea is described both as "a rich man" and as "a disciple of Jesus." So these two were evidently not incompatible. Zacchaeus, the wealthy tax-collector, promised both to pay back to people he had cheated four times what he had taken and to give half of his possessions to the poor, which presumably means that he kept the other half, apart from what he paid back to his victims. Yet Jesus said that salvation had been given to him (Matthew 27:57; Luke 19:8–10). So then, when he said that no one could be his disciple unless he both "renounced" all his possessions and "hated" his parents and other relatives, we shall need to understand both these verbs as dramatic figures of speech. We are not to hate our parents literally nor to renounce all our possessions literally. What we are summoned to is to put Jesus Christ first, above even our family and our property.

The Early Church of Jesus

Luke writes of the first Christian community in Jerusalem that they "had everything in common," that "no one claimed that any of his possessions was his own," that "they shared everything they had" and gave to "anyone as he had need," and that in consequence "there were no needy persons among them" (Acts 2:44–45; 4:32–35). Is Luke setting their common life before us as an example for every church to copy? In the sense that the early Spirit-filled believers loved and cared for one another and eliminated poverty within their fellowship, yes. But is he also advocating the common ownership of goods? Among the Essene groups, especially in their central community of Qumran, this was obligatory, and every novice entering the order had to hand over his property.[25] But it is plain from Luke's narrative that the Christians' selling and sharing were neither universal nor compulsory. For some believers still had houses in which they met. The sin of Ananias and Sapphira was not that they were selfish to withhold some of their property, but that they were deceitful to pretend they had given it all. Peter said to Ananias: "Didn't it belong to you before it was sold? And after it was sold, wasn't the money at your disposal?" (Acts 5:4). Thus the Christian's right to property is affirmed, together with the voluntary nature of Christian giving.

The example, teaching and early Church of Jesus all challenge us to renounce covetousness, materialism and luxury, and to care sacrificially for the poor. But they do not establish the case that all Christians must actually become poor.

If the first option for affluent Christians is to become poor, the second and opposite option is to stay rich. Some seek to defend this stance by an appeal to biblical arguments. Human beings were commanded in the beginning (they rightly say) to subdue and develop the earth, that is, to extract its animal, vegetable and mineral wealth and to harness it for their use. Wealth, moreover, is a sign of God's blessing, and they intend to claim and enjoy it. "The LORD will send a blessing on your barns and on everything you put your hand to. The LORD your God will bless you in the land he is giving you. . . . You will lend to many nations but will borrow from none" (Deuteronomy 28:8, 12). "What could be clearer than that?" they ask.

The most shameless example of this reasoning which I have come across was in the literature of a certain Pentecostal evangelist. He was appealing for funds to enable him to send Christian materials to the Third World. "There's no better way to insure your own financial security," he argued, all in capital letters, "than to plant some seed-money in God's work. His law of sowing and reaping guarantees you a harvest of much more than you sow. . . . Have you limited God to your present income, business, house or car? There's no limit to God's plenty! . . . Write on the enclosed slip what you need from God—the salvation of a loved one, healing, a raise in pay, a better job, newer car or home, sale or purchase of property, guidance in business or investment . . . whatever you need. . . . Enclose your slip with your seed-money. . . . Expect God's material blessings in return."

Our first response to this is vigorously to deny what such Christians are affirming and strenuously to repudiate their false "prosperity" or "health and wealth" gospel. When God's people were a nation, he did indeed promise to reward their obedience with material blessings, but in Christ he has blessed us "with every spiritual blessing" (Ephesians 1:3). Our second response is to draw attention to what they are omitting. For there are other biblical principles which they have overlooked. The earth was to be developed for the common good and its riches shared with all mankind. The Old Testament economy which promised wealth also commanded the care of the poor. And the rich man in the parable of Jesus found himself in hell not because of his wealth but because of his neglect of the beggar at his gate. That is, Dives indulged himself at the very time when Lazarus was starving.

In the light of these additional biblical truths, and of the contemporary destitution of millions, it is not possible for affluent Christians to "stay rich," in the sense of accepting no modification of economic lifestyle. We cannot maintain a "good life" (of extravagance) and a "good conscience" simultaneously. One or the other has to be sacrificed. Either we keep our conscience and reduce our affluence, or we keep our affluence and smother our conscience. We have to choose between God and mammon.

Consider Paul's instruction to Timothy regarding rich people:

> Command those who are rich in this present world not to be arrogant nor to put their hope in wealth, which is so uncertain, but to put their hope in God, who richly provides us with everything for our enjoyment. Command them to do good, to be rich in good deeds, and to be generous and willing to share. In this way they will lay up treasure for themselves as a firm foundation for the coming age, so that they may take hold of the life that is truly life.
>
> 1 Timothy 6:17–19

We observe at once that the apostle does not tell "those who are rich in this present world" to "become poor." But he does not allow them to "stay rich" either. Instead, he first warns them of the spiritual dangers of wealth (as Jesus said, it is not impossible for the rich to enter God's Kingdom but it is hard), and then tells them to be generous with their wealth, which will inevitably result in a lowering of their own standard of living.

The first danger of wealth is pride: "Command those who are rich . . . not to be arrogant." For wealth makes people feel self-important and so "contemptuous of others" (Phillips). Rich people are tempted to boast of their home, car, possessions and gadgets. It is easy for wealthy people to become snobs, to emphasize their social "class" and despise others. James pictures the situation when a rich man enters a Christian assembly wearing fine clothes, and then a poor man in rags comes in. If we behave obsequiously to the rich person and show him to one of the best seats, while rudely telling the poor person to stand on one side or sit on the floor, we have been guilty of class discrimination and so have disrupted the fellowship. It is not difficult to tell whether our affluence has alienated us from our less well-to-do brothers and sisters. If it has, we find ourselves embarrassed in each other's company.

If wealth's first peril is pride, its second is materialism: "Command those who are rich . . . not to put their hope in wealth which is so uncertain, but to put their hope in God." "Materialism" is not the mere possession of material things, but an unhealthy obsession with them. It is but a short step from wealth to materialism, from having riches to putting our trust in them, and many take it. But it is foolish. For there is no security in wealth. It is not for nothing that Paul writes of "uncertain riches." Burglars, pests, rust and inflation all take their toll. Many have gone to bed rich and woken up poor, or, like the rich fool in Jesus' parable, have not woken up at all.

Trust in wealth is not only foolish, it is also unworthy of human beings, since our trust should not be in a thing but in a Person, not in money but in God "who richly provides us with everything for our enjoyment." This is an important addition. For the Christian antidote to materialism is not asceticism; austerity for its own sake is a rejection of the good gifts of the Creator.

Here then are the two main dangers to which rich people are exposed— pride (looking down on the poor) and materialism (enjoying the gift and forgetting the Giver). Wealth can spoil our two noblest relationships. It can make us forget God and despise our fellow human beings. These negative warnings prepare us for the positive instruction which follows.

After considering and rejecting the opposite options of becoming poor and staying rich, we come to the third, which is to be generous and contented. The apostle summons Christian believers to be both. I am not, of course, claiming that this approach by itself will solve the problem of world poverty, but at least it is an appropriate expression of solidarity with the poor.

Take generosity. The skeleton of verses 17 and 18 is striking: "Command those who are rich . . . to be rich." More precisely, "Command those who are rich in this present world . . . to be rich in good deeds." In other words, let them add one kind of wealth to another. Tell them "to do good, to be rich in good deeds, and to be generous and willing to share." Then they will be imitating our generous God "who richly provides us with everything for our enjoyment." They will also store up treasure in heaven (v. 19), as Jesus urged us to do.

It would be impossible, however, to describe as "generous" the voluntary giving to charity of those of us who live in the North of the world. According to the Charities Aid Foundation, in 1993 only 29 percent of all households in Britain were giving to charity. For these 29 percent, average weekly giving was £3.89 per week. Although this shows an increase in giving from past years, the number of households participating has dropped.[26] "The facts appear to be," comments Michael Brophy, Chief Executive of CAF, "that a handful of people are very generous, whilst the majority of us are rather mean." It is interesting to note that UK expenditure on television sets and videos more than doubled between 1976 and 1987.

Next, contentment needs to be added to generosity. For it would be anomalous if generous giving to others resulted in discontent with what we had left. Paul extols contentment in 1 Timothy 6:6–10, as follows:

> But godliness with contentment is great gain. For we brought nothing into the world, and we can take nothing out of it. But if we have food and cloth-

ing, we will be content with that. People who want to get rich fall into temptation and a trap and into many foolish and harmful desires that plunge men into ruin and destruction. For the love of money is a root of all kinds of evil. Some people, eager for money, have wandered from the faith and pierced themselves with many griefs.

We notice that, whereas the other paragraph in 1 Timothy 6 which we considered relates to "those who are rich" (v. 17), this one is addressed to "people who want to get rich" (v. 9), that is, the covetous. Paul sets covetousness and contentment in contrast to one another. Covetousness is a self-destructive passion, a craving which is never satisfied, even when what has been craved is now possessed. As Schopenhauer said, "Gold is like sea water—the more one drinks of it, the thirstier one becomes."[27] "Beware of covetousness," warned Jesus. "Covetousness is idolatry," added Paul (Luke 12:15 RSV; Colossians 3:15; cf. Ephesians 5:5). It seduces the heart from love of God and imprisons it in love for money. It brings much pain and many sorrows, for "the love of money is a root of all kinds of evil" (1 Timothy 6:10).

Contentment, on the other hand, is the secret of inward peace. It remembers the stark truth that "we brought nothing into the world, and we can take nothing out of it" (v. 7). Life, in fact, is a pilgrimage between two moments of nakedness, namely birth and burial. So we should travel light and live simply. Bishop John V. Taylor has put it well: "The word 'poverty' has come to sound so negative and extreme in our ears that I prefer the word 'simplicity,' because it puts the emphasis on the right points. . . . Our enemy is not possessions but excess. Our battle-cry is not 'nothing!' but 'enough!'"[28] Simplicity says "if we have food and clothing, we will be content with that" (v. 8). For Christian contentment is coupled with godliness, the knowledge of God in Jesus Christ, and "godliness with contentment is great gain" (v. 6).

We have looked at the three options which confront all affluent Christians. Should we become poor? No, not necessarily. Though doubtless Jesus Christ still calls some like the rich young ruler to a life of total voluntary poverty, it is not the vocation of all his disciples. Then should we stay rich? No, this is not only unwise (because of the perils of conceit and materialism) but actually impossible (because we are to give generously, which will have the effect of reducing our wealth). Instead of these two, we are to cultivate generosity on the one hand and simplicity with contentment on the other.

At this point the temptation is to lay down rules and regulations, whether for ourselves or others, and so lapse into Pharisaism. This makes three "isms" for us to avoid—materialism (an obsession with things), asceticism (an austerity which denies the good gifts of the Creator) and Pharisaism (binding one another with rules). Instead, we would be wise to stick to principles.

The principle of simplicity is clear. Its first cousin is contentment. It concentrates on what we need, and measures this by what we use. It rejoices in the Creator's gifts, but hates waste, greed and clutter. It says with the Book of Proverbs "give me neither poverty nor riches, but give me only my daily bread," for to have either too much or too little may lead to disowning or dishonoring God (30:8–9). It wants to be free of anything and everything which distracts from the loving service of God and others.

One of the most controversial sections of the Lausanne Covenant, adopted at the conclusion of the International Congress on World Evangelization in 1974, relates to the need for more simple living. It goes like this: "All of us are shocked by the poverty of millions and disturbed by the injustices which cause it. Those of us who live in affluent circumstances accept our duty to develop a simple lifestyle, in order to contribute more generously to both relief and evangelism."[29] It was to elucidate the implications of these sentences that an International Conference on Simple Lifestyle was held in 1980. It issued "An Evangelical Commitment to Simple Lifestyle," whose nine paragraphs deserve careful study. Paragraph 5 is entitled "Personal Lifestyle" and develops the concept of "simplicity." It includes a general resolve to "renounce waste and oppose extravagance in personal living, clothing and housing, travel and church buildings." But it betrays no negative asceticism. On the contrary, it picks up from Dr. Ronald Sider's paper "Living More Simply for Evangelism and Justice" a number of important distinctions: "We also accept the distinction between necessities and luxuries, creative hobbies and empty status symbols, modesty and vanity, occasional celebrations and normal routine, and between the service of God and slavery to fashion."[30] The point is that simple living is not incompatible with careful enjoyment.

But simple living is incompatible with living beyond one's means, that is, borrowing in order to purchase what one cannot afford. As a result of the steady growth of consumer credit in Britain during the 1980s (approximately 10 percent per annum in real terms), more and more people (especially younger and poorer people) have been getting into arrears with their mortgage and purchase repayments and their credit card bills, and so into serious debt. The Jubilee Centre Research Paper No. 7, *Families in Debt*, documents the results of a sample of 1,043 people with multiple debt problems. It also highlights three major biblical principles which "provide a coherent and highly reasonable foundation for policy initiatives" covering the prevention and cure of debt problems, namely "justice" (taking seriously the responsibilities of both lenders and borrowers), "mercy" (lenders giving good advice and being lenient with defaulters) and "hope" (the prospect of ultimate rescue from the debt trap).[31]

If the principle of simplicity is clear, so is the principle of generosity. John expresses it in these terms: "If anyone has material possessions and sees his brother in need but has no pity on him, how can the love of God be in him?" (1 John 3:17). Our God is a generous God. If his love indwells us, we shall relate what we "have" (possessions) to what we "see" (others' needs) and take action.

May God help us to simplify our lifestyle, grow in generosity and live in contentment!

PART 2

Sexual
Issues

5

Women, Men
and God

A schoolgirl was once asked to write an essay on why women outnumber men in the world. "God made Adam first," she wrote. "When he had finished, he looked at him and said to himself, 'Well, I think I could do better than that if I tried again.' So then he made Eve. And God liked Eve so much better than Adam that he has been making more women than men ever since."

The self-confident feminism of that young girl stands out in strong relief against the prevailing attitudes of the centuries. For there is no doubt that in many cultures women have habitually been despised and demeaned by men. They have often been treated as mere playthings and sex objects, as unpaid cooks, housekeepers and baby-sitters, and as brainless simpletons incapable of engaging in rational discussion. Their gifts have been unappreciated, their personality smothered, their freedom curtailed and their service in some areas exploited, in others refused.

The Rise of Feminism

This record of oppression of women has been so longstanding and widespread that there is an evident need for reparation by male-dominated society. Yet in presuming to include a chapter on this topic, I immediately find myself in an unfavorable position. Indeed my maleness, some will say, is more than an initial disadvantage; it constitutes a total disqualification. They may be right. How far can men understand women, let alone make pronouncements about them? Let me make two points in self-defense. First,

I have tried to listen carefully to what feminists (both secular and Christian) are saying, have read a number of their books, and have struggled to understand their hurts, frustration and even rage. At the same time, secondly, I am concerned, on this as on every subject, to listen to what Scripture says. This double listening is painful. But it should save us both from denying the teaching of Scripture in a determination at all costs to be modern, and from affirming it in a way that ignores the modern challenges and is insensitive to the people most deeply affected by them.

The ancient world's scorn for women is well-known. Plato, who believed that the soul is both imprisoned in the body and released only to be reincarnated, went on to suggest that a bad man's fate would be reincarnation as a woman.[1] Aristotle, although respected as the father of biology because of his two works *The History of Animals* and *The Generation of Animals*, regarded a female as "a kind of mutilated male." He wrote: "Females are imperfect males, accidently produced by the father's inadequacy or by the malign influence of a moist south wind."[2]

Such crude male chauvinism was not, unfortunately, limited to the pagan world. Even Jewish writers, whose knowledge of the Old Testament should have given them a better understanding, made derogatory remarks about women. Josephus expressed his opinion that "the woman is inferior to the man in every way."[3] William Barclay sums up the low view of women expressed in the Talmud in these words: "In the Jewish form of morning prayer . . . a Jewish man every morning gave thanks that God had not made him 'a Gentile, a slave or a woman.' . . . In Jewish law a woman was not a person, but a thing. She had no legal rights whatsoever; she was absolutely in her husband's possession to do with as he willed."[4]

It is a further tragedy that some of the early church fathers, influenced more by Greek and Talmudic perspectives than by Scripture, also sometimes spoke disparagingly of women. Tertullian, for example, wrote: "You are the devil's gateway; you are the unsealer of that (forbidden) tree; you are the first deserter of the divine law; you are she who persuaded him whom the devil was not valiant enough to attack. You destroyed so easily God's image, man. On account of your desert—that, is death—even the Son of God had to die."[5]

This kind of exaggerated language is incongruous from the pen of a follower of Jesus, to whom the contemporary liberation of women is largely due. The shame is that it did not come earlier, and that the initiative was not taken more explicitly in his name.

At least during this century the status and service of women have been rapidly changing, especially in the West.[6] Women have now been emancipated from nearly all the restrictions which had previously been imposed upon them. They have obtained the franchise, thanks to the courageous agitation of the suffragettes. In many countries (at least in theory) they receive equal pay for equal work. In Britain the Sex Disqualification (Removal) Act of 1919 opened to them virtually every public function, profession and civil post. By the 1960s only two professions were still closed to them, the London Stock Exchange and the ordained ministry of the historic churches. In 1973, however, the Stock Exchange capitulated. Now it is only ordination which, in some churches, is denied to women.

As the feminist movement gathered momentum, especially in the sixties, the utterances of some of its leaders became more strident.

As an example, take Germaine Greer, the Australian lecturer and author. She regarded her book *The Female Eunuch* (which *Newsweek* called a "dazzling combination of erudition, eccentricity and eroticism") as part of "the second feminist wave." The first had been that of the suffragettes, but their movement had failed because they had never taken advantage of the freedoms they had won. "The cage door had opened, but the canary had refused to fly out." The suffragettes had been content with reform by participation in the existing political system; Germaine Greer called for revolution. Her book contained a chapter entitled "The Middle-Class Myth of Love and Marriage," in which she hinted "that women ought not to enter into socially sanctioned relationships, like marriage, and that once unhappily in, they ought not to scruple to run away." Women "are the true proletariat, the truly oppressed majority; they should rebel, and withdraw their labour."[7]

Christians were offended by her tendency to extreme statement and vulgarity of expression. Yet she was rebelling against the stereotype of a woman as "the Sexual Object sought by all men," whose value is not in herself but in the demand she excites in others. "She is not a woman . . . She is a doll . . . She is an idol . . . Her essential quality is her castratedness."[8] In other words, all that is required of "the female eunuch" is a sexless submission to the sexual desires of men. Was it not right for Germaine Greer to revolt against this demeaning of women? However, since the publication of *The Female Eunuch* (nearly thirty years ago), she has modified both her position and her tone. Her views of men have changed, and so too have her views of marriage and motherhood.[9]

More persuasive was Janet Radcliffe Richards's *The Sceptical Feminist* (1980). She began by describing her book as "a battle on two fronts," since she was combating on the one hand the position which said "there is no justification for the existence of a feminist movement" and on the other hand "a good deal of common feminist dogma and practice."[10] Feminism to her was not an irrational movement by women for women, in which on every single issue (however indefensible) women side with women against men. Instead, it had arisen from the conviction that "women suffer from systematic social injustice because of their sex." Therefore it was "a movement for the elimination of sex-based injustice."[11] This complaint of injustice and cry for justice should be enough to make every Christian sit up and take notice. For justice is concerned with God-given rights.

It would be a mistake, however, to regard feminism as a largely non-Christian movement. Elaine Storkey corrects this error in her fine, largely historical and sociological survey entitled *What's Right with Feminism*.[12] She begins with a thorough, factual account of the inequality and oppression of women in western society. Her case is irrefutable and is calculated to make all readers feel ashamed. She continues with a critical analysis of the three main streams of secular feminism—liberal, marxist and radical. She is prepared to acknowledge what is right in these movements. Yet basically all three are wrong because they have their roots in the Enlightenment and in its fatal confidence in human autonomy. So next she describes the two opposite extremes of Christian response, namely "Christianity against Feminism" (an uncritical and often uninformed rejection, which refuses to take it seriously) and "Salvation through Feminism" (ranging from a "broadly Christian" position, which is selective and even dismissive of Scripture, to a "post-Christian" stance which has attempted to redefine Christianity as a woman-centered religion). Elaine Storkey ends with "A Third Way," which traces biblical feminism back to the Reformation and lays down its theological foundations.

It is clear, then, that feminism in all its forms—whether non-Christian, Christian or post-Christian—presents the Church with an urgent challenge. Feminism cannot be dismissed as a secular bandwagon which trendy churches (in their worldliness) jump on board. Feminism is about Creation and Redemption, love and justice, humanity and ministry. It obliges us to ask ourselves some searching questions. What does "justice" mean in reference to both men and women? What does God intend our relationships and roles to be? What is the meaning of our masculinity or femininity? How are we to discover our true identity and dignity? In endeavoring to summarize and synthesize the biblical teaching on these sensitive topics, I shall focus on four crucial words—*equality, complementarity, responsibility* and *ministry*.[13]

Equality

It is essential to begin at the beginning, namely with the first chapter of Genesis:

> Then God said, "Let us make man in our image, in our likeness, and let them rule over the fish of the sea and the birds of the air, over the livestock, over all the earth, and over all the creatures that move along the ground."
> So God created man in his own image, in the image of God he created him; male and female he created them.

106

God blessed them and said to them, "Be fruitful and increase in number; fill the earth and subdue it. Rule over the fish of the sea and the birds of the air and over every living creature that moves on the ground."

Genesis 1:26–28

If we put together the divine resolve ("Let us make man . . . and let them rule . . ."), the divine Creation ("So God created . . .") and the divine blessing ("Be fruitful . . . fill the earth and subdue it . . ."), we see that the emphasis seems to be on three fundamental truths about human beings, namely that God made (and makes) them in his own image, that he made (and makes) them male and female, giving them the joyful task of reproducing, and that he gave (and gives) them dominion over the earth and its creatures. Thus from the beginning "man" was "male and female," and men and women were equal beneficiaries both of the divine image and of the earthly rule. There is no suggestion in the text that either sex is more like God than the other, or that either sex is more responsible for the earth than the other. No. Their resemblance to God and their stewardship of his earth (which must not be confused, although they are closely related) were from the beginning shared equally, since both sexes were equally created by God and like God.

Moreover, the threefold affirmation of God's Creation in verse 27 is not just poetic parallelism. There is surely a deliberate emphasis here, which we are intended to grasp. Twice it is asserted that God created man in his own image, and the third time the reference to the divine image is replaced by the words "male and female." We must be careful not to speculate beyond what the text warrants. Yet, if both sexes bear the image of God (as is forcefully asserted), then this seems to include not only our humanity (authentic humanness reflecting divinity), but our plurality (our relationships of love reflecting those which unite the persons of the Trinity) and even, at least in the broadest sense, our sexuality. Is it too much to say that since God, when he made humanity in his own image, made them male and female, there must be within the being of God himself something which corresponds to the "feminine" as well as the "masculine" in humankind?

If so, was the National Council of Churches of Christ (USA) justified in publishing *An Inclusive Language Lectionary,* from which all "sexist" or "exclusive" vocabulary had been eliminated? We can certainly applaud their desire "to express the truth about God and about God's inclusive love for all persons" and "to provide to both reader and hearer a sense of belonging to a Christian faith community in which truly all are one in Christ." They were right, therefore, to translate "brethren" as "sisters and brothers," and the generic "man" as "human being" or "humankind," for in so doing they clarified what these words have always meant. I do not think they had the liberty, however, actually to change the biblical text, on the ground that they regarded its language as sometimes "male-biased or otherwise inappropriately exclusive." To call God "the Father (and Mother)" and Jesus Christ his "only Child" is to set aside the concrete historical reality of the Incarnation. This contradicts both the experience and the teaching of Jesus, who addressed God as "Abba Father," knew himself as "the Son," and taught us to call God "our Father in heaven."[14]

What we should do, however, is give full weight to those passages of Scripture which speak of God in feminine—and especially maternal—terms. For these texts help to illumine the nature and quality of his "fatherhood." For example, according to the Song of Moses, Yahweh was not only "the Rock who fathered you" but also "the God who gave you birth." This is a remarkable statement that he was simultaneously Israel's Father and Mother. In consequence, Israel could be sure of God's preserving faithfulness. For though a human mother might "forget the baby at her breast and have no compassion on the child she has borne," yet, Yahweh promised, "I will not forget you!" Instead, he would unfailingly love and console his people: "As a mother comforts her child, so will I comfort you." Moreover, if Yahweh in these texts revealed himself as the mother of his people Israel, the individual Israelite felt at liberty to enter into this relationship. The psalmist dared even to liken his quiet confidence in God to the humble trustfulness of a breast-fed child. Then Jesus himself on occasion used feminine imagery, likening God to a woman who had lost a coin, as well as to a father who had lost a son, and likening himself in his anguish over impenitent Jerusalem to a hen wanting to gather her chicks under her wings (Deuteronomy 32:18; cf. Isaiah 42:14; 49:15; 66:13; Psalm 131:1–3; Luke 15:8–31; Matthew 23:37).

So then, returning to the Creation story, it is clear that from the first chapter of the Bible onwards the fundamental equality of the sexes is affirmed. Whatever is essentially human in both male and female reflects the divine image which we equally bear. And we are equally called to rule the earth, to cooperate with the Creator in the development of its resources for the common good.

This primeval sexual equality was, however, distorted by the Fall. Part of God's judgment on our disobedient progenitors was his word to the woman: "Your desire will be for your husband, and he will rule over you." Thus the sexes would experience a measure of alienation from one another. In place of the equality of the one with the other, and of the complementarity of the one to the other (which we have yet to consider), there would come the rule of the one over the other. Even if (according to Paul) sexual complementarity included from the beginning a certain masculine "headship," to which I will come later, it was never intended to be autocratic or oppressive. The domination of woman by man is due to the Fall, not to the Creation.

Moreover, men have misused this judgment of God as an excuse to maltreat and subjugate women in ways God never intended. Examples could be given from many cultures. I will give four. First, from Gandhi's autobiography: "A Hindu husband regards himself as lord and master of his wife, who must ever dance attendance upon him."[15] Next, consider Sura 4 of the Koran, entitled "Women": "Men have authority over women because Allah has made the one superior to the other. . . . As for those from whom you fear disobedience, admonish them and send them to beds apart and beat them. . . ."[16] My third example comes from the Eskimos. Raymond de Coccola spent twelve years among the "Krangmalit" in the Canadian Arctic, as a Roman Catholic missionary, and got to know them well. He was shocked when an Eskimo hunter used a word of a woman which was also applied to a she-wolf or a bitch. "Trained to do all manner of mean tasks," he reflected, "the Eskimo woman is used to enduring the weaknesses and appetites of men. But I still could not get used to what appeared to be a master-and-slave relationship between the hunter and his wife."[17] As my fourth example I choose pornography, a major symbol of western decadence, in which women are made the objects of male abuse and violence.

These are examples of the unlawful exploitation of women, however. In the Old Testament the husband was certainly the patriarch and *ba'al* (lord or ruler) of his clan. Yet his womenfolk were not despised or ill-treated. They were regarded as an integral part of the covenant community, so that "men, women and children" were together assembled to listen to the public reading of the Torah and to share in the worship (e.g., Deuteronomy 31:12). Marriage was held in high honor, modeled on Yahweh's covenant love to Israel, the beauty of sexual love was celebrated (as in the Song of Songs), the capabilities of a good wife were praised (e.g., Proverbs 31), godly and enterprising women like Hannah, Abigail, Naomi, Ruth and Esther were held up for admiration, and it was constantly emphasized that widows must be cared for.

Yet the prophets looked forward to the days of the New Covenant in which the original equality of the sexes would be reaffirmed. For God would pour out his Spirit on all flesh, including sons and daughters, menservants and maidservants. There would be no disqualification on account of sex.

Then Jesus came in the fullness of time, born of a woman (Galatians 4:4). Although Protestants are anxious to avoid the exaggerated veneration of the Virgin Mary accorded to her in the Roman Catholic and Orthodox Churches, we should also avoid the opposite extreme of failing to honor her. If the angel Gabriel addressed her as "highly favored," and if her cousin Elizabeth called her "blessed . . . among women," we should not be shy to think and speak of her in the same terms, because of the greatness of her Son (Luke 1:28, 42).

It was not only his birth of a woman, however, which restored to women that measure of dignity lost by the Fall, but his attitude to them. In addition to his apostles, who were all men, Jesus was accompanied on his travels by a group of women, whom he had healed and who now provided for him out of their means. Next, he spoke to one at Jacob's well who, as woman, Samaritan and sinner had a threefold disability, but Jesus actually engaged her in a theological discussion. It was similar with the woman who had been caught in the act of adultery; he was gentle with her and refused to condemn her. Then he allowed a prostitute to come behind him as he reclined at table, to wet his feet with her tears, wipe them with her hair, and cover them with kisses. He accepted her love, which he interpreted as gratitude for her forgiveness. In doing so, he risked his reputation and ignored the silent indignation of his host. He was probably the first man to treat this woman with respect; previously men had only used her (Luke 8:1–3; Mark 15:41; John 4:1–26; 8:1–11; Luke 7:36–48).

Here were three occasions on which in public he received a sinful woman. A Jewish male was forbidden to talk to a woman on the street, even if she was his wife, daughter or sister. It was also regarded as impious to teach a woman the law; it would be better for the words of the law to be burned, said the Talmud, than that they should be entrusted to a woman. But Jesus broke these rules of tradition and convention. When Mary of Bethany sat at his feet listening to his teaching, he commended her as doing the one thing that was needed, and he honored another Mary as the very first witness of the Resurrection (Luke 10:38–42; John 20:10–18).[18] All this was unprecedented. Without any fuss or publicity, Jesus terminated the curse of the Fall, reinvested woman with her partially lost nobility, and reclaimed for his new Kingdom community the original creation blessing of sexual equality.

That the apostle Paul had grasped this is plain from his great charter statement of Christian freedom: "There is neither Jew nor Greek, slave nor free, male nor female, for you are all one in Christ Jesus" (Galatians 3:28). This does not mean that Jews and Greeks lost their physical differences, or even their cultural distinctives, for they still spoke, dressed and ate differently; nor that slaves and free people lost their social differences, for most slaves remained slaves and free people free; nor that men lost their maleness and women their femaleness. It means rather that as regards our standing before God, because we are "in Christ" and enjoy a common relationship to him, racial, national, social and sexual distinctions are irrelevant. People of all races and classes, and of both sexes, are equal before him. The context is one of justification by grace alone through faith alone. It affirms that all who by faith are in Christ are equally accepted, equally God's children, without any distinction, discrimination or favoritism according to race, sex or class. So, whatever may need to be said later about sexual roles, there can be no question of one sex being superior or inferior to the other. Before God and in Christ "there is neither male nor female." We are equal.

Sexual equality, then, established by Creation but perverted by the Fall, was recovered by the redemption that is in Christ. What Redemption remedies is the Fall; what it recovers and reestablishes is the Creation. Thus men and women are absolutely equal in worth before God—equally created by God like God, equally justified by grace through faith, equally regenerated by the outpoured Spirit. In other words, in the new community of Jesus we are not only equally sharers of God's image, but also equally heirs of his grace in Christ (1 Peter 3:7) and equally indwelt by his Spirit. This Trinitarian equality (our common participation in Father, Son and Holy Spirit) nothing can ever destroy. Christians and churches in different cultures have denied it; but it is an indestructible fact of the gospel.

Complementarity

Although men and women are equal, they are not the same. Equality and identity are not to be confused. We are different from one another and we complement one another in the distinctive qualities of our own sexuality, psychological as well as physiological. This fact influences our different and appropriate roles in society. As J. H. Yoder has written, "Equality of worth is not identity of role."[19]

When we investigate male and female roles, however, we must be careful not to acquiesce uncritically in the stereotypes which our particular culture may have developed, let alone imagine that Moses brought them down from Mount Sinai along with the Ten Commandments. This would be a serious confusion of Scripture and convention.

Feminists are understandably rebelling against the expectation that women must fit into a predetermined role. For who fixed the mold but men? This is what the American author Betty Friedan meant by "the feminine mystique" in her book of that title (1963). It is the image to which women feel compelled to conform, and which has been imposed on them by a male-dominated society. "It is my thesis," she wrote, "that the core of the problem for women today is not sexual but a problem of identity—a stunting or evasion of growth that is perpetuated by the feminine mystique. . . . Our culture does not permit women to accept or gratify their basic need to grow and fulfill their potentialities as human beings. . . ."[20] Motherhood is indeed a divine vocation, and calls for great sacrifices. But it is not woman's only

111

vocation. There are other equally serious and equally unselfish forms of service to society which she may be called to give.

There is nothing in Scripture to suggest, for example, that women may not pursue their own careers or earn their own living; or that married women must do all the shopping, cooking and cleaning, while their husbands remain noncontributing beneficiaries of their labor; or that child rearing is an exclusively feminine preserve into which men may not trespass. The German saying which restricts the province of women to *Kinder, Küche und Kirche* ("children, kitchen and church") is an example of blatant male chauvinism. Scripture is silent about this kind of division of labor. Does it then say anything about sexual roles and relationships?

It is without doubt by a deliberate providence of God that we have been given two distinct Creation stories, Genesis 2 supplementing and enriching Genesis 1:

> The LORD God said, "It is not good for the man to be alone. I will make a helper suitable for him."
>
> Now the LORD God had formed out of the ground all the beasts of the field and all the birds of the air. He brought them to the man to see what he would name them; and whatever the man called each living creature, that was its name. So the man gave names to all the livestock, the birds of the air and all the beasts of the field.
>
> But for Adam no suitable helper was found. So the LORD God caused the man to fall into a deep sleep; and while he was sleeping, he took one of the man's ribs and closed up the place with flesh. Then the LORD God made a woman from the rib he had taken out of the man, and he brought her to the man.
>
> Genesis 2:18–22

What is revealed in this second story of Creation is that, although God made male and female equal, he also made them different. For in Genesis 1 masculinity and femininity are related to God's image, while in Genesis 2 they are related to each other, Eve being taken out of Adam and brought to him. Genesis 1 declares the equality of the sexes; Genesis 2 clarifies that "equality" means not "identity" but "complementarity" (including, as we shall soon see, a certain masculine headship). It is this "equal but different" state which we find hard to preserve. Yet they are not incompatible; they belong to each other as essential aspects of the biblical revelation.

Because men and women are equal (by Creation and in Christ), there can be no question of the inferiority of either to the other. But because they are complementary, there can be no question of the identity of one with the other. Further, this double truth throws light on male-female relationships and roles. Because they have been created by God with equal dignity, men and women must respect, love, serve and not despise one another. Because they have been created complementary to each other, men and women must recognize their differences and not try to eliminate them or usurp one another's distinctives.

Commenting on the special creation of Eve, Matthew Henry more than three hundred years ago wrote with quaint profundity that she was "not made out of his head to top him, nor out of his feet to be trampled upon by him, but out of his side to be equal with him, under his arm to be protected, and near his heart to be loved." Perhaps he got this idea from Peter Lombard who in about A.D. 1157, just before becoming Bishop of Paris, wrote in his Book of Sentences: "Eve was not taken from the feet of Adam to be his slave, nor from his head to be his lord, but from his side to be his partner."[21]

It is when we try to elaborate the meaning of complementarity, to explain in what ways the two sexes complement each other, and to define the distinctives of men and women, that we find ourselves in difficulties. Feminists become uncomfortable. They are suspicious of attempts to define femininity, partly because the definitions are usually made by men, who have (or at least may have) vested interests in securing a definition congenial to them, and partly because many sexual distinctives, as we have seen, are not intrinsic but established by social pressures. As Janet Radcliffe Richards has put it, feminists consider that it is "not by nature that women are so different from men, but by contrivance."[22]

But inherent sexual differences remain, however much some people wish to abolish them. One author who has emphasized their importance is George F. Gilder in his book *Sexual Suicide* (1973). "The feminists refer often . . . to 'human beings,'" he wrote, "but I do not care to meet one. I am only interested in men and women."[23] Again, "There are no human beings; there are just men and women, and when they deny their divergent sexuality, they reject the deepest sources of identity and love. They commit sexual suicide."[24] They also succeed in "exalting the sexual eccentric—the androgyne."[25] George Gilder quoted Margaret Mead who had said that "if any human society . . . is to survive, it must have a pattern of social life that comes to terms with the differences between the sexes." For, he continued, "the differences between the sexes are the single most important fact of human society."[26] Then in 1986 a revised edition of George Gilder's book was published under the title *Men and Marriage*. In it his position was consolidated (not least on account of his new, or greater, Christian commitment) rather than changed. He was outspoken not only in his description of men as "sexual barbarians" needing to be tamed by the disciplines of marriage and family, but also in his insistence on the mutual sacrifice of the sexes in the marriage covenant as the very foundation of a civilized society.

Although this emphasis on mutuality is welcome, the debate about the distinctions between men and women continues. Are they due to sex (unchanging biological differences between male and female) or to gender (changing cultural differences between masculine and feminine)?

It was a recognition of the differences between the sexes (minimized by feminists) which led to the publication in the early nineties of two books which have been sensational best-sellers. The first was Deborah Tannen's *You Just Don't Understand*, subtitled *Women and Men in Conversation*.[27] Her field in Georgetown and Princeton universities is linguistics, and her basic thesis is that "male-female conversation is cross-cultural communication,"[28] because men and women speak different languages in different ways for different purposes. The fundamental difference between the sexes is that women use language to secure intimacy, while men use language to secure independence. Failure to recognize this leads to misunderstanding and even confusion.

The second book is Dr. John Gray's *Men Are from Mars, Women Are from Venus*. To him the differences between the sexes are so profound that men and women seem to have come from different planets. "Martians" (men) value power and achievement, "Venusians" (women) value love and relationships.[29] Like Professor Tannen, Dr. Gray illustrates the differences from the way people communicate. When a woman is hurting, "she wants empathy, but he thinks she wants solutions."[30] They differ too in how they cope with stress. "Martians go to their caves to solve their problems alone," whereas "Venusians get together and openly talk about their problems."[31] For men are empowered "when they feel needed," women "when they feel cherished."[32] Christians find the book's generalizations somewhat naive and note that its author is descriptive, not evaluative. He does not recommend that we try to change one another; only that we understand and accept one another. But at least he urges us to remember that we are "supposed to be different."[33]

In this connection mention may be made of the remarkable American men's movement called Promise Keepers. Although it is not a self-conscious reaction against feminism, it seems to be responding to the need for men to be men. For example, the second of a Promise Keeper's seven promises is a commitment "to pursuing vital relationships with a few other men, understanding that he needs brothers to help him keep his promises." Since the movement began in July 1991, more than two million men have now attended Promise Keepers stadium conferences. Many thousands of others have formed small men's groups and participated in educational seminars and conferences on men's ministry, men's leadership and building men of integrity.

Responsibility

All students of Genesis agree that chapter 1 teaches sexual equality and chapter 2 sexual complementarity. To these concepts, however, the apostle Paul adds the idea of masculine "headship." He writes both that "the husband is the head of the wife" (Ephesians 5:23) and, more generally, that "the head of every man is Christ, and the head of the woman is man, and the head of Christ is God" (1 Corinthians 11:3). But what does this "headship" mean? And how can it possibly be reconciled with sexual equality and complementarity? These questions still seem to me to lie at the heart of the debate about male-female relationships and about the ordination and ministry of women.

Three attempts to resolve the paradox between sexual equality and masculine headship have been made. Some affirm headship so strongly as to contradict equality (or so it seems). Others deny headship because they see it as incompatible with equality. The third group seeks to interpret headship, and to affirm it in such a way as to harmonize with, and not contradict, equality.

The first of these options could perhaps be called "traditionalist" and even "hardline." It assumes that "headship" equals "lordship," since the husband is said to be head of his wife as Christ is head of the Church. This view understands Paul's prohibition of women speaking in church or teaching men, and his requirement of female submission and silence, as literal, permanent and universal injunctions. It therefore deduces that, although women do have ministries, leadership and decision making in both the church and the home are male prerogatives. The most outspoken and persuasive exposition of this viewpoint is David Pawson's *Leadership Is Male*. He defines "the paradox of gender" in terms of "vertical equality" (equal in relation to God) and "horizontal inequality" (unequal in relation to each other). But "inequality" (even when restricted to the horizontal plane) is a misleading term ("complementarity" is better) and seems impossible to reconcile with that full equality of the sexes which has been established by Creation, Redemption and Pentecost.[34]

Secondly, there are those who go to the opposite extreme. They deny any and every concept of masculine headship as being irreconcilable with the unity of the sexes in Christ. They declare Paul's teaching to be inapplicable on one or the other of four grounds, namely that it is mistaken or confusing or culture-bound or purely situational.

As an example of those who consider Paul's teaching on male headship to be erroneous, I cite Dr. Paul Jewett in his otherwise admirable book *Man as Male and Female*. His thesis can be simply stated. The original "partnership" which God intended for men and women was replaced in Old Testament days by a hierarchical model derived from Israel's cultural milieu. But then with Jesus "a new thing happened: he spoke of women and related to women as being fully human and equal in every way to men. In this respect Jesus was truly a revolutionary."[35] This dialectic between the Old Testament and Jesus was embodied in Paul, who expressed now the one viewpoint, now the other. As the apostle of Christian liberty he "spoke the most decisive word . . . in favour of women's liberation" (namely, Galatians 3:28, "there is neither . . . male nor female"), but as the former Jewish rabbi, following rabbinic interpretation of Genesis 2, he spoke "the most decisive word . . . in favour of woman's subjection" (namely, 1 Corinthians 11:3, "the head of the woman is man").[36] "These two perspectives," Dr. Jewett continues, "are incompatible, there is no satisfying way to harmonize . . . them."[37] Indeed, "female subordination" is "incompatible with (a) the biblical narratives of man's creation, (b) the revelation which is given us in the life of Jesus, and (c) Paul's fundamental statement of Christian liberty" (i.e., Galatians 3:28).[38] This incongruity, he concludes, is due to the fact that Scripture is human as well as divine, and that Paul's "insight" has "historical limitations."[39] In other words, Paul was mistaken. He did not grasp the full implications of his own assertion that in Christ there is neither male nor female. He did not know his own mind. We are therefore free to choose between the apostle of Christian liberty and the unreformed rabbi, and, says Dr. Jewett, we greatly prefer the former.

Now there is much in Dr. Jewett's book which is excellent, especially his exposition of the attitudes and teaching of Jesus. But to abandon the task of harmonization and declare the apostle Paul to be double minded and mistaken is a counsel of despair. It is better to give him credit for consistency of thought. The truth is that submission does not imply inferiority and that distinct sexual identities and roles are not incompatible with equality of worth.

The second way of rejecting the concept of headship is to declare Paul's teaching to be too confusing to be helpful. This is the position adopted by Gretchen Gaebelein Hull in her book *Equal to Serve*. Her study of Pauline "hard passages" led her to the discovery that "there is no scholarly consensus on the meaning or interpretation of these passages."[40] In consequence, she decided to put them aside as peripheral and to focus instead on "the larger truth of women's equal redemption and equal inheritance rights,"[41] and "equal opportunity to serve God."[42] "That all believers are equally redeemed," she writes, "and therefore equally eligible to serve, forms the basis for any philosophy of Christian life and service. God makes no distinction based on race, class or gender."[43] I enjoyed reading Mrs. Hull's book, and particularly appreciated her repeated emphasis on the sacrificial and suffering servanthood to which all Christ's people are called.[44] Yet I do not myself feel able, in the face of difficult texts, to surrender the tasks of interpretation and harmonization. Nor do I think it logical to argue that our equal redemption necessarily implies equal service.

If Paul's teaching was neither mistaken nor too confusing to understand, then was it culture-bound? That is to say, can we argue that his position on masculine headship was valid for his own day, and so for first-century churches in the Greco-Roman world, but that it is not binding on us in the modern world? My immediate response to these questions must be to draw attention to the danger inherent in the argument. If we may reject Paul's teaching on men and women on the ground that it is culture-bound, may we not on the same ground also reject his teaching on marriage, divorce and homosexual relationships, indeed on God, Christ and salvation? If the teaching of the apostles was binding only on their own generation, then none of it has any necessary relevance to us or authority over us. But we have no liberty to engage in cultural rejection (i.e., repudiating God's revelation because of its first-century cultural clothing); our task is rather that of cultural transposition (i.e., guarding God's revelation and translating it into an appropriate modern idiom).

The attempt is sometimes made to strengthen the cultural argument by a reference to slavery. For if Paul told wives to submit to their husbands, he also told slaves to submit to their masters. But slaves have long since been liberated; is it not high time that women were liberated too? This parallel between slaves and women, and between abolitionism and feminism, was made as long ago as 1837, when two American books were published, namely, *The Bible against Slavery* by Theodore Weld and *Letters on the Equality of the Sexes* by Sarah Grimke, his sister-in-law. The key text in their argument was Galatians 3:28, since in it Paul wrote that in Christ on the one hand "there is neither . . . slave nor free" and on the other "there is neither . . . male nor female."[45]

The argument is flawed, however. For the analogy between women and slaves is extremely inexact on two counts. First, women were not chattel property, bought and sold in the marketplace, as slaves were. And secondly, though Paul sought to regulate the behavior of slaves and masters, he nowhere appealed to Scripture in defense of slavery, whereas he did base his teaching about masculine headship on the biblical doctrine of Creation. He drew his readers' attention to the priority of Creation ("Adam was formed first, then Eve," 1 Timothy 2:13), the mode of Creation ("man did not come from woman, but woman from man," 1 Corinthians 11:8) and the purpose of Creation ("neither was man created for woman, but woman for man," 11:9). Thus, according to Scripture, although "man is born of woman" and the sexes are interdependent (11:11–12), yet woman was made after man, out of man and for man. One cannot dismiss these three arguments (as some writers try to) as "tortuous rabbinic exegesis." On the contrary, as Dr. James B. Hurley demonstrates in his *Man and Woman in Biblical Perspective*, they are exegetically well-founded. For (a) by right of primogeniture "the firstborn inherited command of resources and the responsibility of leadership," (b) when Eve was taken out of Adam and brought to him, he named her "woman," and "the power to assign . . . a name was connected with control," and (c) she was made for him neither as an afterthought, nor as a plaything, but as his companion and fellow worker, to share with him "in the service of God and in the custodial ruling of the earth."[46]

It is essential to note that Paul's three arguments are taken from Genesis 2, not Genesis 3. That is to say, they are based on the Creation, not the Fall. And, reflecting the facts of our human creation, they are not affected by the fashions of a passing culture. For what Creation has established, no culture is able to destroy. The wearing of a veil or of a particular hairstyle was indeed a cultural expression of submission to masculine headship and may be replaced by other symbols more appropriate to the twentieth century, but the headship itself is creational, not cultural.[47]

If we may not reject Paul's teaching on masculine headship on the grounds that it is mistaken, unclear or culture-bound, may we do so because it was situational, that is, because it was addressed to highly specific situations which no longer exist today? This argument is similar to the previous one, but differs from it in one important respect. To declare Paul's teaching "culture-bound" is a judgment which we form, namely that it seems to us dated and therefore irrelevant; to call it "culture-specific" is to recognize the particularity of the apostle's instruction, and to argue that he himself did not regard it as applicable to all times and places.

This suggestion is often made with regard to Paul's requirement that "women should remain silent in the churches" and be "not allowed to speak" (1 Corinthians 14:34–35). Again, "I do not permit a woman to teach or to have authority over a man; she must be silent" (1 Timothy 2:12). The scholarly attempt to restrict these prohibitions to particular situations in Corinth and Ephesus is associated with the names of Richard and Catherine Clark Kroeger. They wrote a series of articles for *The Reformed Journal* between 1978 and 1980, whose substance was published in 1992 under the title *I Suffer Not a Woman: Re-thinking 1 Timothy 2:11–15 in Light of Ancient Evidence*.[48] In one article entitled "Pandemonium and Silence in Corinth"[49] they pointed out that ancient Corinth was a well-known center of the worship of Bacchus (identified by the Greeks with Dionysus), which included frenzied shouting, especially by women. They therefore suggest that Paul was urging self-control in worship, in place of wild ecstasies, and that the *lalein* he was forbidding (an onomatopoetic word) was either the mindless ritual shouting of "alala" or the babbling of idle gossip.

The Kroegers also suggest in a subsequent article that a different kind of feminist movement had developed in Ephesus, where Timothy was superintending the churches, and where Diana (Artemis) the great mother goddess reigned, served by her numerous fertility priestesses. They point out that there is a strong emphasis in the Pastoral Epistles on the need to "silence" heretics (e.g., 1 Timothy 1:3; Titus 1:10–11); that the prohibition of women teaching may well refer to their teaching of heresy; and that the heresy which Paul combats in the Pastorals may have been an incipient Gnosticism, whose later developments "based their gnosis on a special revelation given to a woman," notably Eve. For she was the first to eat from the tree of knowledge (gnosis), had also (some taught) enjoyed a prior existence, and was even Adam's creator. She was therefore well qualified to instruct Adam. If such a heresy was already current in Ephesus, then Paul's insistence that Adam was created first and Eve deceived—not enlightened—first (1 Timothy 2:13–14) would certainly take on an extra significance.[50]

As for the verb *authenteo*, whose only New Testament occurrence is in 1 Timothy 2:12, meaning to "domineer," it is argued that it sometimes had sexual overtones. Some scholars have therefore suggested that what Paul was forbidding was the seduction of men which was doubtless common in Ephesian temple prostitution. Catherine Clark Kroeger, however, prefers to translate it "to proclaim oneself the author or originator of something" and to understand it as prohibiting the Gnostic mythology that "Eve predated Adam and was his creator."[51]

These theories have been developed with considerable learning and ingenuity. They remain speculations, however. Not only is it anachronistic to refer to "Gnosticism" as if it were already a recognizable system by the sixties of the first century A.D., but also there is nothing in the text of either 1 Corinthians 14 or 1 Timothy 2 to indicate that Paul was alluding to specific feminist movements in Corinth and Ephesus. On the contrary, the command to "silence" in both passages would seem a strangely roundabout way to prohibit the beliefs and practices which these scholars have described. Besides, Paul gives directions about "a woman" and "women"; his references are generic, not specific. Finally, even if this apostolic instruction can be proved to have been situational, it remains applicable to similar situations today. After all, every New Testament Epistle is an occasional document, which addresses particular problems in particular churches; the Epistles nevertheless continue to speak to our condition today.

So far we have looked at the two opposite viewpoints on relationships between men and women. On the one hand, there are those who affirm masculine headship (rightly, in my view), but do it so strongly as to seem to deny the full equality of the sexes. On the other hand, there are those who deny headship, in order to affirm (rightly, in my view) the equality of the sexes. But, as I have tried to show, all attempts to get rid of Paul's teaching on headship (on the grounds that it is mistaken, confusing, culture-bound or culture-specific) must be pronounced unsuccessful. It remains stubbornly there. It is rooted in divine revelation, not human opinion, and in divine Creation, not human culture. In essence, therefore, it must be preserved as having permanent and universal authority.

Is there, then, no way to resolve the paradox between sexual equality and masculine headship, except by denying one of them? Can they not both be affirmed? Many believe that they can, since Scripture itself does so. The right way forward seems to be to ask two questions. First, what does "headship" mean? Can it be understood in such a way as to be compatible with equality, while at the same time not manipulating it or evacuating it of meaning? Secondly, once headship has been defined, what does it prohibit? What ministries (if any) does it render inappropriate for women? Thus, the meaning and the application of "headship" are crucial to the ongoing debate.

How, then, can we interpret the meaning of headship with care and integrity and allow Scripture to reform our traditions in this respect? We certainly have to reject the whole emotive language of hierarchy, as if headship means patriarchy or patronizing paternalism, autocracy or domination, and as if submission to it means subordination, subjection or subjugation. We must develop a biblical understanding of masculine headship which is fully consistent with the created equality of Genesis 1, the outpouring of the Spirit on both sexes at Pentecost (Acts 2:17–18) and their unity in Christ and in his new community (Galatians 3:28).

Two interpretations of headship are being proposed. The first is that *kephale* ("head") means not "chief" or "ruler" but rather "source" or "beginning," and that Paul was describing man as woman's "origin," referring to the priority of his creation. This view goes back to an article by Stephen Bedale entitled "The Meaning of *Kephale* in the Pauline Epistles," which appeared in the *Journal of Theological Studies* in 1954. It was taken up and endorsed in 1971 by Professors F. F. Bruce and C. K. Barrett in their respective commentaries on First Corinthians, and has been quoted by many authors since then. In 1977, however, Dr. Wayne Grudem published his computerized survey of 2,336 uses of *kephale* in ancient Greek literature, drawn from thirty-six authors from the eighth century B.C. to the fourth century A.D. In this article he rejects Bedale's argument that *kephale* means "source"; he provides evidence that instead it means "authority over."[52] In its turn Dr. Grudem's thesis has been both criticized and reaffirmed.[53] So what *Christianity Today* has called "the battle of the lexicons" continues.[54]

I find myself wondering, however, if this lexical controversy is not to some extent a false trail. To be sure, it is important to determine how *kephale* was used outside the New Testament. Yet much more important is its meaning in the New Testament, and this is determined less by its etymology than by its use in each context. "Headship" seems clearly to imply some kind of "authority," to which "submission" is appropriate, as when "God placed all things under his [Christ's] feet and appointed him to be head over everything for the church" (Ephesians 1:22). But we must be careful not to overly press this. It is true that the same requirement of "submission" is made of wives to husbands, children to parents, slaves to masters and citizens to the state. There must therefore be a common denominator between these attitudes. Yet I cannot believe that anybody conceives the wife's submission to her husband to be identical with the obedience expected of children, slaves or citizens. A very different relationship is in mind. Besides, the word *authority* is never used in the New Testament to describe the husband's role, nor *obedience* the wife's. Nor does *subordination* seem to me to be the right word to describe her submission. Although it would be a formally correct translation of the Greek *hupotage*, it has in modern parlance unfortunate overtones of inferiority, even of military rank and discipline.[55]

How then shall we understand *kephale*, "head," and what kind of masculine headship does Paul envisage? It is unfortunate that the lexical debate confines us to the choice between "source of" and "authority over." There is a third option which contains an element of both. On the one hand, headship must be compatible with equality. For if "the head of the woman is man" as "the head of Christ is God," then man and woman must be equal as the Father and the Son are equal. On the other hand, headship implies some degree of leadership, which, however, is best expressed not in terms of "authority" but of "responsibility." The choice of this word is not arbitrary. It is based on the way in which *kephale* is understood in Ephesians 5 and on the two models Paul develops to illustrate the head's attitude to the body.[56] The first is Christ's attitude to his body, the Church, and the second is the personal concern which we human beings all have for the welfare of our own bodies.

First, "the husband is the head of the wife as Christ is the head of the church, his body, of which he is the Savior" (v. 23). Those last words are revealing. Christ is "head" of the Church in the sense that he is its "Savior." Changing the metaphor, he loved the Church as his bride, "and gave himself up for her to make her holy . . . and to present her to himself . . . holy and blameless" (vv. 25–27). Thus, the very essence of his headship of the Church is his sacrificial love for her.

Secondly, "husbands ought to love their wives as their own bodies. He who loves his wife loves himself. After all, no one ever hated his own body, but he feeds and cares for it [RSV "nourishes and cherishes it"], just as Christ does the church—for we are members of his body" (vv. 28–30). The ancient world did not think of the head's relationship to the body in modern neurological terms, for they did not know about the central nervous system. They thought rather of the head's integration and nurture of the body. So Paul wrote elsewhere of Christ as head of the Church, by whom the whole body is "joined and held together" and through whom it "grows" (Ephesians 4:16; Colossians 2:19).

The husband's headship of his wife, therefore, is a headship more of care than of control, more of responsibility than of authority. This distinction is of far-reaching importance. It takes our vision of the husband's role away from questions of domination and decision making into the sphere of service and nurture. I am glad that John Piper and Wayne Grudem, in their massive symposium *Recovering Biblical Manhood and Womanhood*, have opted for the word *responsibility:* "At the heart of mature masculinity is a sense of benevolent responsibility to lead, provide for and protect women . . ."[57] Similarly, Roy McCloughry in *Men and Masculinity,* subtitled *From Power to Love,* lays his emphasis on Christ's call to self-sacrifice. While conceding that there is "a plurality of masculinities," each shaped by its own culture, yet at all times and in all places masculinity has been associated with power—physical, professional, political and financial. Yet when we see Jesus Christ as "the key to the understanding of what it means to be a man," then masculinity becomes "laying down power to express self-giving love."[58]

Accepting responsibility for her as her "head," her husband gives himself up for her in love, just as Christ did for his body, the Church. And he looks after her, as we do our own bodies. His concern is not to crush her, but to liberate her. As Christ gave himself for his bride, in order to present her to himself radiant and blameless, so the husband gives himself for his bride, in order to create the conditions within which she may grow into the fullness of her womanhood.

But what is "womanhood" that it needs conditions to be created for its flowering? Can "manhood" and "womanhood" be defined in terms of certain invariable distinctives? Many scholars say not, adding that different cultures have arbitrarily assigned different qualities and therefore different roles to their men and women. Margaret Mead, for example, in her classic book *Male and Female: A Study of the Sexes in a Changing World,* compared the perceptions of sexuality among seven South Sea peoples with each other and with that of contemporary America. She showed that the diversity of masculine and feminine traits is enormous, the differences and similarities, the vulnerabilities, handicaps and potentialities all varying from culture to culture. Yet there are some regularities, she added, which seem to go back ultimately to the basic physiological distinctions between male and female, and relate to the tension between activity and passivity, initiative and response, potency and receptivity.[59] Janet Radcliffe Richards is understandably concerned with the same question. She has a chapter entitled "The Feminist and the Feminine," and asks: "What is it that people are afraid of, when they say they are opposed to feminism because it will result in women's ceasing to be feminine?"[60]

At the risk of causing offense, I think it is necessary for us to face the apostle Peter's description of women as "the weaker sex" (1 Peter 3:7). Of course we know that women can be extremely strong. In some cultures they perform all the heavy manual jobs. They are capable of astonishing feats of physical endurance. And there were the Amazons, the women warriors of Greek mythology. Yet even such an ardent feminist as Janet Richards feels bound to concede that "presumably women must in some sense tend to be weaker than men."[61] And Margaret Mead writes: "Still in every society men are by and large bigger than women, and by and large stronger than women."[62] Therefore mining is an occupation reserved for men, and so in most cultures is combatant soldiering. It is also highly significant that in the Olympic Games women do not compete with men. The reason we feel some embarrassment in saying these things is that "weakness" is not a quality which twentieth-century westerners normally admire, because we have absorbed (unconsciously, no doubt) something of the power-philosophy of Nietzsche. In consequence, we tend like him to despise weakness, whereas Peter tells us that it is to be honored. Moreover, a recognition that the woman is "weaker" is not incompatible with Peter's other statement in the same verse that she and her husband are equally "heirs . . . of the gracious gift of [eternal] life."

Under the rubric of "weakness" we should probably include those characteristically feminine traits of gentleness, tenderness, sensitivity, patience and devotion. These are delicate plants, which are easily trodden under foot and which wither and die if the climate is unfriendly. I cannot see that it is demeaning to women to say that male "headship" is the God-given means by which their womanhood is respected, protected and enabled to blossom.

Of course, men are also weak and needy. Weakness is celebrated in Scripture as the human arena in which Christ's power is best displayed (cf. 2 Corinthians 4:7; 12:9–10). Thus, both sexes are weak, fragile, vulnerable, and therefore dependent upon one another. If women need men, men also need women. Indeed, "It is not good for the man to be alone," God said (Genesis 2:18). Without woman, not necessarily as wife but certainly as companion and helper, man is but a pathetic apology for a human being. So we need each other. Yet, because men and women are different, the ways in which we need each other must surely be different too. It seems to me urgent for Christians to research more deeply into the complexity of these differences, in order that we may understand and serve each other better. Meanwhile, "headship" is the biblical term to describe a major way in which women need men and men may serve women. It is intended not to suppress but to support them, and to ensure that they are—and may more fully become—their true selves.

The heartfelt cry of the feminist has been for "liberation." She has felt inhibited by male dominance from discovering her true identity. Letha Scanzoni and Nancy Hardesty, for example, who follow Paul Jewett in his treatment of the biblical material, write this near the beginning of their book *All We're Meant to Be*: "The liberated Christian woman . . . is free to know herself, be herself, and develop herself in her own special way, creatively using to the full her intellect and talents." Then towards the end they write: "What are the basic issues of women's liberation? Do women want to become men? No, we simply want to be full human beings. . . . We only want to be persons, free to give the world all that our individual talents, minds and personalities have to offer."[63] The resolute desire of women to know, be and develop themselves, and to use their gifts in the service of the world, is so obviously God's will for them, that to deny or frustrate it is an extremely serious oppression. It is a woman's basic right and responsibility to discover herself, her identity and her vocation. The fundamental question is in what relationship with men will women find and be themselves? Certainly not in a subordination which implies inferiority to men and engenders low self-esteem. Instead, Letha Scanzoni and Nancy Hardesty insist on "a fully equal partnership." "Equality" and "partnership" between the sexes are sound biblical concepts. But not if they are pressed into denying a masculine headship of protective care. It is surely a distorted headship of domination which has convinced women that they cannot find themselves that way. Only the biblical ideal of headship, which because it is selflessly loving may justly be called "Christ-like," can convince them that it will facilitate, not destroy, their true identity.

Does this truth apply only to married women, whose caring head is their husband? What about single women? Perhaps the reason why this question is not directly addressed in Scripture is that in those days unmarried women were under their father's protective care, as married women were under their husband's. Today, however, at least in the West, it is usual for unmarried women to leave their parents and set up their own home independently. I see no reason to resist this. But I think it would be unnatural for such women to isolate themselves from men altogether, as it would be for single men to isolate themselves from women. For men and women need each other, as we have seen. It would therefore be more conducive to the full flowering of their womanhood if in some context, whether among relatives and friends, or at work, or (if they are Christians) at church, they could experience the respectful and supportive care of a man or men. If it is "not good for man to be alone," without feminine companionship, it is not good for woman to be alone either, without responsible masculine headship.

Ministry

That women are called by God to ministry hardly needs any demonstration. For "ministry" is "service" (*diakonia*), and every Christian, male and female, young and old, is called to follow in the footsteps of him who said he had not come to be served, but to serve (Mark 10:45). The only question is what form women's ministry should take, whether any limits should be placed on it, and in particular whether women should be ordained.

The Roman Catholic and Eastern Orthodox Churches have no women priests; they set themselves firmly against this development. Many Lutheran Churches now have them, for example in Scandinavia, although serious disagreement on the issue continues. The French Reformed Church accepted women ministers in 1965 and the Church of Scotland in 1966. Among the British Free Churches, the Congregationalists have had female ministers since 1917, while Methodists and Baptists have followed suit more recently. In the Anglican Church the pattern is uneven. Bishop R. O. Hall of Hong Kong was the first to ordain a woman priest (that is, presbyter) in 1944. In 1968 the Lambeth Conference (of Anglican bishops) declared that "the theological arguments as at present presented for and against the ordination of women to the priesthood are inconclusive." In 1975, however, the Church of England's General Synod expressed the view that there are "no fundamental objections to the ordination of women to the priesthood." Nevertheless, no women were yet ordained. Then at the 1978 Lambeth Conference the bishops recognized that some Anglican provinces now had women clergy and agreed to respect each other's discipline in this matter. Yet a deep division remains, which is partly theological and partly ecumenical, namely the damage which women's ordination would do to Anglican relationships with the Roman Catholic and Orthodox Churches. A sizeable group has broken away from the American Episcopal Church on this issue, and a similar split has been threatened in the Church of England. In other spheres, however, for example as deaconesses and as pioneer missionaries, women have an outstanding record of dedicated service.

Some Christians, anxious to think and act biblically, will immediately say that the ordination of women is inadmissible. Not only were all the apostles and the presbyters of New Testament times men, but the specific instructions that women must be "silent in the churches" and "not teach or have authority over a man" (1 Corinthians 14:34; 1 Timothy 2:12) settle the matter.

That is only one side of the argument, however. On the other side, a strong prima facie biblical case can be made for active female leadership in the Church, including a teaching ministry. In the Old Testament there were prophetesses as well as prophets, who were called and sent by God to be bearers of his word, women like Huldah, in the time of King Josiah. Before her, Miriam, Moses' sister, was described as a "prophetess," while Deborah was more; she also "judged" Israel for a number of years, settling their disputes, and actually led them into battle against the Canaanites (2 Kings 22:11–20; cf. 2 Chronicles 34:19–28; Exodus 15:20; Judges 4 and 5). In the New Testament, although indeed Jesus had no women apostles, it was to women that he first revealed himself after the Resurrection and entrusted the good news of his victory (John 20:10–18; Matthew 28:8–10). In addition, Acts and the Epistles contain many references to women speakers and women workers. Philip the evangelist's four unmarried daughters all had the gift of prophecy, and Paul refers to women who prayed and prophesied in the Corinthian church. He seems to have stayed on several occasions with Aquila and Priscilla ("my fellow workers in Christ," he called them), and Priscilla was evidently active for Christ in their married partnership, for twice she is named before her husband, and it was together that they invited Apollos into their home and "explained to him the way of God more adequately" (Acts 21:9; 1 Corinthians 11:5; cf. Joel 2:28; Acts 2:17; 18:26). Paul seems to have had women helpers in his entourage, as Jesus had had in his. It is impressive to see the number of women he mentions in his letters. Euodia and Syntyche in Philippi he describes as "fellow workers" (a term he also applied to men like Timothy and Titus), who had "contended" at his side "in the cause of the gospel." And in Romans 16 he refers appreciatively to eight women. He begins by commending "our sister Phoebe, a servant [or perhaps "deacon"] of the church in Cenchrea," who had been "a great help to many people" including Paul himself, and then sends greetings (among others) to Mary, Tryphena, Tryphosa and Persis, all of whom, he says, have worked "hard" or "very hard" in the Lord's service (Philippians 4:2–3; Romans 16:1–12). Then in verse 7 he greets "Andronicus and Junias" and describes them as "outstanding among the apostles." It seems clear (and was assumed by all the early church fathers) that Junias (or Junia) was a woman.[64] But was she an apostle? She may have been an "apostle of the churches" (2 Corinthians 8:23), that is, a kind of missionary, but, since she is otherwise completely unknown, it is extremely unlikely that she belonged to that small and authoritative group, the "apostles of Christ." Paul could equally well have meant that she was well-known among (that is, to) the apostles.

It is true that all the biblical examples in the preceding paragraph are of women's ministries which were either "charismatic" rather than "institutional" (i.e., appointed directly by God, like the prophetesses, not by the church, like presbyters), or informal and private (like Priscilla teaching Apollos in her home) rather than official and public (like teaching during Sunday worship). Nevertheless, if God saw no impediment against calling women into a teaching role, the burden of proof lies with the Church to show why it should not appoint women to similar responsibilities.

There is another argument in favor of women's ministry (including leadership and teaching) which is more general than these specific references, however. It is that on the Day of Pentecost, in fulfillment of prophecy, God poured out his Spirit on "all people," including "sons and daughters" and his "servants, both men and women." If the gift of the Spirit was bestowed on all believers of both sexes, so were his gifts. There is no evidence, or even hint, that the charismata in general were restricted to men, although apostleship does seem to have been. On the contrary, the Spirit's gifts were distributed to all for the common good, making possible what is often called an "every-member ministry of the Body of Christ" (Acts 2:17–18; 1 Corinthians 12:4–11). We must conclude, therefore, not only that Christ gives charismata (including the teaching gifts) to women, but that alongside his gifts he issues his call to develop and exercise them in his service and in the service of others, for the building up of his body.

This much is clear. But now we return to the double command to women to be silent in the public assembly. How shall we handle these texts? In 1 Corinthians 14 Paul is preoccupied with the building up of the Church (vv. 3–5, 26) and with the "fitting and orderly" conduct of public worship (v. 40). Perhaps, then, his command to silence is addressed more to loquacious women in the congregation than to all women. It certainly was not absolute, since he assumed that some women would pray and prophesy publicly (1 Corinthians 11:5). Rather, just as tongue-speakers should "keep quiet in the church" if there is no interpreter (1 Corinthians 14:28), and a prophet should stop talking if a revelation is given to somebody else (v. 30), so too talkative women should "remain silent in the churches" and, if they have questions, put them to their husbands when they get home (vv. 34–35). For (and this is the principle which seems to govern all public behavior in church) "God is not a God of disorder but of peace" (v. 33). It can hardly be a prohibition of all talking by women in church, since Paul has not only referred earlier to prophetesses (11:5) but here allows "everyone" to contribute "a hymn, or a word of instruction, a revelation, a tongue or an interpretation" (v. 26), without explicitly restricting these to men.

What about 1 Timothy 2:11–15?[65] The attempt to limit these verses to particular, heretical, feminist movements has not succeeded in gaining widespread acceptance. The apostle is giving directions about public worship and about the respective roles in it of men (v. 8) and women (vv. 9–12). His instruction sounds quite general: "A woman should learn in quietness and full submission. I do not permit a woman to teach or to have authority over a man; she must be silent." What strikes me about these sentences (and about 1 Corinthians 14:34), which has not been sufficiently considered by commentators, is that Paul expresses two antitheses, the first between to "learn in quietness" or "be silent" and "to teach," and the second between "full submission" and "authority." The latter is the substantial point, confirms Paul's constant teaching about female submission to male headship and is firmly rooted in the biblical account of Creation ("for Adam was formed first, then Eve"). But the other instruction (the requirement of silence and the prohibition of teaching), in spite of the controversial reference to the fact that Eve was "deceived," not Adam, seems to be an expression of the authority-submission syndrome, rather than an addition to it. There does not appear to be anything inherent in our distinctive sexualities which makes it universally inappropriate for women to teach men. So is it possible (I ask myself) that, although the requirement of "submission" is of permanent and universal validity, because grounded in creation, the requirement of "silence," like that of head covering in 1 Corinthians 11, was a first-century cultural application of it? Is it further possible, then, that the demand for female silence was not an absolute prohibition of women teaching men, but rather a prohibition of every kind of teaching by women which attempts to reverse sexual roles and even domineer over men?

My tentative answer to my own two questions is in the affirmative. I believe that there are situations in which it is entirely proper for women to teach, and to teach men, provided that in so doing they are not usurping any improper authority over them. For this to be so, three conditions need to be fulfilled, relating to the content, context and style of their teaching.

First, the content. Jesus chose, appointed and inspired his apostles as the infallible teachers of his Church. And they were all men, presumably because their foundational teaching required a high degree of authority. The situation today is entirely different, however. The canon of Scripture has long ago been completed, and there are no living apostles of Christ comparable to the Twelve or Paul. Instead, the primary function of Christian teachers is to "guard the deposit" of apostolic doctrine in the New Testament and to expound it. They do not therefore claim authority for themselves, but put themselves and their teaching under the authority of Scripture. This being so, women may surely be numbered among them. Moreover, if the reference to Eve being deceived (1 Timothy 2:14) is intended to mean that women are vulnerable to deception, then their determination to teach only from the Bible should be an adequate safeguard against it.

Secondly, there is the context of teaching, which should be a team ministry in the local church. Whether directly or indirectly, Paul appointed "elders" (plural) in every church (e.g., Acts 14:23; 20:17; Philippians 1:1; Titus 1:5). Many local churches in our day are repenting of an unbiblical one-man ministry and returning to the healthy New Testament pattern of a plural pastoral oversight. Members of a team can capitalize on the sum total of their gifts, and in it there should surely be a woman or women. But, in keeping with biblical teaching on masculine headship, I still think that a man should be the team leader. The practice of "cultural transposition" seeks to clothe the unchanged essence of divine revelation in new and appropriate cultural dress. In the first century masculine headship was expressed in the requirement of female head coverings and in the prohibition of women teaching men; could it not be expressed today, in a way that is both faithful to Scripture and relevant to the twentieth century, in terms of female participation in team ministries of which men are leaders? The team concept should also take care of the problem of ecclesiastical discipline. Discipline involves authority, it is rightly said, and should therefore not be exercised by a woman. But then it should not be exercised by a man on his own either. Discipline (especially in its extreme form of excommunication) should ideally be administered by the whole local church membership, and before the ultimate is reached by a team of leaders or elders together (e.g., Matthew 18:17; 1 Corinthians 5:4–5; Hebrews 13:17).

The third condition of acceptable teaching by women concerns its style. Christian teachers should never be swashbucklers, whether they are men or women. The humility of Christian teachers is to be seen both in their submission to the authority of Scripture and in their spirit of personal modesty. Jesus warned his apostles against imitating either the vainglorious authoritarianism of the Pharisees, or the power-hungry bossiness of secular rulers (Matthew 23:1–36 and Mark 10:42–45). And the apostle Peter, sensitive to the temptation to pride which all Christian leaders face, urged his fellow elders to put on the apron of humility, not lording it over those entrusted to their pastoral care, but rather being examples to Christ's flock (1 Peter 5:1–4). This instruction to men will be even more clearly exemplified in women who have come to terms with their sexual identity and are not trying to be, or behave like, men.

It seems then to be biblically permissible for women to teach men, provided that the content of their teaching is biblical, its context a team and its style humble. For in such a situation they would be exercising their gift without claiming a responsible "headship" which is not theirs. Does this mean, then, that women could and should be ordained? The difficulty I have in giving a straight answer to this question is due to the layers of muddle which have been wrapped round it. But if ordination publicly recognizes God's call and gifts, and authorizes the person concerned to exercise the kind of ministry described above, there is no a priori reason why women should not be ordained. It remains my view that the best way to reconcile women's ministry with masculine headship is to ordain women for ministry in a local team situation. Then they have ample opportunity to exercise their God-given gifts, while at the same time recognizing masculine headship. The fact that in recent years in the Anglican Communion some women have been appointed rectors or vicars and that, at the time of writing, eleven have become bishops (seven diocesan and four suffragan), has not changed my mind about the ideal arrangement. Now that we have been overtaken by events, however, how should we respond? We should surely avoid the two extreme reactions. We should neither make an unprincipled surrender to cultural pressure, nor give up and secede from the Church. What then? We should continue the dialogue, refusing to regard the issue as settled. Meanwhile, we should encourage ordained women to exercise their ministry voluntarily in ways which recognize masculine headship, for example in team situations.

If what I have written above about "cultural transposition" is correct, then we need to go on searching for appropriate visible symbols of masculine headship. Yet in the end the reality is more important than its symbols, and the reality we need to clarify concerns the essential nature of the ordained ministry and its relationship to masculine headship.

Those who begin with the Catholic view of the priest as an icon of Christ (who was male), representing God to us and us to God, conclude that it is impossible for a woman to fulfill this role.[66]

Those who begin instead with the Reformed view of the presbyter as a dominant figure, responsible for the teaching and discipline of the Church, conclude that it would be inappropriate for a woman to fulfill such an inherently authoritative role.

Supposing, however, that the Church oversight envisaged by the New Testament is neither priestly in the Catholic sense but pastoral, nor presbyteral in the fixed Reformed sense but more fluid, modest and varied, offering different kinds and degrees of ministry? Supposing that we begin instead with the teaching of Jesus Christ about the servant-leader? True, pastors are said to be "over" the congregation in the Lord, and the people are to "obey" their leaders (1 Thessalonians 5:12; Hebrews 13:17). But this was not Jesus' main emphasis. He described two communities, secular and godly, each with its distinctive leadership style. In the world "rulers of the Gentiles lord it over them, and their high officials exercise authority over them." But, he added immediately, "not so with you." "Instead, whoever wants to become great among you must be your servant," for he himself had come not to be served, but to serve (Mark 10:42–45). Thus, Jesus introduced into the world an altogether new style of leadership.

If then our fundamental vision of church leadership is neither the priest of Catholic tradition, nor the presbyter of Reformed tradition, but the servant described by Jesus, why should women be disqualified? If the essence of pastoral care is love, and its style is humility, then no biblical principle is infringed if women are welcomed to share in it. The fundamental issue is neither "ordination" nor "priesthood," but the degree of authority which necessarily inheres in the presbyterate. It may be difficult for us to envisage presbyters (even rectors and bishops), whose whole lifestyle exemplifies the humble servanthood of the Kingdom of God, for church history illustrates the constant tendency towards autocracy and prelacy, and we know the pride of our own hearts. But this is the reality we should be seeking, namely a ministry characterized by humility, not authority. For men it will mean expressing their God-appointed headship in self-sacrificial service. For women it will mean submitting to this headship and not attempting to discard or usurp it. Then men will remain men, and women women, and an unbiblical confusion will be avoided.

Our Christian struggle, in the midst of and indeed against the prevailing secularism, is to bear witness to the twin biblical principles of sexual equality and male headship, in Church and society as well as in the home, even as we continue to debate how this can best and most appropriately be done. Dr. J. I. Packer has expressed this tension well. Scripture continues to convince him, he writes, "that the man-woman relationship is intrinsically non-reversible. . . . This is part of the reality of creation, a given fact that nothing will change. Certainly, redemption will not change it, for grace restores nature, not abolishes it." We need, therefore, to "theologize reciprocity, spiritual equality, freedom for ministry, and mutual submission and respect between men and women within this framework of non-reversibility. . . . It is important that the cause of not imposing on women restrictions that Scripture does not impose should not be confused with the quite different goals of minimizing the distinctness of the sexes as created and of diminishing the male's inalienable responsibilities in man-woman relationships as such."[67]

I conclude with some central simplicities. If God endows women with spiritual gifts (which he does), and thereby calls them to exercise their gifts for the common good (which he does), then the Church must recognize God's gifts and calling, must make appropriate spheres of service available to women, and should "ordain" (that is, commission and authorize) them to exercise their God-given ministry, at least in team situations. Our Christian doctrines of Creation and Redemption tell us that God wants his gifted people to be fulfilled not frustrated, and his Church to be enriched by their service.

Marriage
and Divorce

Marriage is in all societies a recognized and regulated human institution. But it is not a human invention. Christian teaching on this topic begins with the joyful affirmation that marriage is God's idea, not ours. As the preface to the 1662 Prayer Book Marriage Service says, it was "instituted by God himself in the time of man's innocency"; it was "adorned and beautified" by Christ's presence when he attended the wedding at Cana; and it symbolizes "the mystical union betwixt Christ and his church." In these ways God has shaped, endorsed and ennobled marriage. True, he calls some people to forgo it and remain single in this life (Matthew 19:11–12; 1 Corinthians 7:7), and in the next world after the Resurrection it will be abolished (Mark 12:25). Nevertheless, while the present order lasts, marriage is to be "honored by all"; those who "forbid people to marry" are false teachers who have been misled by deceiving spirits (Hebrews 13:4; 1 Timothy 4:1–5). Moreover, because it is a "creation ordinance," preceding the Fall, it is to be regarded as God's gracious gift to all humankind.

Classical theology has followed the biblical revelation in identifying three main purposes for which God ordained marriage. It has also usually listed them in the order in which they are mentioned in Genesis 1 and 2, while adding that priority of order does not necessarily signify priority of importance. The first command to the male and female whom God had made in his own image was "Be fruitful and increase in number" (Genesis 1:28). So the procreation of children has normally headed the list, together with their upbringing within the love and discipline of the family.[1]

Secondly, God said, "It is not good for the man to be alone. I will make a helper suitable for him" (Genesis 2:18). Thus, God intended marriage (to quote the 1662 Book of Common Prayer again) for "the mutual society, help

133

and comfort that the one ought to have of the other both in prosperity and adversity." Dr. Jack Dominian uses more modern phraseology when he writes that husband and wife can give each other "sustenance" (supporting and "cherishing" one another), "healing" (for married life is the best context in which early childhood hurts may be healed by love), and "growth" or fulfillment (stimulating each other to develop the individual potential of each and so become a mature person).[2]

Thirdly, marriage is intended to be that reciprocal commitment of self-giving love which finds its natural expression in sexual union, or becoming "one flesh" (Genesis 2:24).

These three needs have been strengthened by the Fall. The loving discipline of family life has become all the more necessary because of the waywardness of children, mutual support because of the sorrows of a broken world, and sexual union because of temptation to immorality. But all three purposes existed before the Fall and must be seen as part of God's loving provision in the institution of marriage.

The higher our concept of God's original purpose for marriage and the family, the more devastating the experience of divorce is bound to be. A marriage which began with tender love and rich expectations now lies in ruins. Marital breakdown is always a tragedy. It contradicts God's will, frustrates his purpose, brings to husband and wife the acute pains of alienation, disillusion, recrimination and guilt, and precipitates in any children of the marriage a crisis of bewilderment, insecurity and often anger.[3]

Changing Attitudes

Yet, in spite of the suffering involved, the number of divorces continues to be high. In 1994 in the United States there were 2.4 million marriages and 1.2 million divorces. This means that a marriage took place every 13 seconds and a divorce every 26.[4] The total number of divorced people in the U.S. was 17.4 million in 1994.[5] One in every two marriages now ends in divorce. In the UK the picture is not much brighter. In 1994 there were 338,000 marriages, over a third of which were remarriages, and just under 180,000 divorces.[6] Almost four in ten marriages end in divorce. This is the highest rate in the European Union.[7]

The sociological reasons for the growth in divorce are many and varied. They include the emancipation of women, changes in the pattern of employment (both parents working), the pressures on family life exerted by unemployment and financial anxiety and of course the provisions of the civil law for easier divorce. But undoubtedly the greatest single reason is the decline of Christian faith in the West, together with the loss of commitment to a

Christian understanding of the sanctity and permanence of marriage, and the growing non-Christian assault on traditional concepts of sex, marriage and family. A clear indication of secularization in this area is the fact that, whereas in 1850 only 4 percent of British marriages took place in a Registry Office (as opposed to a church, chapel or synagogue), by 1993 the percentage had risen to 51. Further, the proportion of women aged 18 to 49 who were cohabiting without being married tripled between 1979 and 1992.[8]

Consider as an example of changed attitudes the book by George and Nena O'Neill entitled *Open Marriage: A New Lifestyle for Couples*. They confidently declare that monogamous marriage is obsolete and urge their readers to replace an "archaic, rigid, outmoded, oppressive, static, decaying, Victorian" institution with one that is "free, dynamic, honest, spontaneous, creative." They refuse to glorify either traditional marriage or motherhood, and regard partners as equal, independent individuals who enjoy complete and unfettered role reversibility.[9]

If each partner comes to regard marriage as primarily a quest for his or her self-fulfillment, rather than as an adventure in reciprocal self-giving, through which parents and children grow into maturity, the outcome is bound to be bleak. Yet it is this self-centered attitude to marriage which is being debated by many today. Here is an unabashed quotation from the book *Divorce: How and When to Let Go* by John H. Adam and Nancy Williamson Adam.[10] It appeared in the June 1982 issue of *New Woman:*

> Yes, your marriage can wear out. People change their values and lifestyles. People want to experience new things. Change is a part of life. Change and personal growth are traits for you to be proud of, indicative of a vital searching mind. You must accept the reality that in today's multi-faceted world it is especially easy for two persons to grow apart. Letting go of your marriage— if it is no longer good for you—can be the most successful thing you have ever done. Getting a divorce can be a positive, problem-solving, growth-oriented step. It can be a personal triumph.

Here is the secular mind in all its shameless perversity. It celebrates failure as success, disintegration as growth, and disaster as triumph.

Not only is the Christian view of marriage as a lifelong commitment or contract now a minority view in the West, but the Church is in danger of giving in to the world. For among Christian people, too, marriages are no longer as stable as they used to be, and divorces are becoming almost commonplace. Even some Christian leaders divorce their spouses and remarry, the while retaining their position of Christian leadership. In this area also the Christian mind is showing signs of capitulating to secularism. The dominant worldview seems to be one of selfish individualism.[11]

My concern in this chapter is with the Christian understanding of marriage as set forth in Scripture. Politico-legal issues (like the place of matrimonial offense in the concept of irretrievable breakdown, justice in financial settlements, custody of and access to children) are very important. So are social and psychological questions, some of which I have already mentioned. And I shall come to personal and pastoral matters at the end. But of primary importance for the Christian mind are the biblical questions. Even the painful trauma of a failed marriage cannot be made an excuse for avoiding these. What has God revealed to be his will in regard to marriage, and the possibility of divorce and remarriage? And how can we frame our policies and practice in accordance with biblical principles? To be sure, there are no easy answers. In particular, the Church feels the tension between its prophetic responsibility to bear witness to God's revealed standards and its pastoral responsibility to show compassion to those who have been unable to maintain his standards. John Williams is right to bid us remember that "the same God who said through Malachi 'I hate divorce' (2:16) also said through Hosea (whose partner had been blatantly immoral) 'I will heal their waywardness and love them freely, for my anger has turned away from them' (14:4)."[12]

Old Testament Teaching

The nearest the Bible comes to a definition of marriage is Genesis 2:24, which Jesus himself was later to quote, when asked about permissible grounds for divorce, as a word of God (Matthew 19:4–5). Immediately after Eve has been created and brought to Adam, and Adam has recognized her (in an outburst of love poetry) as his God-given spouse, the narrator comments: "For this reason a man will leave his father and mother and be united to his wife, and they will become one flesh."

From this we may deduce that a marriage exists in God's sight when a man leaves his parents, with a view not merely to living apart from them but to "cleaving" to his wife, and becomes one flesh with her. The "leaving" and the "cleaving" belong together, and should take place in that order. They denote the replacement of one human relationship (child-parent) by another (husband-wife). There are some similarities between these relationships, for both are complex and contain several elements. These are physical (in one case conception, birth and nurture; in the other sexual intercourse), emotional ("growing up" being the process of growing out of the dependence of childhood into the maturity of partnership) and social (children inheriting an already existent family unit, parents creating a new one). Yet there is an essential dissimilarity between them too. For the biblical expression "one flesh" clearly indicates that the physical, emotional and social unity of husband and wife is more profoundly and mysteriously personal than the relationship of children to parents. It is increasingly recognized that development as a human being necessitates a measure of emotional separation from parents, and that, as Dr. Jack Dominian has put it, "the failure to achieve a minimum of emotional independence is one of the main causes of marital breakdown."[13]

So Genesis 2:24 implies that the marriage union has at least five characteristics. It is an exclusive man-woman relationship ("a man . . . his wife . . ."), which is publicly acknowledged at some social event ("leaves his parents"), permanent ("cleaves to his wife"), and consummated by sexual intercourse ("they will become one flesh"). A biblical definition of marriage might then be as follows: Marriage is an exclusive heterosexual covenant between one man and one woman, ordained and sealed by God, preceded by a public leaving of parents, consummated in sexual union, issuing in a permanent mutually supportive partnership and normally crowned by the gift of children.

With this definition of marriage in our minds, we are in a position to evaluate cohabitation, that is, the practice of living together as man and wife without being married. This has become an increasingly popular lifestyle. In fact, "it is estimated that by the year 2000 four out of five couples (in the UK) will cohabit before they marry."[14] The report of a Church of England working party entitled *Something to Celebrate* (1995), and subtitled *Valuing Families in Church and Society*, included a ten-page section on this topic. It is a great pity that serious reflection on it has been inhibited by a diversion tactic on the part of the media. They seized on the statement that the Church should "abandon the phrase 'living in sin,'" but failed to appreciate the reason for the report's recommendation, namely that the expression reduced a complexity of issues to "a single sensationalist category."[15] The working party deserved better treatment, and in my view was right to listen open-mindedly, even sympathetically, to those who are unwilling to condemn cohabitation out of hand.

For cohabitation is at least to some degree a protest by the rising generation against the marriage conventions, hypocrisies and failures of their parents' generation. They have no wish to repeat their mistakes. "Marriage is only a piece of paper," they cry dismissively, meaning that the quality of their relationship is more important. We could perhaps affirm their concern as follows. If a man and a woman find themselves marooned on a desert island, they can undoubtedly enter into a valid marriage in the sight of God, even though all the trappings of a traditional wedding are unavailable to them. For what constitutes marriage before God is neither a legal document nor a church service nor an elaborate reception nor a shower of gifts, but a reciprocal covenant, pledging lifelong fidelity and consummated in sexual union.

In the light of this, some cohabitation may almost be regarded as marriage by another name, since the essence of marriage (a covenant commitment) is there. Nevertheless, two essential elements are usually missing from a situation of cohabitation. The first is the promise of a lifetime commitment. Too much cohabitation is an open-ended arrangement, a kind of trial marriage, in which the permanent commitment of marriage has been replaced by a temporary experiment. This cannot be called marriage; moreover, its provisional nature is bound to destabilize the relationship. "The period of cohabitation tends to be short-lived. One third of couples cohabit for less than a year, and only 16 per cent live with their partner for more than 5 years."[16] Further, the commonly made claim that a trial period will make a later marriage more stable is not borne out by the facts. "Those couples marrying in the 1980s, having first cohabited, were 50 per cent more likely to have divorced within 5 years of marrying than those who did not previously cohabit."[17] No relationship may be called marriage which does not include the intention to be faithful to one another for life. "What God has joined together," Jesus said, "let man not separate" (Matthew 19:6).

The second missing element in cohabitation is the public context in which marriage is undertaken. We have seen that the biblical definition of marriage (Genesis 2:24) includes the leaving of parents. In the culture of those days such a departure will not have been private, let alone clandestine, but public. In our day it cannot be applied to a casual leaving of home, as when a single student goes up to university. It indicates rather a definitive move away from dependence on parents in the home of one's childhood, in order to marry and so establish a new and independent home. A public relationship like this (a man and a woman living together as partners) needs to have a public beginning. This would of course be impossible on a desert island, but in society, family and friends have a right to know what kind of relationship exists, so that they can adjust to it. They would naturally also desire an opportunity to say good-bye, to celebrate and to promise support in the future. It is neither fair nor kind to leave the families in the dark and in the cold.

It is not parents only, however, nor only a wider circle of family and friends, who have a right to know about and share in the new relationship, but society as a whole. Sexual intimacy is of course essentially private, but not the relationship within which it takes place. Yet cohabitees do not make this distinction and make the mistake of regarding their whole relationship as an entirely private affair. Marriage, however, is public—both the event which initiates it and the relationship to which it leads. And although its due recognition by the law is not essential to the marriage itself (desert island marriages being registered in heaven but not on earth), its legal enactment is certainly advantageous. For a solemn pledge can hardly be regarded as "binding" without the sanctions of law. Moreover, a couple who commit themselves to each other need the protection which the law gives them.

From the family and the law we come to the Church. To be sure, a church service is no more essential to a marriage in God's sight than the corresponding secular formalities. Neither church nor registry office is to be found on a desert island. Nevertheless, since lifelong vows are solemn and should if possible be made publicly, a church service is most appropriate, especially for Christian believers. For it sets the reciprocal pledges in the presence of God and his people. Although marriage is not a "sacrament" in the sense that baptism is, yet both include a public commitment, which should be made in the presence of chosen witnesses.

To sum up, we should be able to agree that a couple could marry validly in the sight of God on a desert island, provided that they make lifelong vows to one another, even though no representatives of family, law or Church are present to witness them. But in the real world in which we live, a couple's commitment needs to be public as well as permanent, and the role of the family, the law and the Church make the difference between marriage and cohabitation.

In my view, therefore, *Something to Celebrate* was unwise to take a "both-and" approach, and to recommend Christians "both to hold fast to the centrality of marriage and at the same time to accept that cohabitation is, for many people, a step along the way towards that fuller and more complete commitment."[18] In their both-and approach, and in their laudable desire to be sympathetic and nonjudgmental, the authors of the report have blurred the distinction between marriage and cohabitation. It is more accurate and more helpful to speak of cohabitation as falling short of marriage, than as a stepping-stone towards it. Our imaginary visit to a desert island should have helped us to clarify theologically what the essence of marriage is in the sight of God. But our responsibility is to stay in the real world and to maintain without compromise the biblical definition of marriage, including its public and permanent nature.

Then we can affirm what Dr. George Carey, Archbishop of Canterbury, said during the General Synod debate on *Something to Celebrate:*

> Cohabitation is not, and cannot be, marriage in all but name. Marriage is public and formal, whereas . . . cohabiting relationships . . . remain private and provisional in status. . . . Marriage, not cohabitation, is the institution which is at the heart of the good society, and let us not be reluctant to say so. I do not say this in condemnation, I say it as an invitation to a better way . . .[19]

We come now in our survey of biblical teaching to Deuteronomy 24:1–4, which is of particular importance because it is the only Old Testament passage which refers to grounds or procedures for divorce.

If a man marries a woman who becomes displeasing to him because he finds something indecent about her, and he writes her a certificate of divorce, gives it to her and sends her from his house, and if after she leaves his house she becomes the wife of another man, and her second husband dislikes her and writes her a certificate of divorce, gives it to her and sends her from his house, or if he dies, then her first husband, who divorced her, is not allowed to marry her again after she has been defiled. That would be detestable in the eyes of the LORD. Do not bring sin upon the land the LORD your God is giving you as an inheritance.

Three particular points need to be clarified about this legislation. The first concerns its thrust and purpose. It neither requires, nor recommends, nor even sanctions divorce. Its primary concern is not with divorce at all, nor even with certificates of divorce. Its object is to forbid a man to remarry his former spouse, if he has divorced her, since this would be "detestable in the eyes of the LORD." It is thought that the ruling was intended to protect the woman from a capricious and perhaps cruel former husband. At all events, the first three verses are all the protasis or conditional part of the sentence; the apodosis or consequence does not begin until verse 4. The law is not approving divorce; what it says is that if a man divorces his wife, and if he gives her a certificate, and if she leaves and remarries, and if her second husband dislikes and divorces her, or dies, then her first husband may not marry her again.

Secondly, although divorce is not encouraged, yet if it happens, the ground on which it takes place is that the husband finds "something shameful" (NEB, RSV) or "something indecent" (NIV) in his wife. This cannot refer to adultery on her part, for this was punishable by death, not divorce (Deuteronomy 22:20–21; cf. Leviticus 20:10). So what was it? During the first century B.C. the rival Pharisaic parties led by Rabbi Shammai and Rabbi Hillel were debating this very thing. Shammai was strict and understood "something indecent" (whose Hebrew root alludes to "nakedness" or "exposure") as a sexual offense of some kind which, though left undefined, fell short of adultery or promiscuity. Rabbi Hillel, by contrast, was lax. He picked on the phrases which said that the wife "becomes displeasing" to her first husband (v. 1) or that her second husband "dislikes" her (v. 3), and interpreted them as including even the most trivial misdemeanors; for example, if she spoiled the food she was cooking for him or was quarrelsome or if he came across a woman more beautiful than she, and so lost interest in her.[20] In fact, according to Hillel, "anything which caused annoyance or embarrassment to a husband was a legitimate ground for a divorce suit."[21]

A third point from these Deuteronomy verses, which is noteworthy, is that if divorce was allowed, so evidently was remarriage. For the text presupposes that, once the woman had received her certificate of divorce and been sent from the house, she was free to remarry, even though in this case she was the guilty party, having done "something indecent" on account of which she had been divorced. In fact, so far as is known, the cultures of the ancient world all understood that divorce carried with it the permission to remarry; *divortium a thoro et mensa* (from bed and board), namely a legal separation, without being also a *vinculo matrimonii* (from the marriage bond itself), was not contemplated. Dr. James B. Hurley summarizes the marriage and divorce laws of the Code of Hammurabi, who was king of Babylon in the early eighteenth century B.C. when Abraham left Ur, and also the harsher Assyrian laws at the time of Israel's exodus from Egypt.[22] And Dr. Gordon Wenham has added information from the fifth century B.C. papyri at Elephantine, a small Jewish garrison town in southern Egypt, as well as from Philo, Josephus and the Greek and Roman world.[23] All these cultures supply evidence for divorce by the husband, and in some cases by the wife as well, with liberty to remarry. Usually the divorced wife had her dowry returned to her, and received some divorce money as well. If divorce was comparatively infrequent in the ancient world, it was because the termination of one marriage and the arrangement of a second would have been financially crippling.

The Teaching of Jesus

Our Lord's instruction on marriage and divorce was given in response to a question from the Pharisees. Mark says they posed their question in order to "test" him (10:2), and Matthew elaborates what the test question was: "Is it lawful for a man to divorce his wife for any and every reason?" (19:3). Perhaps behind their question was the public scandal of Herodias, who had left her husband Philip in order to marry King Herod Antipas. John the Baptist had courageously denounced their union as "unlawful" (Mark 6:17–20), and had been imprisoned as a result. Would Jesus be equally outspoken, especially when, as seems probable, he was at the time within the jurisdiction of Herod (Mark 10:1)? Certainly the Pharisees wanted to embroil him in the Shammai-Hillel debate, already mentioned. Hence the emphasis in their question on the "reasons" or "causes" which justify divorce.

> Some Pharisees came to him to test him. They asked, "Is it lawful for a man to divorce his wife for any and every reason?"
>
> "Haven't you read," he replied, "that at the beginning the Creator 'made them male and female,' and said, 'For this reason a man will leave his father and mother and be united to his wife, and the two will become one flesh'? So

141

they are no longer two, but one. Therefore what God has joined together, let man not separate."

"Why then," they asked, "did Moses command that a man give his wife a certificate of divorce and send her away?"

Jesus replied, "Moses permitted you to divorce your wives because your hearts were hard. But it was not this way from the beginning. I tell you that anyone who divorces his wife, except for marital unfaithfulness, and marries another woman commits adultery."

The disciples said to him, "If this is the situation between a husband and wife, it is better not to marry."

Jesus replied, "Not everyone can accept this word, but only those to whom it has been given. For some are eunuchs because they were born that way; others were made that way by men; and others have renounced marriage because of the kingdom of heaven. The one who can accept this should accept it."

Matthew 19:3–12

It is clear that Jesus disassociated himself from the laxity of Rabbi Hillel. He had already done so in the Sermon on the Mount. His teaching on divorce in that passage was given as one of his six antitheses, introduced by the formula "you have heard that it was said . . . but I tell you . . ." What he was opposing in these antitheses was not Scripture ("it has been written") but tradition ("it has been said"), not the revelation of God but the perverse interpretations of the scribes. The object of their distortions was to reduce the demands of the law and make them more comfortable. In the divorce antithesis the scribal quotation ("It has been said, 'Anyone who divorces his wife must give her a certificate of divorce'" appears to be a deliberately misleading abbreviation of the Deuteronomy 24 passage. It gives the impression that divorce was readily permissible, even for trivial reasons (as Hillel taught), provided only that a certificate was given. Jesus categorically rejected this. What did he teach?

First, Jesus endorsed the permanence of marriage. It is significant that he did not give the Pharisees a direct answer to their question about divorce. Instead, he spoke to them about marriage. He referred them back to Genesis 1 and 2 and asked incredulously if they had not read these chapters. He drew their attention to the two facts that human sexuality was a divine creation and that human marriage was a divine ordinance. For he bracketed two texts (Genesis 1:27 and 2:24) and made God the author of both. For the same Creator who "at the beginning . . . 'made them male and female,'" also said (in the biblical text) "'For this reason a man will leave his father and mother and be united to his wife and they will become one flesh.'" "So," Jesus went on, adding his own explanatory assertion, "they are no longer two, but one." And, "Therefore," adding his own prohibition, "what God has joined together [literally, "yoked together"], let man not separate."

142

The teaching is unambiguous. The marriage bond is more than a human contract: it is a divine yoke. And the way in which God lays this yoke upon a married couple is not by creating a kind of mystical union but by declaring his purpose in his Word. Marital breakdown, even the so-called "death" of a relationship, cannot then be regarded as being in itself a ground for dissolution. For the basis of the union is not fluctuating human experience ("I love you, I love you not") but the divine will and Word (they "become one flesh").

Secondly, Jesus declared the Mosaic provision of divorce to be a concession to human sinfulness. The Pharisees responded to his quotations from Genesis by asking a second question: "Why then did Moses command that a man give his wife a certificate of divorce and send her away?" To this Jesus replied: "Moses permitted you to divorce your wives because your hearts were hard. But it was not this way from the beginning." Thus, what they had termed a "command" Jesus called a "permission," and a reluctant permission at that, due to human stubbornness rather than divine intention.[24]

Since Jesus referred to the Mosaic provision as a concession to human sin, which was also intended to limit its evil effects, it cannot possibly be taken as indicating God's approval of divorce. To be sure, it was a divine concession, for according to Jesus whatever Moses said, God said. Yet the divine concession of divorce was contrary to the divine institution of marriage "from the beginning." The rabbis' error lay in ignoring the distinction between God's will (Genesis 1 and 2) and his legal provision for human sinfulness (Deuteronomy 24). "Human conduct which falls short of the absolute command of God is sin and stands under the divine judgement. The provisions which God's mercy has designed for the limitation of the consequences of man's sin must not be interpreted as divine approval for sinning."[25]

Thirdly, Jesus called remarriage after divorce "adultery." Putting together his teaching from the Synoptic Gospels, and leaving aside for the moment the exceptive clause, we may summarize it as follows: a man who divorces his wife, and then remarries, both commits adultery himself (Matthew 19:9; Mark 10:11; Luke 16:18) and, because it is assumed that his divorced wife will also remarry, causes her to commit adultery as well (Matthew 5:32). A woman who divorces her husband and remarries similarly commits adultery (Mark 10:12). Further, a man (and presumably a woman too, assuming reciprocity in this situation as in others) who marries a divorcee commits adultery (Matthew 5:32; Luke 16:18). These are hard sayings. They expose with candor the logical consequences of sin. If a divorce and remarriage take place, which have no sanction from God, then any new union which follows, being unlawful, is adulterous.

Fourthly, Jesus permitted divorce and remarriage on the sole ground of immorality *(porneia)*. It is well-known that Matthew 5:32 and 19:9 both contain an "exceptive clause," whose purpose is to exempt one category of divorce and remarriage from being branded "adultery." Much controversy has raged round this clause. I do not think I can do more than indicate three conclusions which I have reached about it.

(1) The exceptive clause should be accepted as an authentic utterance of Jesus. Because it does not occur in the parallel sayings in Mark and Luke, many scholars have been too ready to dismiss it. Some suggest that it was an early scribal interpolation and not part of Matthew's original text. But there is no manuscript evidence that it was a gloss; even the alternative reading of Codex Vaticanus, retained in the RSV margin, does not omit the clause. Other scholars attribute the clause to Matthew himself, and/or to the church in which he was writing, but deny that Jesus ever spoke it. But its omission by Mark and Luke is not in itself a sufficient ground for rejecting it as an editorial invention or interpretation by the first evangelist. It is perfectly possible to suppose that Matthew included it for his Jewish readership who were very concerned about the permissible grounds for divorce, whereas Mark and Luke, writing for Gentile readers, did not have the same concern. Their silence is not necessarily due to their ignorance: it may equally well be that they took the clause for granted. Pagan cultures regarded adultery as a ground for divorce. So did both the Jewish schools of Hillel and Shammai, in spite of their disagreements on other points. This was not in dispute.

(2) The word *porneia* means sexual immorality. In deciding how to translate *porneia*, we need to avoid both extremes of too much laxity and too much rigidity.

Several "rigid" views have been held, which identify *porneia* as one particular sexual sin—either "fornication" in the sense of the discovery of premarital immorality, or a marriage within prohibited familial relationships, or postmarriage adultery. The main reason for rejecting any of these translations is that, although *porneia* could mean all of them, it would not be understood as referring to any one of them if there were no further qualification. *Porneia* was, in fact, a generic word for sexual infidelity or "marital unfaithfulness" (NIV), and included "every kind of unlawful sexual intercourse" (Arndt-Gingrich).

The "lax" view is that *porneia* includes offenses which may be regarded as broadly "sexual" in psychological rather than physical terms and so embraces even a basic temperamental incompatibility. Now it may be possible to use other arguments for the legitimacy of divorce on such grounds as these, but it is not possible to do so from the meaning of the word *porneia*. *Porneia* means physical sexual immorality; the reason why Jesus made it the sole permissible ground for divorce must be that it violates the "one flesh" principle which is foundational to marriage as divinely ordained and biblically defined.

(3) Divorce for immorality is permissible, not mandatory. Jesus did not teach that the innocent party must divorce an unfaithful partner, still less that

sexual unfaithfulness ipso facto dissolves the marriage. He did not even encourage or recommend divorce for unfaithfulness. On the contrary, his whole emphasis was on the permanence of marriage in God's purpose and on the inadmissibility of divorce and remarriage. His reason for adding the exceptive clause was to clarify that the only remarriage after divorce which is not tantamount to adultery is that of an innocent person whose partner has been sexually unfaithful, for in this case the infidelity has already been committed by the guilty partner. Jesus' purpose was emphatically not to encourage divorce for this reason, but rather to forbid it for all other reasons. As John Murray wrote: "It is the one exception that gives prominence to the illegitimacy of every other reason. Preoccupation with the one exception should never be permitted to obscure the force of the negation of all others."[26]

After this long excursus on the meaning of the exceptive clause and the permissible ground for divorce, it is important to come back to where we began. Although Jesus knew the realities of the Fall and of the hardness of human hearts, he recalled his contemporaries to the norm of the Creation and the unchanging purpose of God. He stressed reconciliation not separation, marriage not divorce. We must never move out of earshot of his ringing cry: "What God has joined together, let no one separate."

The Teaching of Paul

The teaching of Paul which we have to consider occurs in 1 Corinthians 7:10–16, and concerns in particular the so-called "Pauline privilege":

> To the married I give this command (not I, but the Lord): A wife must not separate from her husband. But if she does, she must remain unmarried or else be reconciled to her husband. And a husband must not divorce his wife.
> To the rest I say this (I, not the Lord): If any brother has a wife who is not a believer and she is willing to live with him, he must not divorce her. And if a woman has a husband who is not a believer and he is willing to live with her, she must not divorce him. For the unbelieving husband has been sanctified through his wife, and the unbelieving wife has been sanctified through her believing husband. Otherwise your children would be unclean, but as it is, they are holy.
> But if the unbeliever leaves, let him do so. A believing man or woman is not bound in such circumstances; God has called us to live in peace. How do you know, wife, whether you will save your husband? Or, how do you know, husband, whether you will save your wife?

We need to observe, first, that Paul is giving authoritative, apostolic instruction. The antithesis he makes between verse 10 ("I give this command—not I, but the Lord") and verse 12 ("To the rest I say this—I, not the Lord") has been much misunderstood. It is quite mistaken to imagine that he is setting Christ's teaching and his own in opposition to each other, with the further implication that Christ's has authority, whereas his has not. No, his contrast is not between divine, infallible teaching (Christ's) and human, fallible teaching (his own), but between two forms of divine and infallible teaching, the one dominical (the Lord's) and the other apostolic (his own). There can be no doubt that this is correct, for Paul continues to use the authoritative apostolic ego "I" in this chapter, in verse 17 ("This is the rule I lay down in all the churches"), verse 25 ("I have no command from the Lord," i.e., no recorded saying of Jesus, "but I give judgment as one who by the Lord's mercy is trustworthy") and verse 40 ("I think that I too have the Spirit of God"). Later and similarly, he puts his authority above that of prophets and declares his instruction to be the Lord's command: "If anybody thinks he is a prophet or spiritually gifted, let him acknowledge that what I am writing to you is the Lord's command" (14:37).

Secondly, Paul echoes and confirms Jesus' prohibition of divorce. In verses 10 and 11, as in his teaching in Romans 7:1–3, and as in the Lord's teaching recorded by Mark and Luke, the prohibition of divorce is stated in absolute terms. "A wife must not separate from her husband. . . . And a husband must not divorce his wife." This is because he is expressing the general principle. It is not necessary to suppose that he knew nothing of the Lord's exceptive clause.

In verse 11 he adds an important parenthesis to the effect that if a wife does "separate" from her husband, "she must remain unmarried or else be reconciled to her husband." Now the verb Paul uses for "separate" (*chorizo*) could refer to divorce and was so used both in marriage contracts in the papyri and by some early church fathers (Arndt-Gingrich). But the context suggests that Paul is not referring to divorce. He seems rather to be envisaging a situation in which the husband has not been sexually unfaithful and the wife is therefore not at liberty to divorce him. Some other reason (unstated) has prompted her to "separate" from him. So Paul emphasizes that in this case she is not free to remarry. Her Christian calling is either to remain single or to be reconciled to her husband, but not to remarry.

Thirdly, Paul permits divorce after a believer has been deserted by an unbelieving partner. He addresses three successive paragraphs "to the unmarried and the widows" (vv. 8–9), "to the married" (vv. 10–11) and "to the rest" (vv. 12–16). The context reveals that by "the rest" he has in mind a particular kind of mixed marriage. He gives no liberty to a Christian to marry a non-Christian, for a Christian woman "is free to marry anyone she wishes, but he must belong to the Lord" (v. 39). And the converse is equally true of Christian men (2 Corinthians 6:14–16). Paul is rather handling the situation which arises when two non-Christians marry, one of whom is subsequently converted. The Corinthians had evidently sent him questions about this. Was the marriage unclean? Should the Christian partner divorce the non-Christian? What was the status of their children? Paul's reply is clear.

If the unbelieving partner "is willing to live with" the believing, then the believer must not resort to divorce. The reason given is that the unbelieving partner "has been sanctified" through his or her believing spouse, and so have the children. The "sanctification" in mind is clearly not a transformation of character into the likeness of Christ. As John Murray puts it, "the sanctification of which Paul speaks . . . must be the sanctification of privilege, connection and relationship."[27]

But if, on the other hand, the unbelieving partner is unwilling to stay, and decides to leave, then "let him do so. A believing man or woman is not bound in such circumstances." The reasons given are that God has called us to live in peace, and that the believer cannot guarantee to win the unbeliever by insisting on perpetuating a union which the unbeliever is not willing to continue.[28]

It is important to grasp the situation which the apostle envisages, and not to draw unwarrantable deductions from his teaching. He affirms that, if the unbeliever refuses to stay, the believer "is not bound," that is, bound to hold on to him or her, indeed, bound to the marriage itself.[29] Several negative points need to be made about the freedom which the believing partner is here given.

(1) The believer's freedom is not due to his or her conversion, but rather to the partner's nonconversion and unwillingness to remain. Christians sometimes plead for what they call "gospel realism," arguing that because conversion makes all things new, a marriage contracted in preconversion days is not necessarily still binding and in its place a new beginning may be made. This is dangerous reasoning, however. Are all preconversion contracts cancelled by conversion, including all one's debts? No, Paul's teaching lends no possible support to such a view. On the contrary, he contradicts it. His teaching is not that after conversion the believing partner is defiled by the unbeliever, and should therefore extricate himself or herself from the relationship. It is the opposite, that the unbelieving partner has been "sanctified" by the believer, and that therefore the believer should not seek to escape. Further, Paul urges in verses 17–24 that Christians should remain in the state in which they were when God called them, and that we are able to do so because now we are there "with God."

(2) The believer's freedom is not due to any resolve of his own to begin divorce proceedings, but only to his reluctant acquiescence in his partner's "desertion," or unwillingness to stay. The initiative must not be the believer's. On the contrary, if the unbelieving partner is willing to remain, "he must not divorce her" and "she must not divorce him" (vv. 12–13). The

furthest Paul goes is to say that if the unbeliever insists on leaving, "let him do so" (v. 15). Perhaps this is the way to reconcile the apparently inconsistent statements that (a) Jesus permitted divorce on one ground only and (b) Paul added another. The first is a case of divorce; the second is an acquiescence in desertion.

(3) The believer's freedom is not due to "desertion" of any and every kind, nor to desertion for any form of unbelief (e.g., the Roman Catholic Church's view that marriage is not ratum if a partner is unbaptized), but only to the specific unwillingness of an unconverted person on religious grounds to continue living with his or her now-converted partner. The "Pauline privilege" provides no basis, therefore, for divorce on the general grounds of desertion; this is not a Christian option.

Summing up what Scripture teaches in the passages so far considered, we may make the following three affirmations:

(1) God created humankind male and female in the beginning, and himself instituted marriage. His intention was and is that human sexuality will find fulfillment in marriage, and that marriage will be an exclusive, loving and lifelong union. This is his purpose.

(2) Divorce is nowhere commanded, and never even encouraged, in Scripture. On the contrary, even if biblically justified, it remains a sad and sinful declension from the divine norm.

(3) Divorce and remarriage are permissible (not mandatory) on two grounds. First, an innocent person may divorce his or her partner if the latter has been guilty of serious sexual immorality. Secondly, a believer may acquiesce in the desertion by his or her unbelieving partner, if the latter refuses to go on living with him or her. In both cases, however, the permission is given in negative or reluctant terms. Only if a person divorces his or her partner on the ground of marital unfaithfulness is his or her remarriage not adulterous. Only if the unbeliever insists on leaving, is the believer "not bound."

Irretrievable Breakdown

My position, as defined above, was criticized by Dr. David Atkinson in his book *To Have and to Hold* (1979). He called it "legislative" and expressed his uneasiness in the following terms:

> The difficulty with this view is that in pastoral practice it can lead to the sort of casuistry which can become negatively legalistic. It concentrates on physical adultery but neglects other "unfaithfulness," and can mean that the Church's blessing for second marriage is reserved only for those who are for-

tunate [!] enough to have had their former partner commit adultery against them. It raises the question as to what breaks the marriage bond.[30]

It is, indeed, because of the practical problems which beset us when we insist on a "matrimonial offense" as the only legitimate ground for divorce, that an alternative and more flexible approach has been sought. The Church of England report *Putting Asunder* (1966) recommended the concept of "irretrievable breakdown" as an alternative, and the 1969 Divorce Reform Act was based upon it. It nevertheless required that irretrievable breakdown be proved by one of five evidences, three being faults (adultery, desertion and unreasonable behavior), and two indicating de facto separation (for two years if the couple agree to divorce, and for five years if they do not). Then the Church of England Commission which was presided over by Canon Professor Howard Root, and which reported in *Marriage, Divorce and the Church*,[31] investigated further the concept that some marriages "die" even while both married partners are still alive. And a few years later the Commission chaired by Bishop Kenneth Skelton of Lichfield, which reported in *Marriage and the Church's Task*,[32] took a similar line.

In 1990 the Law Commission's report *Family Law: The Ground for Divorce* proposed that all reference to fault be dropped; that irretrievable breakdown become the sole ground for divorce; and that such breakdown be proved by the passage of twelve months (minimum) in which the couple may reflect, voluntarily seek counsel and conciliation, and make adequate arrangements for custody, home and finance. These proposals with modifications were embodied in the Family Law Act, which became law in 1996 and went into effect in 1998. It is based on the no-fault principle, and extends the minimum period of waiting for reflection and consideration to eighteen months. Lord Mackay emphasized that the purpose of the Act is to support marriage and stem the rising tide of divorce. The Church of England's General Synod debated and approved his proposals.

One can understand the motives behind this development, in particular the desire to avoid the need to establish culpability. But the arguments against it do not seem to have been adequately considered. The concept of "irretrievable breakdown" has undesirable consequences. (1) It makes divorce too easy; it virtually opens the door to divorce on demand. (2) It represents marriage in terms of self-fulfillment, instead of self-giving. If it does not deliver what we had expected, then, instead of working at it, we declare that it doesn't work for us. (3) It gives the impression that marriages break down by themselves. It makes marriage the scapegoat and exonerates the married partners. But if the essence of marriage is a commitment of love and faithfulness, then only a failure in these will threaten it. By adopting the secular approach of no-fault breakdown, Dr. Alan Storkey has written, the churches have locked themselves into a contradiction, "affirming

. . . one view of marriage, while accepting a competely different dynamic behind divorce reform."[33] (4) It is an expression of secular pessimism. If two persons are "incompatible," and a breakdown is "irretrievable," what has become of the grace of God and the gospel of reconciliation?

Here then are two different approaches to the vexed question of divorce—"fault" and "no-fault," human culpability and irretrievable breakdown. Are we obliged to choose between them? Or is there a third way which embraces the best in both concepts? Perhaps the answer lies in the biblical notion of "covenant" and "covenant faithfulness." It could be described as a third way in the sense that the ground for divorce is neither a breakdown for which nobody accepts responsibility, nor a particular individual fault which has to be proved, but rather a culpable breach of the marriage covenant.

It is clear that Scripture regards marriage as a covenant, indeed—although between two human beings—as a "covenant of God" (Proverbs 2:17 literally), instituted and witnessed by him. In a letter which I received some years ago, Roger Beckwith, Warden of Latimer House, Oxford, summarized what he saw to be the five terms of the marriage covenant: (1) Love (as in every covenant), but married love involving specific obligations; (2) living together as a single household and family; (3) faithfulness to the marriage bed; (4) provision for the wife by the husband; and (5) submission to the husband by the wife.

In his book *To Have and to Hold,* subtitled *The Marriage Covenant and the Discipline of Divorce,* David Atkinson develops the covenant idea further. He defines a covenant as "an agreement between parties based on promise, which includes these four elements: first, an undertaking of committed faithfulness made by one party to the other (or by each to the other); secondly, the acceptance of that undertaking by the other party; thirdly, public knowledge of such an undertaking and its acceptance; and fourthly, the growth of a personal relationship based on and expressive of such a commitment."[34] It is not difficult to apply such a definition of "covenant" to marriage, especially because human marriage is used in Scripture as a model of God's covenant with his people, and God's covenant as a model for human marriage.[35] David Atkinson goes on to quote Professor G. R. Dunstan's development of this analogy, in that God's covenant and human marriage both have (1) an initiative of love, inviting a response, and so creating a relationship, (2) a vow of consent, guarding the union against the fitfulness of emotion, (3) obligations of faithfulness, (4) the promise of blessing to those who are faithful to their covenant obligations, and (5) sacrifice, the laying down of life in death, especially in this case death to the old independence and self-centeredness.[36]

David Atkinson goes on to argue that "the covenant structure of marriage lends weight to the view . . . that marriage is not a metaphysical status which cannot be destroyed; it is rather a moral commitment which should be honoured."[37] Yet a covenant can be broken. "Covenants do not just 'break down'"; however, "they are broken; divorce expresses sin as well as tragedy." So then "from a biblical moral perspective, we cannot dissolve the category of 'matrimonial offense' without remainder into the less personally focused concept of 'irretrievable breakdown.'"[38] Instead, "the covenant model for marriage places the question of divorce in the area of moral responsibility."[39] And his conclusion is that "any action which constitutes unfaithfulness to the marriage covenant so persistent and unrepentant that reconciliation becomes impossible may be sufficient to break the bond of marriage and so may release the other partner from their covenant promise."[40]

There is much in the covenant model of marriage which is compelling. To begin with, it is a thoroughly biblical notion. It also emphasizes the great solemnity both of covenant making and of covenant breaking—in the former case emphasizing love, commitment, public recognition, exclusive faithfulness and sacrifice, and in the latter the sin of going back on promises and rupturing a relationship of love. I confess, however, that my problem is how to fuse the concepts of covenant loyalty and matrimonial offense. I can understand the reasons for not wanting to build permission to divorce on two offenses. But if Scripture regards the marriage covenant as capable of being broken in several ways, how shall we explain the single offense mentioned in our Lord's exceptive clause? Certainly the covenant relationship envisaged in marriage (the "one flesh" union) is far deeper than other covenants, whether a suzerainty treaty, a business deal or even a pact of friendship. May it not be, therefore, that nothing less than a violation (by sexual infidelity) of this fundamental relationship can break the marriage covenant?

God's marriage covenant with "Jerusalem" (personifying his people), described at length in Ezekiel 16, is germane to this issue. God says to her: "I gave you my solemn oath and entered into a covenant with you . . . and you became mine" (v. 8). But Jerusalem "played the harlot," or rather (because she gave hire rather than receiving it) was a wife guilty of promiscuous adultery (vv. 15–34). Therefore, God said he would sentence her to "the punishment of women who commit adultery" (v. 38). Nevertheless, although her behavior was worse even than her "younger sister Sodom" (vv. 46–52), and although she had despised God's oath "by breaking the covenant" (v. 59), yet God said: "I will remember the covenant I made with you in the days of your youth, and I will establish an everlasting covenant with you" (v. 60), bringing forgiveness and penitence.

It seems to me that we must allow these perspectives of God's covenant to shape our understanding of the marriage covenant. The marriage covenant is not an ordinary human contract which, if one party to it reneges, may be renounced by the other. It is more like God's covenant with his people. In this analogy (which Scripture develops) only fundamental sexual unfaithfulness breaks the covenant. And even this does not lead automatically or necessarily to divorce; it may rather be an occasion for reconciliation and forgiveness.

Personal and Pastoral Realities

This has been a long chapter. Some readers will have been provoked by it, finding it dryly academic, or unfeeling towards the profound sufferings of those whose marriages break down, or remote from the realities of the contemporary western world, or all three. I can understand their reactions. Yet it has been necessary to give the biblical material a thorough examination, for this book is about developing a Christian mind on current issues. Conscientious disciples of Jesus know that Christian action is impossible without Christian thought; they resist the temptation to take shortcuts. At the same time, the process of "making up one's mind" means reaching a decision which has practical consequences. What then are these likely to be? Because of the great seriousness with which Scripture views both marriage and divorce, I conclude with four urgent pastoral needs.

First, there is the need for thorough biblical teaching about marriage and reconciliation. Pastors must give positive instructions on both these subjects. In sermons, Sunday school and confirmation classes we have to hold before the congregation we serve the divine intention and norm of exclusive, committed, lifelong faithfulness in marriage. We ought also to give clear and practical teaching on the duty and the way of forgiveness. For reconciliation lies at the very heart of Christianity. For some years now I have followed a simple rule, that whenever anybody asks me a question about divorce, I refuse to answer it until I have first talked about two other subjects, namely, marriage and reconciliation. This is a simple attempt to follow Jesus in his own priorities. When the Pharisees asked him about the grounds for divorce, he referred them instead to the original institution of marriage. If we allow ourselves to become preoccupied with divorce and its grounds, rather than with marriage and its essentials, we lapse into Pharisaism. For God's purpose is marriage not divorce, and his gospel is good news of reconciliation. We need to see Scripture as a whole, and not isolate the topic of divorce.

Secondly, there is the need for preparation for marriage. Couples preparing for marriage usually cherish high ideals for the future, and are ready, even anxious, for help. Yet hard-pressed clergy can often manage to give each couple no more than a single interview, and even then legal and social questions sometimes crowd out the spiritual and moral dimensions of marriage. Some clergy arrange courses for groups of engaged couples or encourage them to attend appropriate weekend conferences. Others give couples a book or a short annotated list of recommended reading.[41] Best of all, perhaps, is the resolve to harness the services of mature lay couples in the congregation, who would be willing to spend several evenings with an engaged couple, meet them again after the wedding and continue to keep in touch with them during the early days of adjustment.

Thirdly, there is the need for a reconciliation ministry. In the UK, during the eighties both in-court and out-of-court conciliation services were developed, and there has been a growing desire to see conciliation attempts built into the initial stages of legal proceedings, so that an adversarial approach is avoided. At present, probation officers appear to be more involved than anybody else with married couples and families who need help. There are also voluntary organizations like RELATE, the Catholic Marriage Advisory Council, the Family Discussion Bureau, and Marriage Resource (a network of Christian marriage-support groups, which sponsor National Marriage Week). I wish the churches were yet more actively involved in this ministry, especially at the local level. Christians are supposed to be in the reconciliation business. Many more people would seek help, and seek it early when it is most needed, if they knew where they could turn for sympathy, understanding and advice. Sometimes expert marital therapy will be necessary, but at other times a listening ear may be enough. As Dr. Jack Dominian writes, "Marital reconciliation ultimately depends on the ability of the spouses to change sufficiently to meet each other's minimal needs."[42] But a friend can often be the catalyst to help people see the need for change and want it.

American Christians are in advance of Britain in this area. Partly as a result of the epidemic of suing (in 1982 22,000 law suits were being filed every day), the Christian Legal Society took the initiative in 1977 to set up the Christian Conciliation Service. Responding to Christ's call to his followers to be peacemakers, to his teaching in Matthew 18:15–17 and to Paul's in 1 Corinthians 6:1–8, they are seeking to resolve conflicts and settle disputes (in business, marriage and other fields) out of court. So they offer mediation, reconciliation and (if these fail) arbitration, as alternatives to the adversarial approach of the civil courts.[43]

Fourthly, there is the need for pastoral ministry to the divorced. Because marriage is a "creation ordinance," God's purposes for it do not vary; they are the same for the world as for the Church. The non-Christian world will often be unable and unwilling to fulfill them because of the hardness of human hearts, and so is likely to have its own legislation for divorce. It is right, however, to expect higher standards in the new community of Jesus. He repeatedly told his followers not to follow the way of the world. "It shall not be so among you," he said. In marriage, therefore, the Church's calling is not to conform to popular trends, but to bear witness to God's purpose of permanence.

Nevertheless, "hardness of heart" is not confined to the non-Christian world. As with the Old Testament people of God, so with the people of the New Covenant, some concession to human fallibility and failure will be needed, and each church or denomination will have to make its own regulations. The sustained policy of the Church of England for several decades has been to refuse to marry in church any person who has a previous spouse still living, while at the same time seeking to offer a ministry of pastoral compassion and care to those who have been divorced. In 1981, however, reversing a vote taken in 1978, the General Synod resolved that "there are circumstances in which a divorced person may be married in church during the lifetime of a former partner." What those "circumstances" are has until now not been agreed. Yet it is hoped that the deep division in the Church on this issue will be overcome, and that the Church will distinguish between those who cause divorce and those who are victims of it. For if Jesus and his apostle Paul did allow divorce and remarriage in certain circumstances, then this permission of a new beginning needs what Professor Oliver O'Donovan has called "institutional visibility."[44]

What institutional arrangements should the Church make? Professor O'Donovan continues: "The primary question is how it may find some arrangement that will give adequate form both to its beliefs about the permanence of marriage and to its belief about the forgiveness of the penitent sinner."[45] It could express this ambivalence either by permitting the remarriage in church (emphasizing the gospel of redemption), while adding some kind of discipline (recognizing God's marriage norm), or by refusing the remarriage in church (emphasizing the norm), while adding some expression of acceptance (recognizing the gospel). I myself incline to the former. But before any church service for the marriage of a divorced person is permitted, the Church must surely exemplify its adherence to the revelation of God in two ways. It must satisfy itself first that the remarriage comes within the range of the biblical permissions, and secondly that the couple concerned accept the divine intention of marriage permanence.

In this case the church service could not with integrity be identical with a normal marriage ceremony. Some expression of penitence should be included, either in a private preliminary (as suggested by the Root Report in paragraphs 143–47) or in the public service itself. Either way would be an acknowledgment that every divorce, even when biblically permissible, is a declension from the divine norm. This is not to stand in judgment on the people concerned in any proud or paternalistic way; it is rather to confess the universal taint of sin, in which we ourselves, as well as they, are personally involved.

In all this we continue to be caught in the tension between law and grace, witness and compassion, prophetic ministry and pastoral care. On the one hand, we need the courage to resist the prevailing winds of permissiveness and to set ourselves to uphold marriage and oppose divorce. The state will continue to frame its own divorce laws, but the Church also has its own witness to bear to the teaching of its divine Lord, and must exercise its own discipline. On the other hand, we shall seek to share with deep compassion in the suffering of those whose marriages have failed, and especially of those whom we cannot conscientiously advise to seek an escape by divorce. We may on occasion feel at liberty to advise the legitimacy of a separation without a divorce, or even a divorce without a remarriage, taking 1 Corinthians 7:11 as our warrant. But we have no liberty to go beyond the permissions of our Lord. He knew his Father's will and cared for his disciples' welfare. Wisdom, righteousness and compassion are all found in following him.

7

Abortion
and Euthanasia

The debates over abortion and euthanasia are admittedly complex. They have medical, legal, theological, ethical, social and personal aspects. They are highly emotional subjects, for they touch on the mysteries of human sexuality and reproduction, life and death. Both often involve acutely painful dilemmas.

Yet Christians cannot opt out of personal decision making or public discussion regarding these topics merely because of their complexity. Instead, two factors should bring them to the top of our agenda.

First, what is involved in the abortion and euthanasia debate is nothing less than our Christian doctrines of both God and humanity, or, more precisely, the sovereignty of God and the sanctity of human life. All Christian people believe that Almighty God is the only giver, sustainer and taker-away of life. On the one hand "he himself gives all men life and breath and everything else," and "in him we live and move and have our being." On the other, as the psalmist says to God, "when you take away their breath, they die and return to the dust." Indeed, whenever anybody dies, Christian faith struggles to affirm with Job: "The LORD gave and the LORD has taken away; may the name of the LORD be praised" (Acts 17:25, 28; Psalm 104:29; Job 1:21). To the Christian, then, both life-giving and life-taking are divine prerogatives. And although we cannot interpret "You shall not kill" as an absolute prohibition, since the same law which forbade killing also sanctioned it in some situations (e.g., capital punishment and holy war), yet the taking of human life is a divine prerogative which is permitted to human beings only by specific divine mandate. Without this, to terminate human life is the height of arrogance. Hence Mother Teresa's strong feelings about the evil of abortion:

... only God can decide life and death. .... That is why abortion is such a terrible sin. You are not only killing life, but putting self before God; yet people decide who has to live and who has to die. They want to make themselves almighty God. They want to take the power of God in their hands. They want to say, "I can do without God. I can decide." That is the most devilish thing that a human hand can do . . .[1]

The questions of abortion and euthanasia concern our doctrine of humanity as well as our doctrine of God. For, however undeveloped the embryo may still be, and however mentally absent an elderly person may be, everybody agrees that they are living and that the life they possess is human. So in whatever way we decide to formulate the relationship between newborn and unborn children, or those with a life "worth living" and those "not worth living," our evaluation of human life is inevitably involved. Abortion and euthanasia reflect a rejection of the biblical view of human dignity. It is this aspect of the situation which most concerned Francis Schaeffer and C. Everett Koop in their book and film *Whatever Happened to the Human Race?* which dealt with abortion, infanticide and euthanasia. They rightly traced "the erosion of the sanctity of human life" to "the loss of the Christian consensus."[2]

So then, if both divine sovereignty and human dignity are being challenged by the abortion and euthanasia debates, no conscientious Christian can stand aside from them. We will look primarily at abortion and the discussion that surrounds it, returning at the end of the chapter to euthanasia and some of the particular problems which it raises.

The Revolution in Public Attitudes

The second reason for taking these questions seriously concerns the revolution which has recently taken place in public attitudes. Whether or not doctors have actually subscribed to the ancient Hippocratic Oath (fifth century B.C.), it has been generally assumed that they took its main undertakings for granted:

I will follow that method of treatment which, according to my ability and judgment, I consider for the benefit of my patients, and abstain from whatever is deleterious and mischievous. I will give no deadly drug to anyone if asked, nor suggest any such counsel; and in like manner I will not give to a woman a pessary to procure abortion.

Since some other clauses of the Oath are decidedly antiquated, the Declaration of Geneva (1948) updated it, while at the same time taking care to include the promise: "I will maintain the utmost respect for human life from the time of conception."

One would not necessarily expect a country like Japan, whose Christian population numbers less than 1 percent, to reflect a biblical view of the sanctity of human life (although of course the Buddhist tradition professes all life to be sacred). So we are not altogether surprised by the statistics which followed their liberalization of abortion legislation in 1948. In the first eight years no fewer than 5 million abortions were performed, and in the year 1972 1.5 million were carried out.[3]

But one's expectations of the situation in the West, the heir of many centuries of Christian tradition, are naturally higher. In Britain abortion remained illegal until the Infant Life (Preservation) Act of 1929 provided that no action would be punishable "when done in good faith with the intention of saving the life of the mother." David Steel's 1967 Abortion Act appeared to many to be only a cautious extension of this. Two registered medical practitioners were required to express their opinion, "formed in good faith," that the continuance of the pregnancy would involve either (1) risk to the life of the pregnant woman, or (2) and (3) risk of injury to her or her existing children's physical or mental health, "greater than if the pregnancy were terminated," or (4) "substantial risk that if the child were born it would suffer from such physical or mental abnormalities as to be seriously handicapped." Whatever the intentions were of the Abortion Law Reform Association (who masterminded the Bill), it seems clear that its catastrophic consequences were not foreseen by its parliamentary sponsors. Before the Act became law, the number of legal abortions carried out annually in the hospitals of the National Health Service in England and Wales had crept up slowly to 6,100 (1966).[4] In 1968, however, the number was already 24,000, in 1973 it was 167,000 and in 1983 over 184,000, an increase on the previous decade of about 8 percent. By 1983 over 2 million legal abortions had been performed since the 1967 Act was passed, and by 1995 over 4.5 million.[5]

Since 1967 several unsuccessful attempts have been made to tighten our much-too-liberal abortion legislation. But in April 1990 the time limit was successfully reduced from twenty-eight weeks to twenty-four. This victory was extremely modest, however, (1) because very few abortions are performed after twenty-four weeks anyway (only twenty-three in 1988) and (2) because at the same time (by an oversight, it seems) no abortion time limit at all was set where there is substantial risk that, if born, the child would suffer serious physical or mental handicap.

The situation in the United States is worse. In 1970 a Texan woman (who used the pseudonym Jane Roe) became pregnant and decided to fight the antiabortion legislation of her state. She took Henry Wade, the Dallas district attorney, to court. In January 1973 in the now notorious *Roe v. Wade* case, the United States Supreme Court declared by seven votes to two that the Texas law was unconstitutional.[6] Its judgment inhibited all regulation of abortion during the first three months of pregnancy, and during the second and third trimesters regulated it only in relation to the mother's physical or mental health. This ruling implicitly permitted abortion on demand at every stage of pregnancy. The number of legal abortions in the United States in 1969 was less than 20,000. In 1975 it passed the million mark, and in 1980 reached more than 1.5 million. Throughout the 1980s it remained at about this number every year. This means that during this period, for every 1,000 "births" (natural and induced), 300 were abortions. In fact, over 4,250 babies are aborted daily, 177 hourly, or 3 every minute. In 1996 1,400,000 abortions were performed, bringing the total since 1973 to an estimated 32.5 million.[7]

Although *Roe v. Wade* has not been overturned, in July 1989 a divided Supreme Court, hearing the case of *Webster v. Reproductive Health Services*, decided to allow states to limit a woman's access to abortion and outlawed it in all public institutions. Meanwhile, the nationwide debate has grown into a deeply held confrontation. Abortion is always a major election issue, and both pro-life and pro-choice groups have annual marches on Washington. The March for Life in 1996 had an estimated attendance of 125,000.

The total number of legal and illegal abortions throughout the world was estimated in 1968 to be between 30 million and 35 million.[8] Today the estimate is that as many as 55 million abortions take place each year,[9] which means that more than one abortion occurs every second.

These figures are so staggering as to defy the imagination. I do not think Francis Schaeffer and Everett Koop were exaggerating when they wrote of "The Slaughter of the Innocents," or John Powell, SJ, when he entitled his moving book *Abortion: The Silent Holocaust*.[10] To make his point yet more forcefully, he introduced his book with a chart of "war casualties," on which each cross represented 50,000 American combatants killed. The Korean and Vietnam wars had only one cross each. World War I had two and a half, and World War II eleven. But "the War on the Unborn" had no fewer than 240 crosses, representing the 12 million legal American abortions up to the beginning of 1981.

Any society which can tolerate these things, let alone legislate for them, has ceased to be civilized. One of the major signs of decadence in the Roman Empire was that its unwanted babies were "exposed," that is, abandoned and left to die.[11] Can we claim that contemporary western society is any less decadent because it consigns its unwanted babies to the hospital incinerator instead of the local rubbish dump? Indeed modern abortion is even worse than ancient exposure because it has been commercialized and has become, at least for some doctors and clinics, an extremely lucrative practice. But reverence for human life is an indisputable characteristic of a humane and civilized society.

The Key Issue

Those who campaign for a lax policy on abortion, and those who campaign for a strict one, begin their argument from opposite positions.[12]

Proabortionists emphasize the rights of the mother, and especially her right to choose; antiabortionists emphasize the rights of the unborn child, and especially his or her right to live. The first see abortion as little more than a retroactive contraceptive, the second as little less than prenatal infanticide. The appeal of proabortionists is often to compassion (though also to the justice of what they see as a woman's right); they cite situations in which the mother and/or the rest of the existing family would suffer intolerable strain if an unwanted pregnancy were allowed to come to term. The appeal of antiabortionists is usually also and especially to justice; they stress the need to defend the rights of unborn children who are unable to defend themselves.

Those who oppose easy abortion are not lacking in compassion, however. They recognize the hardships, and even tragedies, which the arrival of an unplanned baby often brings. Consider some examples. An expectant mother is already worn out by a large and demanding family. Their home is already overcrowded and their budget overstretched. It would be financially crippling to have another mouth to feed. The family simply could not cope with another child. Or the mother is herself the wage earner (because she is widowed or divorced, or her husband is sick or unemployed); to have another child would ruin the family. Or the husband is violent or cruel, perhaps an alcoholic or even a psychopath, and his wife dare not allow another child to come under his influence. Or she is unmarried and feels she cannot face either the stigma or the disadvantage which she and her child would have to endure as a single-parent family. Or she is a schoolgirl or student, and a continued pregnancy would interfere with her education and her career. Or perhaps her pregnancy is due to adultery or incest or rape, and these tragedies are great enough in themselves without adding to them an unplanned, unwanted child. Or she has contracted rubella, or had a prenatal scan, and fears that her child will have Down's syndrome or be defective in some other way.

All these cases, and many more, cause great personal suffering and arouse sincere Christian compassion. It is easy to understand why some women in such situations opt for the abortion which seems to them the only escape, and why some doctors interpret the law as liberally as they can, in order to justify one.

But Christians who confess Jesus as Lord, and who desire to live under the authority of his truth, justice and compassion, can never be pure pragmatists. We have to ask ourselves what principles are involved. Our compassion needs both theological and moral guidelines. If it is expressed at the expense of truth or justice, it ceases to be genuine compassion.

The key issue, then, is a moral and theological one. It concerns the nature of the fetus (*foetus* is Latin for "offspring"). How are we to think of the embryo in the mother's womb? For it is our evaluation of the fetus which will largely determine our attitude to abortion.

The first view (which Christians reject as totally false and utterly abhorrent) is the notion that the fetus is merely a lump of jelly or blob of tissue, or a growth in the mother's womb, which may therefore be extracted and destroyed like teeth, tumors or tonsils. Yet some adopt this extreme position. For example, K. Hindell and Madelaine Simms (proabortion campaigners) have written that "medically and legally the embryo and fetus are merely parts of the mother's body, and not yet human."[13] Such people insist that the fetus belongs to the woman who bears it; that it cannot be regarded as in any sense independent of her or as human in its own right; that to have it removed is no more significant than the surgical removal of some other unwanted tissue; and that the decision to abort or not to abort rests entirely with the woman. Since it is her body, it is also her choice. Nobody else (and certainly no man, feminists would add) has any say in the matter. A liberated woman cannot be forced to bear a child; she has absolute control over her own reproductive powers and processes.

After a mass rally in Hyde Park, arranged by the Society of the Protection of Unborn Children in June 1983, we were walking to 10 Downing Street, in order to present a petition to the Prime Minister, when at the top of Whitehall a group of young women started chanting:

> Not the Church, not the State,
> Let the woman decide her fate.

I went over to talk to them and quietly remonstrated that it was not the woman's fate we were concerned about in our rally and march, so much as her unborn child's. Their only reply was to shout unprintable obscenities at me and to make the rather obvious point that I would not be able to give birth to a child in a million years. I am not saying that they were wholly wrong. For I recognize that abortion is more a woman's issue than a man's. It is she who has been made pregnant, perhaps without her consent, who has to bear the pregnancy and who will carry the burden of early child care. It is all too easy for men to forget these facts. But we should remember them.

162

We should also be "pro-choice" in the sense that we recognize a woman's right to decide whether to have a baby or not. But the time for her to exercise her right and make her choice (still assuming that she has not been forced) is before conception, not after. Once she has conceived, her child has independent rights both before and after birth, and it was these rights which those young women in Whitehall did not acknowledge.

That an embryo, though carried within the mother's body, is nevertheless not a part of it, is not only a theological but a physiological fact. This is partly because the child has a genotype distinct from the mother's, but also because the whole process of gestation, from ovulation to birth, may be seen as a kind of "expulsion" of the child with a view to its ultimate independence.

A second group of people seeks the decisive moment of the embryo's "humanization" at some point between conception and birth. Some opt for implantation when the egg, six days after fertilization, descends the fallopian tube and becomes attached to the wall of the uterus. And it is true both that implantation is an indispensable stage in the development of the fetus, and that the greatest number of spontaneous abortions (often due to fetal abnormality) take place before this moment. Nevertheless, implantation changes only the environment of the fetus, not its constitution. In former generations "quickening" was regarded by many as the moment of, or at least the evidence for, the "ensoulment" of the embryo, but we now know that this new beginning is not of the child's movement but of the mother's perception of it. A third option is "viability," the time when the fetus, if born prematurely, would be able to survive. But modern medical techniques are constantly bringing this moment forward. The fourth option is to regard birth itself as the crucial moment. This was the position adopted by Rex Gardner in his *Abortion: The Personal Dilemma* (1972). "My own view," he wrote, "is that while the fetus is to be cherished increasingly as it develops, we should regard its first breath at birth as the moment when God gives it not only life, but the offer of Life." He quoted Genesis 2:7 as biblical evidence, when God breathed into man's nostrils "the breath of life." He appealed also to common human experience: "An audible sigh of relief goes round the delivery room when the baby gives that first gasp."[14] It is certainly true that no funeral is held for a stillborn child, and that Scripture usually speaks of "new life" beginning at "new birth." Yet this does not settle the matter, since Scripture also speaks of God "begetting" us and of the implanted "seed" which leads to new birth (see, e.g., James 1:18; 1 Peter 1:23–25; and 1 John 3:9). In addition, pictures of the child just before birth reveal that there is no fundamental difference between the unborn and the newly born: both are dependent on their mother, even if in different ways.

The third group of people, which I think should include all Christians, although they use different formulations and draw different deductions, looks back to conception or fusion as the decisive moment when a human being begins. This is the official position of the Roman Catholic Church. Pope Pius XII, for example, in his Address to the Italian Catholic Society of Midwives in 1951, said, "The baby, still not born, is a man (that is, a human being) in the same degree and for the same reason as the mother."[15] Similarly, many Protestants, although some find difficulty with the nonrecognition of "degree," yet similarly affirm that there is no point between conception and death at which we can say, "After that point I was a person, but before it I was not." For certainly the conceptus is alive, and certainly the life it possesses is human life. Indeed, many medical people who make no Christian profession recognize this fact. Thus, the First International Conference on Abortion, meeting in 1967 in Washington, D.C., declared: "We can find no point in time between the union of sperm and egg and the birth of an infant at which point we can say that this is not a human life."[16]

There is now a fourth view, which deliberately avoids making a decision about the precise identity of the fetus. It has been persuasively put forward by Professor Ronald Dworkin in his influential book *Life's Dominion*, subtitled *An Argument about Abortion and Euthanasia*. What readers have found appealing about Professor Dworkin's approach is that he tries to break the deadlock between the "conservative" pro-life and the "liberal" pro-choice lobbies, to get behind the "screaming rhetoric" of the debate, and to reformulate the fundamental moral issue.

There is both agreement and disagreement between the two positions, he claims. On the one hand, both (he alleges) believe that "our lives have intrinsic, inviolable value,"[17] so that to extinguish a human life is "intrinsically a bad thing, a kind of cosmic shame."[18] On the other hand, the crucial difference between them lies in their understanding of the "value" of human life. Conservatives tend to regard the fetus as being from conception "a person with rights and interests of its own," whereas liberals affirm "the sanctity of life understood in a more impersonal way."[19] The former he calls the "derivative" view, because it is derived from the nature of the fetus and its supposed rights. The latter he calls the "detached" view, because it regards human life as sacred in itself, without any presupposition about rights and interests.[20]

When Professor Dworkin comes to explain the "value" of human life, however, he seems to be in difficulties. Human lives are intrinsically valuable as great paintings are. Their value is measured by the degree of "investment" contributed to their creation (both natural and human) and by the degree of "waste" involved in their destruction. For example, should a seriously deformed fetus be allowed to be born or be aborted? Either way there would be a serious "frustration of life." Abortion would mean the destruction of life. Birth "would add, to the sad waste of a deformed human's biological creation, the further heartbreaking waste of personal emotional investment made in that life by others, but principally by the child himself before his inevitable early death."[21] Which is the greater "investment"? Which would be the greater "waste"?

While appreciating Professor Dworkin's emphasis on the "value" of the fetus, Christians will feel very uneasy about the way he develops his thesis. (1) He is much too optimistic in his assessment of the liberals' position. They do not appear to affirm (as he says they do) the "sanctity," let alone the "inviolability," of the life of the unborn. (2) His personification of "nature" (e.g., "not destroying what nature has created," p. 76) lacks plausibility. The better and biblical way of explaining the intrinsic value of the human fetus is to acknowledge God as Creator and ourselves as the bearers of his image. It is not "investment" but "creation" which establishes the innate worth of human beings. (3) Professor Dworkin's vocabulary of "investment" and "waste" seems inappropriate in relation to human beings. "Waste" suggests the loss of a commodity, and an "investment" is an outlay with a view to a profit. But it is of the essence of love to give without expecting any return.

The Biblical Basis

To me the firmest foundation in Scripture for the third view is to be found in Psalm 139, in which the author marvels at God's omniscience and omnipresence, and in the course of his meditation makes important statements about our prenatal existence. To be sure, Psalm 139 makes no claim to be a textbook of embryology. It employs poetical imagery and highly figurative language (e.g., verse 15, "I was woven together in the depths of the earth"). Nevertheless, the psalmist is affirming at least three important truths.

The first concerns his creation. "You created my inmost being; you knit me together in my mother's womb" (v. 13). Two homely metaphors are used to illustrate God's creative skill, namely those of the potter and the weaver. God is like a skilled artisan, who "created" him ("formed" is a better word) as the potter works the clay. The same thought recurs in Job 10:8, where Job affirms that God's hands had "fashioned and made" him (RSV) or "shaped and modelled" him (JB). The other picture is that of the weaver who "knit" him together (v. 13), which the NASB renders "thou didst weave me." Similarly Job asks: "Did you not . . . clothe me with skin and flesh and knit me together with bones and sinews?" (10:10–11). In consequence, the psalmist goes on: "For all these mysteries I thank you, for the wonder of myself, for the wonder of your works" (v. 14 JB).

Though not intending to give a scientific account of fetal development, the biblical authors are nevertheless affirming (in the familiar imagery of the ancient Near East) that the process of embryonic growth is neither haphazard nor even automatic, but a divine work of creative skill.

The psalmist's second emphasis is on continuity. He is now an adult, but he looks back over his life until before he was born. He refers to himself both before and after birth by the same personal pronouns "I" and "me," for he is aware that during his antenatal and postnatal life he was and is the same person. He surveys his existence in four stages. First (v. 1), "you have searched me" (the past). Secondly (vv. 2–3), "you know when I sit and when I rise . . . you are familiar with all my ways" (the present). Thirdly (v. 10), "your hand will guide me, your right hand will hold me fast" (the future). And fourthly (v. 13), "you knit me together in my mother's womb" (the prenatal stage). Yet in all four stages (before birth, from birth to the present, at the present moment, and in the future), he refers to himself as "I." He who is thinking and writing as a grown man has the same personal identity as the fetus in the womb. He is aware of no discontinuity between his antenatal and postnatal being. On the contrary, in and out of his mother's womb, before and after his birth, as embryo, baby, youth and adult, he is conscious of being the same person.

The third truth the psalmist expresses I will term communion, for he is conscious of a very personal and particular communion between God and himself. It is the same God who created him, who now sustains him, knows him and loves him, and who will forever hold him fast. Psalm 139 is perhaps the most radically personal statement in the Old Testament of God's relationship to the individual believer. The "I-you" relationship is expressed in almost every line. Either the pronoun or the possessive in the first person ("I-me—my") comes forty-six times in the psalm, and in the second person ("you—your") thirty-two times. More important than the "I-you" relationship is his awareness of the "you-me" relationship, of God knowing him, surrounding him, holding him (vv. 1–6), and of God sticking to him in covenant faithfulness and never leaving him or letting him go (vv. 7–12).

Indeed, "communion" may not be the best description of this third awareness, because the word implies a reciprocal relationship, whereas the psalmist is bearing witness to a relationship which God has established and which God sustains. Perhaps, therefore, "covenant" would be a better word, indeed a unilateral covenant, or covenant of "grace" which God initiated and which God maintains. For God our Creator loved us and related himself to us long before we could respond in a conscious relationship to him. What makes us a person, then, is not that we know God, but that he knows us; not that we love God but that he has set his love upon us. So each of us was already a person in our mother's womb, because already then God knew us and loved us.

It is these three words (creation, continuity and communion or covenant) which give us the essential biblical perspective from which to think. The fetus is neither a growth in the mother's body, nor even a potential human being, but already a human life who, though not yet mature, has the potentiality of growing into the fullness of the individual humanity he or she already possesses.

Other biblical passages express the same sense of personal continuity due to divine grace. Several times in the Wisdom Literature of the Old Testament the conviction is expressed that it is God who "made me in the womb" (Job 31:15; Psalm 119:73), even though we do not know how (Ecclesiastes 11:5), who "brought me out of the womb," and who therefore "from my mother's womb" has been my God (Psalm 22:9–10; 71:6). The prophets shared the same belief, whether of the individual like Jeremiah ("Before I formed you in the womb I knew you," 1:5), or of "the Servant of the Lord" (whom the Lord both formed and called in the womb, Isaiah 49:1, 5) or by analogy of the nation of Israel (Isaiah 46:3–4). The implications of these texts for personal continuity cannot be avoided by analogy with New Testament assertions that God "chose" us in Christ and "gave" us his grace in Christ "before the creation of the world" (e.g., Ephesians 1:4; 2 Timothy 1:9). The argument would then be that, just as we did not exist before the beginning of time except in the mind of God, so we had no personal existence in the womb, although God is said to have "known" us in both cases. The analogy is inexact, however, for the situations are different. In passages which relate to election, the emphasis is on salvation by grace not works, and therefore on God's choice of us before we existed or could do any good works. In passages which relate to vocation, however (the calling whether of prophets like Jeremiah or of apostles like Paul—cf. Galatians 1:16), the emphasis is not only on God's gracious choice but on his "forming" or "fashioning" them for their particular service. This was not "before the creation of the world," nor even "before conception," but rather "before birth," before they were yet fully "formed," that is, while they were still being "fashioned" in the womb. Personal continuity before and after birth is integral to this teaching.

There is only one Old Testament passage which some interpreters have thought devalues the human fetus, namely Exodus 21:22–25.[22] The situation envisaged is not in dispute. While two men are fighting, they accidentally hit a pregnant woman with the result that she either miscarries or "gives birth prematurely" (NIV). The penalty laid down depends on the seriousness of any injury sustained. If the injury is not serious, a fine is to be imposed; if it is serious, there is to be exact retribution, "life for life" etc. Some have argued that the first category (no serious injury) means the death of the child, while the second is serious harm to the mother, and that therefore the mere imposition of a fine in the former case indicates that the fetus was regarded as less valuable than the mother. This is a gratuitous interpretation, however. It seems much more probable that the scale of penalty was to correspond to the degree of injury, whether to the mother or to her child, in which case mother and child are valued equally.

Turning to the New Testament, it has often been pointed out that when Mary and Elizabeth met, both being pregnant, Elizabeth's baby (John the Baptist) "leaped in her womb" in salutation of Mary's baby (Jesus) and also that Luke here uses the same word *brephos* of an unborn child (1:41, 44) as he later uses of the newborn baby (2:12, 16) and of the little ones whom people brought to Jesus to be blessed by him (18:15).

It is fully in keeping with all this implied continuity, that Christian tradition affirms of Jesus Christ in the Apostles' Creed that he was "conceived by the Holy Spirit, born of the Virgin Mary, suffered under Pontius Pilate, was crucified, dead and buried . . . and on the third day he rose again." Throughout these events, from beginning to end, from conception to resurrection, it is the very same person, Jesus Christ, in whom we believe.

Modern medical science appears to confirm this biblical teaching. It was only in the 1960s that the genetic code was unraveled. Now we know that the moment the ovum is fertilized by the penetration of the sperm, the twenty-three pairs of chromosomes are complete, the zygote has a unique genotype which is distinct from both parents, and the child's sex, size and shape, color of skin, hair and eyes, temperament and intelligence are already determined. Each human being begins as a single fertilized cell, while an adult has about thirty million million cells. Between these two points (fusion and maturity) forty-five generations of cell division are necessary, and forty-one of them occur before birth.

Prenatal medical photography has further disclosed the marvels of fetal development. I have in mind particularly the strikingly beautiful pictures in the Swedish photographer Lennart Nilsson's book *A Child Is Born*.[23] At three to three and a half weeks the tiny heart begins to beat. At four, though the fetus is only about a quarter of an inch long, the head and body are distinguishable, as are also the rudimentary eyes, ears and mouth. At six or seven weeks brain function can be detected, and at eight (the time most abortions begin to be performed) all the child's limbs are apparent, including fingers, fingerprints and toes. At nine or ten weeks the baby can use his or her hands to grasp and mouth to swallow, and can even suck his thumb. By thirteen weeks, the completion of the first trimester, the embryo is completely organized, and a miniature baby lies in the mother's womb; he can alter his position, respond to pain, noise and light, and even get a fit of hiccups. From then on the child merely develops in size and strength. By the end of the fifth month and beginning of the sixth (before the second trimester is complete, and while the pregnancy is not yet two-thirds complete), the baby has hair, eyelashes, nails and nipples, and can cry, grip, punch and kick (which sometimes happens after an abortion has been performed by hysterotomy, to the extreme distress of the medical team).

Expectant mothers endorse from their own experience their sense of bearing a living child. True, parents sometimes give their little one a humorous nickname, especially if they do not know which sex it will turn out to be. But they also say with pride, "We have a baby on the way." During pregnancy one mother said she "felt herself to be the mother of a person, with certain motherly responsibilities before birth, and others after birth." Another wrote: "My feelings know that this is a person, and thus has his or her own independent rights before God."

A Contemporary Christian Debate

It would not be honest to claim that all Christians see eye to eye on this issue, even all Christians who seek to submit to the authority of Scripture. An apparently sharp difference of opinion surfaced when an interdisciplinary seminar of theologians and doctors was held in 1983, jointly sponsored by the London Institute for Contemporary Christianity and the Christian Medical Fellowship. The keynote address was given by Canon Oliver O'Donovan, Regius Professor of Moral and Pastoral Theology at Oxford, under the title "And Who Is a Person?" His starting point was the Parable of the Good Samaritan. Just as Jesus declined to answer the question "And who is my neighbor?" by providing a set of criteria, so there are no criteria (whether self-consciousness or reason or responsive love) by which to decide who is a "person." Instead, the Good Samaritan identified his neighbor by caring for him, since "the truth of neighborhood is known in engagement." Just so, the question, "Who is a person?" cannot be answered speculatively. Instead, we come to recognize someone as a person "only from a stance of prior moral commitment to treat him or her as a person." Then later we come to know him or her as a person, as he or she is disclosed to us in personal relationships. It is not that personhood is conferred on someone by our resolve to treat him as a person, but that personhood is disclosed that way. Personhood becomes apparent in personal relationships, although it is not established by them. At the same time, before we commit ourselves to the service of a person, it is right to look for evidence that it is appropriate to do so, either by appearance or (in the case of a fetus) by our scientific knowledge of its unique genotype. There are thus three stages. First, there must be recognition, making it appropriate to engage with a person as person. Next follows commitment, caring for him as a person. And thirdly there comes encounter: "Those whom we treat as persons when they are yet unborn, become known to us as persons when they are children." These three stages acknowledge the gradualness of development into personal encounter, while affirming the reality of personhood from the moment of conception.[24]

In an unpublished essay entitled "The Logic of Beginnings" the late Professor Donald MacKay, formerly director of the Research Department of Communication and Neuroscience at Keele University, took issue with Professor O'Donovan's argument. "Things come into existence in various ways," he wrote. For example, artifacts (like a car) are assembled piece by piece, rain clouds form by condensation, an explosive mixture of gas and air develops gradually, while plants and animals grow. Each of these processes has an end product (a car, a rain cloud, an explosion, a mature plant or an animal), but it is difficult for us to perceive either the exact moment when this comes into being or the exact nature of the change which takes place when it does. This led Donald MacKay to criticize the language of "potentiality." To be sure, the beginning of every process has the potentiality to reach the end product, granted the enabling conditions, but this does not justify ontological assertions about the earlier stages. For example, various components will become a car, if they are assembled properly, but we do not refer to them as a "potential car," because they might instead end up on the scrap heap. May we then refer to a fertilized ovum as a "potential human being"? Yes, in the sense that it will lead to maturity if gestation proceeds normally, but not if this leads us to attribute to the ovum specific properties of the end product. The value of "potentiality" language is that it emphasizes the importance of beginnings, expectations and resulting obligations; its danger is to imagine that all the attributes and rights of the end product already belong to the beginning. They do not, even if there is a direct line of continuity between the two.

In particular, Donald MacKay concluded, before the fetus may rightly be considered a "conscious personal agency," there are certain information-processing requirements which are necessary for human self-supervision. This is not to reduce a person to a brain, but to say that a person cannot be embodied in a structure which lacks a self-supervisory system, because it lacks adequate brain development. "The capacity to sustain conscious personhood is a systemic property of the central nervous system." On the one hand, the fertilized ovum is a "physical structure with the richest and most strangely mysterious repertoire known to man," for it can develop into "the embodiment of a new human being in the image of God, loved by God, replete with potentialities of not merely earthly but eternal significance." On the other, to treat it as "a person with the rights of a person" is a conspicuous example of "thin-end-of-the-wedgery."[25]

In summary, Oliver O'Donovan insisted that the fetus has "personhood" from the moment of fusion, and that therefore we must commit ourselves to its care, although only later will its personhood be revealed in personal relationships. Donald MacKay agreed that from the moment of fusion the conceptus has biological life and a marvelous repertoire of potentiality, but added that it only becomes a person possessing rights and demanding care when brain development makes self-supervision possible.

The conflict between the two learned professors sounds irreconcilable. Yet I believe that there may be more common ground between them than appears at first sight, and I do not believe that either is altogether denying what the other affirms. Donald MacKay emphasizes the development of the fetus, while not denying that already the fertilized ovum has a rich repertoire. Oliver O'Donovan emphasizes that from the very beginning the conceptus has a unique and complete genotype, and indeed personhood, while not denying that its destiny is to reach human maturity. Is this not at base the old tension (with which the New Testament has made us familiar) between the "already" and the "not yet"? Tertullian expressed it as early as the end of the second century: "He also is a man who is about to be one; you have the fruit already in its seed."[26] In our own day Paul Ramsey has put it like this: "The human individual comes into existence as a minute informational speck. . . . His subsequent prenatal and postnatal development may be described as a process of becoming what he already is from the moment he was conceived."[27] Lewis Smedes calls the status of a fetus a "deep ontological ambiguity—the ambiguity of not being something yet and at the same time having the makings of what it will be."[28] It is the language of "potentiality" in relation to the embryo which has confused us. Professor Thomas F. Torrance has clarified it by explaining that "the potentiality concerned is not that of becoming something else but of becoming what it essentially is."[29]

This brings me back to Psalm 139 and to the reason for the psalmist's sense of continuity of being, namely God's steadfast love. Indeed, it is God's loving, personal commitment to the unborn child which makes me uncomfortable with Donald MacKay's nonpersonal analogies (material artifacts, clouds, gases, plants and animals). The sovereign initiative of God in creating and loving is the biblical understanding of grace. Donald MacKay declines to attribute personhood to the newly conceived fetus because as yet it has no brain to sustain either self-supervision or conscious relationships. But supposing the vital relationship which confers personhood on the fetus is God's conscious, loving commitment to him, rather than his to God? Such a one-sided relationship is seen in parents who love their child, and commit themselves to its care and protection, long before it is able to respond. And a unilateral initiative is what makes grace to be grace. It is, in fact, God's grace which confers on the unborn child, from the moment of its conception, both the unique status which it already enjoys and the unique destiny which it will later inherit. It is grace which holds together this duality of the actual and the potential, the already and the not yet.

Human Fertilization

The ethical debate has to some extent shifted from the deliberate destruction of unwanted fetuses to the artificial creation of embryos for married couples who desperately want to have a child. One feels instinctive sympathy for a couple who began their married life with the intention and expectation of having children, only to discover that they cannot. Scripture itself speaks positively of parenthood as the natural crown of marriage, summons us to praise the God who "settles the barren woman in her home as a happy mother of children" (Psalm 113:9) and views childlessness as a painful, personal tragedy.

It is understandable, therefore, that fertility clinics have been set up and that a variety of techniques have been developed, not only medical and surgical but also biogenetic, in order to help infertile couples to have children. These procedures have provoked public reactions ranging from "pride" in technological achievement and "pleasure" in overcoming infertility to "unease" over the lack of social controls.[30] What should Christians think of modern fertilization techniques?

At the risk of serious oversimplification, one might say that normal and natural procreation depends on four parental contributions—the father's sperm, the mother's egg, fallopian tubes which connect her ovaries to her womb and where fusion takes place, together with her womb in which the embryo develops. But one or more of these four (sperm, egg, tubes and womb) may be in some way defective. For example, a common cause of infertility is the blocking of the fallopian tubes, which in many cases can be rectified by surgery. In other situations artificial insemination may be used, namely the insertion of the husband's sperm ("AIH") through a plastic tube directly into his wife's cervix or uterus.

An alternative way of bringing about the fusion of sperm and ovum, outside rather than inside the mother's body, is in vitro fertilization ("IVF"), followed by embryo transfer ("ET"). This double technique was first developed in Britain by Dr. Robert Edwards, a Cambridge University physiologist, and Mr. Patrick Steptoe, a gynecologist. Their first "test-tube baby" was Louise Brown, who was born in 1978, and they celebrated their one hundredth birth by this means in 1983. It was reckoned at that time that perhaps another one hundred IVF babies had been born worldwide. By now the number is much higher, since IVF is also practiced in Australia, the United States, France, West Germany, Israel and other countries.[31]

The moral dicussion surrounds not only the IVF technique itself, but also the uses to which it is being put. If damage to the fallopian tubes is one cause of infertility, others are a defect or deficiency in the husband's sperm or in the wife's ova or womb, so that the proposed solution involves in each case the "donation" by an outside or third party of the missing component.

First, if it is the husband who is infertile, sperm donation is possible, either by direct insemination ("AID") or by IVF. In the latter case the wife's egg is fertilized by an outside donor's sperm, followed a few days later by ET into the wife's womb.

Secondly, if it is the wife who is infertile, then egg donation by another woman (perhaps her sister) is possible, the outside donor's egg being fertilized by the husband's sperm through IVF, followed again by ET into the wife's womb.

Thirdly, if both husband and wife are infertile, it is possible for them to commission another married couple to contribute their sperm and ovum, which would then be fused through IVF and placed in the wife's womb. This would be a case of embryo donation.

Fourthly, it may be that, although neither husband nor wife is infertile, her womb has been damaged so that she cannot bear her own child. In this case, it is suggested, his sperm and her egg could through IVF and ET be inserted into another woman, who would carry and in due course give birth to their child and then surrender him or her to them, the genetic parents. This could be called womb donation, although it is commonly referred to as "surrogate motherhood."

These are the four main procedures which are being recommended, although additional permutations and combinations are possible. What is common to all four is the use of IVF together with the donation (which IVF makes possible) of sperm, egg, embryo or womb, in each case by a third party or outside donor.

Although the brief of the Warnock Committee included "consideration of the social, ethical and legal implications" of the new technologies for assisted reproduction, the weakest feature of its Report is its failure to contribute a coherent or comprehensive moral basis for its proposals. The Committee even acknowledges its decision to go "straight to the question of how it is right to treat the human embryo" without first considering "when life or personhood begin."[32] Before we are ready, however, to enter into the moral debate, here is a summary of those main recommendations of the Report which are germane to our discussion. It was recommended

- that sperm, egg and embryo donation should be permitted, provided that they are properly controlled by a statutory licensing authority (A 4–7)
- that couples and donors (of sperm and ova) should remain permanently unknown to each other, although a confidential central register should be maintained (B 18, 24)

173

- that donors should have no parental rights or obligations (E 51, 54, 55)
- that children born as a result of donation should have their birth registered as if the couple were their parents (though with "by donation" added if desired) and should never be entitled to know the identity of their biological parents except, on reaching the age of eighteen, their "ethnic origin and genetic health" (E 53–54; 4.17, 21, 25)
- that, although surrogate motherhood should not be made a criminal offense, surrogacy agencies, arrangements and contracts should (E 56–58)
- that research on human embryos (both "spare" and specially procured embryos) should be permitted under license for up to fourteen days after fertilization and on condition of informed parental consent. However, three committee members opposed all experimentation, and four more were opposed to the deliberate production of embryos for research purposes (A 11–14, D 43–44)

A few months after the publication of the Warnock Report Mr. Enoch Powell MP tabled his private member's Unborn Children (Protection) Bill, which would have prohibited the production of human embryos by IVF solely for research and subsequent destruction. Although it attracted considerable support, it ran out of parliamentary time. In 1987 the government published a White Paper which prepared the way for its Human Fertilization and Embryology Research Bill, which was first introduced to Parliament in November 1989. Then in April 1990 in a free vote MPs endorsed by almost two to one the practice of research on human embryos up to fourteen days old.

What, then, are the ethical issues which make Christians uneasy about (to say the least), and even totally hostile to, these developments? The question of fertilization is a debate about relationships—between husband and wife, parents and children, doctors and family, donors and recipients, the natural and the artificial. In particular, Christians see in the new reproductive technologies a threefold intrusion or interference.

First, IVF may involve an intrusion into the process of procreation. Some Christians are just able to come to terms with IVF and ET when they concern the husband's sperm and the wife's ovum and womb. Yet even in this case, when no external donation is involved, the sacredness of human reproduction has been moved from the bedroom into the laboratory, and from a God-designed process to a human technique, as fusion takes place no longer unwitnessed within the mother's body but on a glass dish carefully monitored by scientists. It was this which led Professor Oliver O'Donovan to entitle his 1983 London Lectures *Begotten or Made?* "That which we beget," he said, "is like ourselves. . . . But that which we make is unlike ourselves." Consequently, "that which is made rather than begotten becomes something that we have at our disposal, not someone with whom we can engage in brotherly fellowship."[33] It is, in fact, on account of "the extent of medical intervention and control" in the process of IVF, that Dr. Richard Higginson called his fine book on the ethics of IVF *Whose Baby?* Is an IVF child in some sense "the doctor's baby" or "the donor's baby," or still truly "God's baby"?[34]

Moreover, IVF separates what God has united. His purpose from the beginning was that marriage, love, sex and procreation should belong together, and in particular that "baby-making" (better, "baby-getting") should be the consequence of lovemaking. The Vatican's 1987 Instruction makes this one of the main grounds of its unequivocal rejection of IVF. It quotes from Pope Paul VI's *Encyclical Humanae Vitae* (1968) that there is an "inseparable connection, willed by God and unable to be broken by man on his own initiative, between the two meanings of the conjugal act: the unitive meaning and the procreative meaning."[35] Protestants are less dogmatic, however, on the inseparability of sexual intercourse and the procreation of children. Since contraception (which they tend to allow), whether natural or mechanical, separates sex from procreation, it would be illogical to condemn IVF for separating procreation from sex. Nevertheless, we agree that God did unite the two. In consequence, parents who decide on IVF will want to ensure (as far as possible) that its whole context is one not of clinical efficiency only but of caring, conjugal love.[36]

Secondly, IVF may involve an intrusion into the bonds of marriage and parenthood. Marriage is a permanent covenant between one man and one woman, which demands uncompromising faithfulness. But all forms of donation introduce a third party (the donor) into this relationship. When sperm or egg donation by outside donor is achieved by sexual intercourse, we condemn it as "adultery." If the donation is made externally, without intercourse, is it entirely free from the taint of adultery? It is certainly incompatible with the view of marriage as an exclusive relationship which admits of no third-party intrusion. In surrogacy too, even if both sperm and ovum are contributed by the married couple, a physical and emotional bonding takes place between the "mother" and the child she is carrying, which may later be hard to break.

The fundamental inappropriateness of all donation arrangements is seen in the consequent muddle between biological and social parents and the tensions which this is bound to cause either between husband and wife (since one has contributed to their child's procreation while the other has not), or between the two mothers, or between the parents and the child. As for the secrecy which surrounds these transactions, it is enough in itself to outlaw them. All children have a fundamental right to know their own identity, which includes the identity of their parents. It would certainly be shameful to lie to them about their genetic parents. The Warnock Report at least provides, as we have seen, for the optional addition of the words "by donation" on the birth certificate and for the availability to the child when eighteen years old of some information. But children should surely have access to all the information they wish to be given. One reason why fostering and adoption belong to a different category is that they are not shrouded in secrecy or spoiled by deception.

Thirdly, IVF may involve an intrusion into the integrity of the embryo, since a living human embryo is now available for research and/or experimentation outside the mother's body and in a laboratory. Indeed, several embryos are usually available, since the custom is to induce super-ovulation in the mother so that the doctor can recover about half a dozen eggs, either in case first attempts at fertilization or implantation fail or in order that some eggs may be frozen for possible future use. Should spare embryos be used for research? Two arguments are used to defend this practice. First, research is necessary, the pioneers are saying, in order to perfect the IVF technique, to discover the causes of infertility, early miscarriage, genetic disorders and hereditary diseases, to be able to use embryonic tissue for transplant and to test drugs. However, Professor Jerome Lejeune, the French geneticist, wrote to *The Times* on 26 March 1985 that equivalent research could be performed on laboratory mammals instead, and that in any case the human embryo of less than fourteen days is too underdeveloped for some research into genetic disabilities. It is true that Dr. Andrew Huxley, President of the Royal Society, expressed his disagreement in a letter which appeared on 6 April. But other scientists have sided with Professor Lejeune. So the experts are not at one on the necessity of embryonic research.

The second argument is that up to fourteen days the embryo is so minute as to be invisible to the naked eye, and that therefore it should not be given the total or absolute protection which is given to a mature human being or even to the fetus at later stages of its development. But this begs the question of the status of the embryo from the moment of fusion.

The Warnock Report agreed "that the embryo of the human species ought to have a special status," which "should be enshrined in legislation" and should carry with it "some protection in law."[37] That is good, but not enough, as the three dissentients saw. They rightly said that the embryo's special status and legal protection should not be made dependent on a technical decision about "personhood": "Clearly, once that status [of personhood] has been accorded, all moral principles and legal enactments which relate to persons will apply. But before that point has been reached the embryo has a special status because of its potential for development to a stage at which everyone would accord it the status of a human person."[38] So then, both those who accord "personhood" to human embryos and those who do not should be able to agree (1) that they are at least in the process of developing into their full potential (which indeed is the popular understanding of the adjective "embryonic") and (2) that they are therefore inviolable.

176

Once this special status of the human embryo is acknowledged, it will follow that "experimentation" should be forbidden and that permissible "research" should be most carefully defined. The Vatican's Instruction (1987) is quite clear: "No objective, even though noble in itself, such as a foreseeable advantage to science, to other human beings or to society, can in any way justify experimentation on living human embryos."[39] The only justification would be when the work "is clearly therapeutic for the subject himself."[40] This is in keeping with the fundamental principle that human beings must be regarded and treated as ends in themselves, and not as means to some other end, however good.

Techniques and Exceptions

How will our evaluation of the uniqueness of the human fetus (however we decide to formulate it) affect our thinking and acting, especially in relation to abortion?

To begin with, it will change our attitudes. Since the life of the human fetus is a human life, with the potential of becoming a mature human being, we have to learn to think of mother and unborn child as two human beings at different stages of development. Doctors and nurses have to consider that they have two patients, not one, and must seek the well-being of both. Lawyers and politicians need to think similarly. As the United Nations' "Declaration of the Rights of the Child" (1959) put it, the child "needs special safeguards and care, including appropriate legal protection, before as well as after birth." Christians would wish to add "extra care before birth." For the Bible has much to say about God's concern for the defenseless, and the most defenseless of all people are unborn children. They are speechless to plead their own cause and helpless to protect their own life. So it is our responsibility to do for them what they cannot do for themselves.

All Christians should therefore be able to agree that the human fetus is in principle inviolable. Lord Ramsey, when as Archbishop of Canterbury he was addressing the Church Assembly in 1967, said, "We have to assert as normative the general inviolability of the fetus. . . . We shall be right to continue to see as one of Christianity's great gifts to the world the belief that the human fetus is to be reverenced as the embryo of a life capable of coming to reflect the glory of God . . ."

It is the combination of what the human fetus already is and what it one day could be which makes the realities of abortion so horrific. How can anybody possibly reconcile the brutal techniques of abortion with the concept of the abortus as a potential mirror of God's glory?

The most common method of abortion is vacuum aspiration, which is used in pregnancies up to twelve to fourteen weeks. In this operation the cervix is dilated and a tube connected to a suction pump is inserted into the womb. The fetus is sucked from the womb and collected in a jar where body parts must be accounted for to ensure full removal.

A second, older method is "D and C," dilation and curettage. The cervix is dilated to facilitate the insertion of an implement, either a "curette" with which the wall of the womb is scraped until the fetus is cut into pieces and removed, or, in later pregnancies, sponge forceps and a plier-like instrument by which it is torn into pieces. In either case a violent and bloody dismemberment takes place.

A third method (employed between twelve and sixteen weeks) is to inject a toxic (usually saline) solution by a long needle inserted through the mother's abdomen into the amniotic sac enveloping the fetus, which is thus poisoned, burned and killed, and then "spontaneously" ejected. At a later stage of pregnancy surgery is used, either a hysterotomy which resembles a cesarean section (except that in this case the baby is taken from the womb to be killed, not saved) or a complete hysterectomy by which womb and fetus are removed together and discarded together (this is rarely used).

Yet another method, developed in the United States but legal in Britain as well, is dilation and extraction (D and X), commonly known as "partial birth abortion." This procedure is performed in late-term pregnancies when fetal tissues have become too strong for easy dismemberment. In this abortion the child is manipulated into a breech birth position and partially delivered feet-first until the head alone remains in the womb. The doctor then inserts a pair of scissors into the base of the skull, followed by a suction catheter that removes the brain, causing the skull to collapse and facilitating the removal of the now dead baby. Because of the barbaric nature of this method it is currently under intense debate in the United States, and the discussion grows louder in Britain.

An alternative to surgery in the first few months of pregnancy is the use of the drug RU 486 in conjunction with prostaglandins. The RU 486 drug was licensed for use in 1991 by the Department of Health and is now in fairly common use. It can be taken up to nine weeks of pregnancy and procures an abortion by destroying the lining of the womb. RU 486 is used in conjunction with prostaglandin, a drug which facilitates the evacuation of the contents of the womb.

A final method of abortion is the "morning after" pill. If a woman has had intercourse without contraception and fears pregnancy she can be prescribed a "morning after" pill to be taken within seventy-two hours of intercourse. This is a high-dose estrogen pill that prevents implantation by disrupting the lining of the womb. Because this method is not covered by the

Abortion Act, the pill can be prescribed by a single doctor, even one's family doctor.

A factual knowledge of these procedures should lead us to revise our vocabulary. For the popular euphemisms make it easier for us to conceal the truth from ourselves. The occupant of the mother's womb is not a "product of conception" or "gametic material," but an unborn child. Even "pregnancy" tells us no more than that a woman has been "impregnated," whereas the truth in old-fashioned language is that she is "with child." How can we speak of "the termination of a pregnancy" when what is terminated is not just the mother's pregnancy but the child's life? And how can we describe the average abortion today as "therapeutic" (a word originally used only when the mother's life was at stake), when pregnancy is not a disease needing therapy, and what abortion effects nowadays is not a cure but a killing? And how can people think of abortion as no more than a kind of contraceptive, when what it does is not prevent conception but destroy the conceptus? We need to have the courage to use accurate language. Induced abortion is feticide, the deliberate destruction of an unborn child, the shedding of innocent blood.

Is abortion, then, never justified? To answer this question in a way that is both faithful and realistic, theologians and doctors need each other. More interdisciplinary consultation is necessary. For doctors are understandably impatient with theologians because they tend to be unpractical, making ivory-tower pronouncements unrelated to painful clinical dilemmas. Theologians, on the other hand, are understandably impatient with doctors because they tend to be pragmatists, making clinical decisions uncontrolled by theological principle. The principle on which we should be able to agree is well expressed as the first aim of the Society for the Protection of Unborn Children, namely "that human life ought not to be taken except in cases of urgent necessity." Professor G. R. Dunstan is probably right that there is an ethic of "justifiable feticide," by analogy with "justifiable homicide."[41] But if we accept the general inviolability of the human fetus, then every exception has to be rigorously and specifically argued. Ever since the Infant Life (Preservation) Act (1929) an abortion to save the mother's life has been legal in England, though not condoned by the Roman Catholic Church. With improved modern medical techniques, however, this case seldom arises, although one could imagine a borderline situation in which an unwanted pregnancy threatened an overburdened and neurotic mother with such a complete breakdown that she would become "a physical and mental wreck,"[42] or would be in imminent danger of taking her own life. According to Christian tradition human life may be taken to protect and preserve another life—for example, in self-defense; but we have no liberty to introduce death into a situation in which it is not already present, either as a fact or as a threat.

What about the "substantial risk" of the child to be born being "seriously handicapped," which is the fourth clause of the 1967 Abortion Act? Antenatal screening and amniocentesis (tapping and testing the amniotic fluid) can now reveal abnormalities in the fetus at about the fourth month. Is an abortion then morally justified? Many think so. Dr. Glanville Williams has expressed himself forcefully on this issue: "To allow the breeding of defectives is a horrible evil, far worse than any that may be found in abortion."[43] In discussing the tragic predicament of a mother who gives birth to "a viable monster or an idiot child," he even wrote: "An eugenic killing by a mother, exactly paralleled by the bitch that kills her misshapen puppies, cannot confidently be pronounced immoral."[44] How should a Christian conscience react to this possibility? Surely with horror. The only exceptions might be an anencephalic child (born without a brain) or a child so completely malformed as to be incapable of independent survival; these could be allowed to die.

But there are at least three reasons why such a drastic procedure must be reserved for only the most exceptional cases and must not be extended to other—even severe—abnormalities. First, it is now frequently said that the issue is not the "sanctity" of life but the "quality" of life, and that the life of a severely handicapped person is not worth living. But who can presume to decide this? To me the most moving speech at the Hyde Park Rally in June 1983, which I have already mentioned, was made by Alison Davis, who described herself as "a happy spina bifida adult" and spoke from a wheelchair. "I can think of few concepts more terrifying," she said, "than saying that certain people are better off dead, and may therefore be killed for their own good." One doctor, on hearing her say that she was glad to be alive, "made the incredible observation that no one can judge their own quality of life, and that other people might well consider a life like mine miserable!" On the contrary, she insisted, "most handicapped people are quite contented with the quality of their lives." After all, it is love which gives quality to life and makes it worth living, and it is we—their neighbors—who can choose whether to give love to the handicapped or withhold it. The quality of their life is in our hands.

Secondly, once we accept that a handicapped child may be destroyed before birth, why should we not do it also after birth? Indeed, the practice of infanticide has already begun. Doctors of course do not use this word, and some try to persuade themselves that starving babies to death is not killing them, but "I'd like to bet they'd change their minds," said Alison Davis, "if we did it to them!" The solemn fact is that if society is prepared to kill an unborn child on the sole ground that it will be handicapped, there is no logical reason why we should not go on to kill the deformed newborn, the comatose victim of a car crash, the imbecile and the senile. For the handicapped become disposable when their lives are judged "worthless" or "unproductive," and we are back in Hitler's horrible Third Reich.

Christians will rather agree with Jean Rostan, the French biologist, who wrote:

> For my part I believe that there is no life so degraded, debased, deteriorated or impoverished that it does not deserve respect and is not worth defending with zeal and conviction. . . . I have the weakness to believe that it is an honour for our society to desire the expensive luxury of sustaining life for its useless, incompetent, and incurably ill members. I would almost measure society's degree of civilization by the amount of effort and vigilance it imposes on itself out of pure respect for life.[45]

A third reason for not aborting the handicapped is that to do so would be for fallible mortals to play God. We do not have that authority, and those who arrogate it to themselves are bound to make grave mistakes. Maurice Baring used to tell the story of one doctor who asked another: "About the termination of a pregnancy, I want your opinion. The father was syphilitic, the mother tuberculous. Of the four children born the first was blind, the second died, the third was deaf and dumb, and the fourth also tuberculous. What would you have done?" "I would have ended the pregnancy." "Then you would have murdered Beethoven."[46]

In this whole discussion we have to be on our guard against selfish rationalizations. I fear that the real reason why we say that serious handicap would be an unbearable burden for a child, if it were allowed to be born, is that it would be an unbearable burden for us. But Christians must remember that the God of the Bible has expressed his special protective care for the handicapped and the weak.

A Call to Action

What then shall we do? First, we need to repent. I agree with Raymond Johnston, the late founder director of CARE Trust, when he wrote in a newspaper article: "I personally am convinced that the destruction of the unborn on this massive, deliberate scale is the greatest single offence regularly perpetrated in Britain today, and would be the first thing an Old Testament prophet redivivus would reproach us for." Dr. Francis Schaeffer and Dr. Everett Koop dedicated their book and film *Whatever Happened to the Human Race?* "to those who were robbed of life, the unborn, the weak, the sick, the old, during the dark ages of madness, selfishness, lust and greed for which the last decades of the twentieth century are remembered." Were they right to condemn our "enlightened" western civilization as "the dark ages"? At least in this matter I think they were, and I for one am ashamed that we Christians have not been "the light of the world" which Jesus intended us to be. We also need to repent of our tendency to selective campaigning. We lack integrity if we fight for the life of the unborn and care little for the life of the born—for example, of abused or neglected children, battered and abandoned mothers, slum dwellers or refugees. Christians are committed to human life, both to defending its sanctity and to promoting its quality.

Secondly, we need to accept full responsibility for the effects of a tighter abortion policy, if it can be secured. To agitate for it without being prepared to bear its costs would be sheer hypocrisy. We must not occasion an increase of illegal "back-street" abortions. Instead, we shall want to help the pregnant woman to overcome any reluctance she feels to have her baby, and see that she is given every possible personal, medical, social and financial support. For God tells us to "carry each other's burdens, and in this way . . . fulfill the law of Christ" (Galatians 6:2). We shall want to ensure that, although some babies are unwanted (and even unloved) by their parents, no baby is unwanted by society in general and by the Church in particular. We should not hesitate to oppose the abortion, and urge the birth, of every child. Pregnancy is a time of emotional instability, so that the minds and feelings of expectant mothers sometimes change. Rex Gardner refers to two reports about women who have been refused an abortion. In one case 73 percent of them, in the other 84 percent, said they were glad the pregnancy had not been terminated. He also quotes Sir John Stallworthy, who has said that some of the happiest people he knows are those who have said to him: "You don't remember, but the first time I came wanting an abortion. Thank God you did not agree, because this child has brought the greatest joy into our home that we have ever known."[47] As for those who would find the strain of keeping their child too great, there is a lengthy queue of married but infertile couples who are longing for the chance to adopt. As Mother Teresa used to say, "We are fighting abortion by adoption."

I thank God for the organizations which have been pioneering a supportive ministry for pregnant women, like "Birthright" and CareNet in Canada and the United States, "Alternatives to Abortion International" (whose publication is called *Heartbeat*), and LIFE and SPUC (Society for the Protection of Unborn Children) in Britain.[48] In different ways they are offering a caring service, such as counseling women with an unplanned pregnancy, offering emergency help to those in despair, giving advice on practical problems, finding accommodation for mothers both before and after their child's birth, helping to secure employment for them, granting financial help, and providing personal support groups. As Louise Summerhill, founder of "Birthright," has written, "We help rather than abort; we believe in making a better world for babies to come into, rather than killing them."[49]

Thirdly, we need to support a positive educational and social campaign, not least in schools. Christians must not be shy to teach thoroughly and constantly the biblical understanding of humanness and of the value, indeed the sacredness, of human life. We have to recognize that all abortions are due to unwanted pregnancies, and that all unwanted pregnancies are due to a failure of some kind.

Often it is sexual failure, whether lack of sexual self-control (especially in men, who usually escape the tragic consequences of their action) or lack of a responsible use of contraceptives. The Church of England General Synod's Board for Social Responsibility has called for "a major effort at social education" (and moral education too, we might add), in order "to reduce the number of unwanted pregnancies," "to undermine the habit of mind which leads straight from the recognition of pregnancy to resort to an abortionist," and to move the public "to find a better solution."[50] This is "The Better Way" of which Rex Gardner writes in his chapters 28 and 29.[51]

Unwelcome pregnancies are also often due to social failure, to such conditions as poverty, unemployment and overcrowding. So for this reason we too should be working for a better society. Social evils are to be fought; they will not be solved by more abortions.

In the Third World large families are a kind of insurance against old age. Only a measurable reduction of infant mortality will give parents confidence to have smaller families, and only the development of a simple, safe, cheap contraceptive will help them to do so.

More important in the end than either social education or social action, vital as they both are, is the good news of Jesus Christ. He came to bind up the brokenhearted and support the weak. He calls us to treat all human life with reverence, whether in the unborn, the infant, the handicapped or the senile.

I have no desire to stand in personal judgment either on the women who have resorted to an abortion, or on the men whose sexual self-indulgence is responsible for most unwanted pregnancies. I want to say to them instead, "There is forgiveness with God" (see Psalm 130:4). For Christ died for our sins and offers us a new beginning. He rose again and lives, and by his Spirit can give us a new, inward power of self-control. He is also building a new community characterized by love, joy, peace, freedom and justice. A new beginning. A new power. A new community. This is the gospel of Christ.

Euthanasia

The obvious parallels between abortion and euthanasia make it appropriate for them to be discussed in the same chapter. For, although abortion relates to the beginning of a human life, and euthanasia to its end, both are decisions for death. Both therefore raise the same urgent question whether it may ever be morally justifiable to terminate life and precipitate death.

The euthanasia debate can be traced back at least to the heyday of Greek philosophy. But a number of factors have combined to bring it to the forefront of public concern in our day—advances in medical technology which prolong life and so are responsible for an aging population, the AIDS epidemic, some particularly poignant and well-publicized cases which seemed to cry out for euthanasia on compassionate grounds, and the persuasive campaigning of EXIT (previously the Voluntary Euthanasia Society) in the UK and the Hemlock Society, its equivalent in the United States.

A widely accepted definition of euthanasia, which has been adopted for example by HOPE ("Healthcare Opposed to Euthanasia"), is as follows: "Euthanasia is the intentional killing by act or omission of a person whose life is considered not to be worth living."

This is popularly called "mercy killing," and is divided between "voluntary euthanasia" ("assisted suicide," the death occurring at the explicit plea of the patient) and "involuntary euthanasia" (the death occurring by someone else's decision when the patient is incapable of giving consent). It is essential to clarify that euthanasia, whether voluntary or involuntary, is intentional killing. It deliberately introduces death into a situation in which it did not previously exist. But to withhold or withdraw useless treatment from a terminally ill patient is not euthanasia. Nor is the administration of painkillers to a dying patient which may incidentally accelerate death, but whose primary intention is to relieve pain. In both these cases death is already irreversibly present. To intervene with further treatment would only prolong the process of dying. Although this distinction is not always amenable to precise definition, there is a fundamental difference between causing somebody to die (which is euthanasia) and allowing him or her to die (which is not). During Dr. Martyn Lloyd-Jones's final illness in hospital, there came a moment when he refused further treatment, complaining to his doctor "You are keeping me from the glory!"

There seem to be three basic issues in the euthanasia debate, which I will call *value* (what value has a human life?), *fear* (what are the main fears which euthanasia is intended to relieve?) and *autonomy* (what right do we have over our own life?).

First, there is the question of value. Some contemporary non-Christian writers flatly deny that human life has any absolute or intrinsic value. Notable among them is Professor Peter Singer in his book *Rethinking Life and Death: The Collapse of Our Traditional Ethics*. He is well-known for his rejection of "speciesism," namely "discrimination against or exploitation of certain animal species by human beings, based on an assumption of mankind's superiority" (OED). Accepting both the Darwinian view that

184

"we are animals too" and the corresponding view that the higher animals are "persons" too,[52] he argues that we must "abandon the distinction between humans and non-human animals." Since then "neither a newborn human infant nor a fish is a person,"[53] we can imagine the logical consequences of such a position for both abortion and euthanasia.

There are other non-Christian scholars, however, who still maintain, albeit not on biblical grounds, that human beings have a unique value. For example, as with abortion so with euthanasia, Professor Dworkin is able to affirm "the intrinsic cosmic importance of human life itself."[54] So far we have seen that, in relation to abortion, he has formulated a person's value in terms of the "investment," both natural and human, which has been made in him or her, adding that the natural investment in a human life is more important than the human. It can therefore be argued that death would frustrate nature's investment and so "cheat nature."[55] Now, however, in relation to euthanasia, Professor Dworkin develops a view of human "value" which is based on our "best interests," distinguishing between "experiential" interests (what causes pleasure or pain) and "critical" interests (what gives life meaning). Only after he has made this distinction is he able to ask the question whether death could ever be in someone's "best interests." Certainly our life's conclusion needs to be consonant with the convictions and commitments which have motivated it throughout, since "none of us wants to end our lives out of character."[56] On the contrary, this would compromise our dignity, our sense of being "someone with critical interests."[57]

These concepts of "investment" and "critical interests" are valiant attempts to construct a secular understanding of human value. They fail to convince, however, and seem too abstract to have popular appeal. The Christian alternative, which we need to defend and promote with increasing determination, is that we have intrinsic value because God has created us in his own image. Human beings are Godlike beings, possessing a cluster of unique faculties (rational, moral and social) which distinguish us from animals. In particular, there is our capacity for the relationships of love, since God is love.

But this raises a problem. Is not love an essentially reciprocal relationship? How can we love a person who is unable to respond to our love, for example somebody in a "persistent vegetative state" or indeed an unborn fetus? Does not their unresponsiveness disqualify them from being regarded and treated as human beings? No, this is where grace comes in. For grace is precisely love to the unresponsive. Grace is love taking a unilateral initiative. Grace is God's free, spontaneous, unsolicited, even unreturned love, which finds its origin in itself, not in its object. We looked earlier at Psalm 139, in which the psalmist affirms that at every stage of his life (as fetus, baby, youth and adult) he is the same person with the same identity. He is also aware of a special personal relationship to God, which God has initiated and which God sustains. He finds his humanity and dignity not in his knowing and loving God, but in the fundamental truth that God knows and loves him, whether he responds to God or not. This same divine unilateral love binds a mother to her unborn child, and young people to their frail, elderly, and perhaps demented relatives. It is not responsiveness which makes people human; it is love, not loving only but being loved.

Secondly, the specter of fear haunts the euthanasia debate. One of the strongest incentives of those campaigning for euthanasia is that (understandably) they are afraid of what they see as the only alternative, namely having to endure (or see loved ones endure) the horrors of a lingering, distressing, anguished, messy end. Professor John Wyatt, consultant neonatal pediatrician at University College Hospital, in his 1997 London Lectures in Contemporary Christianity (Matters of Life and Death) analyzed this often inarticulate fear. First, it is fear of uncontrollable and unbearable pain. Secondly, it is fear of indignity, of being subjected to the dehumanizing effect of modern medical technology, "with tubes in every orifice." Thirdly, it is fear of dependence. We want to "write our own script and determine our own exit" and not suffer the ultimate humiliation of total helplessness.

Further, if we are to have a balanced understanding of the place of fear in the euthanasia debate, we need to add a fourth fear, although this is experienced not by those who advocate euthanasia, but by those who oppose it. It is the fear that their doctor might become their killer. A crucial clause in the Hippocratic Oath is the following: "I will use treatment to help the sick according to my judgment and ability, but I will never use it to injure or wrong them." This general promise to heal and not to hurt accounts for the two particular rejections which follow, namely assisted suicide and abortion, although both were very common in the ancient world: "I will not give poison to anyone, even though asked to do so. . . . I will not give a pessary to a woman to cause abortion." Here is a clear recognition that the vocation of a doctor is to be a healer. There is therefore a fundamental anomaly about a healer becoming a killer at either end of human life. It undermines the doctor-patient relationship, which is based on trust, not fear. Doctors are the servants of life; they must not become the agents of death.[58]

Reverting to the fears which surround the process of dying, many see euthanasia as the only way to escape this threefold trauma (pain, indignity and dependence). But there is an alternative, which Christians want to promote, namely modern palliative care. One of its Christian pioneers was Dame Cicely Saunders, founder of the St. Christopher's Hospice in South London.[59] Another is Dr. Robert Twycross, who since 1971 has been a full-time hospice doctor. He says to his patients: "Not only will we enable you to die with dignity, but we will enable you to live before you die." But it appears that large numbers of doctors do not know about this development. It is significant that Dr. Nigel Cox, who in 1992 gave a lethal injection to his longstanding patient Lilian Boyes, was rebuked by the General Medical Council for being unaware of the available resources of palliative medicine and was ordered to take a course in this area. It is now claimed that more than 90 percent of pain can be controlled by analgesia. And Christian people can and should be more actively involved in giving love and support to terminally ill patients in their nearest hospice.

The third issue involved in the euthanasia debate is the question of human autonomy or self-determination. The advocates of euthanasia insist, often in strident tones, that all human beings (provided that they are rational and competent) have the right to make their own decisions and dispose of their own life, and that no institution or individual has the authority to deny them that right.

It is certainly a fundamental biblical truth that God has made us rational and volitional beings. That is, we have a God-given mind and will of our own. Consequently, it is an essential aspect of our identity and maturity as human beings that we live by choice and not by coercion, and that we are accountable to God for our decisions. Indeed, this is the meaning of freedom. Freedom presupposes choice, and "freedom is the cardinal absolute requirement of self-respect."[60] While stating in general terms the goodness of choice, however, we need immediately to qualify our assertion in relation to freedom, dependence and life.

First, freedom has limits. The notion of absolute freedom is an illusion. Even God, who is perfect in his freedom, is not free to do absolutely anything. This is not the meaning of his omnipotence. Scripture itself mentions several things God "cannot" (because he will not) do, especially that he cannot deny or contradict himself (2 Timothy 2:13), for God's freedom is limited by his nature. He is free to do absolutely anything which is consistent with his nature to do. The same principle applies to human beings. Human freedom is not unlimited. We find our freedom only in living according to our God-given nature, not in rebellion against it. The notion of total human autonomy is a myth.

Secondly, dependence can be good, even though it is the opposite of autonomy. It is highly significant that Jesus chose little children as his model of humility. For the "humility" of children is not in their character (which is often self-centered and stubborn) but in their status (dependent on their parents). Just so, we human beings are to acknowledge humbly our dependence on God, not only for the sustaining of our physical existence, but also for our salvation, which is due to his grace, not our achievement. The proclamation of our autonomy in this area, claiming that we can know and reach God by our own effort, is the essence of sin, not of maturity. Dependence is far from being the unmitigated, undignified evil some fear.

Thirdly, life is a gift of God. "I know, O LORD," cried Jeremiah, "that a man's life is not his own" (Jeremiah 10:23). He was right; it is God's. According to a long, consistent, biblical tradition, God is the creator, giver, sustainer and taker-away of life. He said in the Song of Moses: "There is no god besides me. I put to death and I bring to life" (Deuteronomy 32:39; cf. Genesis 39:2; 1 Samuel 2:6; Job 1:21). Similarly, the king of Israel was indignant when the king of Syria wrote to him about Naaman's leprosy: "Am I God? Can I kill and bring back to life?" (2 Kings 5:7). Moreover, having received this gift from his hands, we are trustees and guardians of it, and he invites us to cooperate with him in fostering it. This includes curing and caring, looking after those who cannot look after themselves, and seeking to restore to health those who are sick. For human beings are not animals, *pace* Professor Peter Singer and others who reject "speciesism." When necessary, we "put down" or "put to sleep" a favorite pet, but we may not use this vocabulary in relation to the handicapped or the senile, the unborn or the dying. The doctor must not think or behave like a vet.

Yet "there exists in contemporary culture," Pope John Paul II has written, "a certain Promethean attitude which leads people to think that they can control life and death by taking the decisions about them into their own hands."[61] The proper name for this frame of mind is not autonomy but hubris, presumption before God. Although the lines of demarcation between God's responsibility and ours are not always sharp, and although God does call us into a privileged partnership with himself, yet we human beings may not trespass into his territory or assume his prerogatives. Instead, we must let God be God in his unique majesty and power and humble ourselves before him in worship.

8

Same-Sex Partnerships?

Because of the explosive nature of this topic, let me begin by describing the proper context of our thinking about it and by affirming a number of truths about my readers and myself which I am taking for granted as I write.

The Context for Discussion

First, we are all human beings. That is to say, there is no such phenomenon as "a homosexual." There are only people, human persons, made in the image and likeness of God, yet fallen, with all the glory and the tragedy which that paradox implies, including sexual potential and sexual problems. However strongly we may disapprove of homosexual practices, we have no liberty to dehumanize those who engage in them.

Secondly, we are all sexual beings. Our sexuality, according to both Scripture and experience, is basic to our humanness. Angels may be sexless; we humans are not. When God made humankind, he made us male and female. So to talk about sex is to touch a point close to the center of our personality. A vital part of our identity is being discussed, and perhaps either endorsed or threatened. So the subject demands an unusual degree of sensitivity.

Moreover, not only are we all sexual beings, but we all have a particular sexual inclination. The American zoologist Alfred C. Kinsey's famous investigation into human sexuality led him to place every human being somewhere on a spectrum from 0 (an exclusively heterosexual bias, attracted only to the opposite sex) to 6 (an exclusively homosexual bias, attracted

189

only to the same sex, whether homosexual males or "lesbians," as homosexual females are usually called). In between these poles he plotted varying degrees of bisexuality, referring to people whose sexual inclination is either dual or indeterminate or fluctuating.

Since the publication in 1948 of Kinsey's report on male sexual behavior,[1] he has been widely quoted as having found that 10 percent of American men (at least of white American males) are exclusively homosexual throughout their lives. This is a serious misquotation, however. Ten percent was his figure for men who are predominantly homosexual for up to three years between the ages of sixteen and sixty-five. His figure for lifelong and exclusive homosexual men was 4 percent, and even this has been challenged on the ground that his sampling was not representative. More recent studies have found the incidence of homosexual practice to be lower still. According to four surveys conducted by the U.S. National Opinion Research Center between 1970 and 1990, the number of men who had ever had a homosexual encounter was 6 percent and during the previous year 1.8 percent, while the percentage of the population who had adopted a consistently homosexual lifestyle was between 0.6 and 0.7 percent. A 1990–91 British survey found similarly that 1.1 percent had had a homosexual partner during the previous year. These studies suggest that in the western world less than 2 percent of the male population, and less than 1 percent of the female, are exclusively homosexual in inclination and practice.

Thirdly, we are all sinners. We are frail and vulnerable. We are pilgrims on our way to God. We are very far from having arrived. We are engaged in an unremitting conflict with the world, the flesh and the devil. Not yet have we conquered. Perfection awaits the Parousia. In addition and in particular, we are all sexual sinners. The doctrine of total depravity asserts that every part of our human being has been tainted and twisted by sin, and that this includes our sexuality. Dr. Merville Vincent, of the Department of Psychiatry at Harvard Medical School, was surely correct when he wrote: "In God's view I suspect we are all sexual deviants. I doubt if there is anyone who has not had a lustful thought that deviated from God's perfect ideal of sexuality."[2] Nobody (with the sole exception of Jesus of Nazareth) has been sexually sinless. There is no question, therefore, of coming to this study with a horrid "holier-than-thou" attitude of moral superiority. Because all of us are sinners, we all stand under the judgment of God and we are all in urgent need of the grace of God. Besides, sexual sins are not the only sins, nor even necessarily the most sinful; pride and hypocrisy are surely worse.

Fourthly, in addition to being human, sexual and sinful creatures, I take it that we are all Christians. At least the readers I have in mind in this chapter are not people who reject the lordship of Jesus Christ, but rather those who earnestly desire to submit to it, believe that he exercises it through

Scripture, want to understand what light Scripture throws on this topic, and have a predisposition to seek God's grace to follow his will when it is known. Without this kind of commitment, it would be more difficult for us to find common ground. To be sure, God's standards are the same for everybody, but non-Christian people are less ready to accept them.

Having delineated the context for our discussion, I am ready to ask the question: are same-sex partnerships a Christian option? I phrase my question advisedly. It introduces us to three necessary distinctions.

First, at least since the Wolfenden Report of 1957 and the resultant Sexual Offences Act of 1967, we have learned to distinguish between sins and crimes. Adultery has always (according to God's law) been a sin, but in most countries it is not an offense punishable by the state. Rape, by contrast, is both a sin and a crime. What the Sexual Offences Act of 1967 did was to declare that a homosexual act performed between consenting adults over twenty-one in private should no longer be a criminal offense. "The Act did not in fact 'legalize' such behaviour," wrote Professor Sir Norman Anderson, "for it is still regarded by the law as immoral, and is devoid of any legal recognition; all the Act did was to remove the criminal sanction from such acts when performed in private between two consenting adults."[3]

Secondly, we have grown accustomed to distinguish between a homosexual inclination or "inversion" (for which people may not be responsible) and homosexual physical practices (for which they are). The importance of this distinction goes beyond the attribution of responsibility to the attribution of guilt. We may not blame people for what they are, though we may for what they do. And in every discussion about homosexuality we must be rigorous in differentiating between this "being" and "doing," that is, between a person's identity and activity, sexual preference and sexual practice, constitution and conduct.

But now we have to come to terms with a third distinction, namely between homosexual practices which are casual (and probably anonymous) acts of self-gratification and those which (it is claimed) are just as expressive of authentic human love as is heterosexual intercourse in marriage. No responsible homosexual person (whether Christian or not) is advocating promiscuous "one-night stands," let alone violence or the corruption of young people and children. What some are arguing, however, especially in the Lesbian and Gay Christian Movement, is that a heterosexual marriage and a homosexual partnership are "two equally valid alternatives,"[4] being equally tender, mature and faithful. In May 1989 Denmark became the first country to legalize homosexual marriages. The previous year Bishop John S. Spong of Newark, New Jersey, urged the Episcopal Church "to bless and affirm the love that binds two persons of the same gender into a life-giving relationship of mutual commitment."[5]

The question before us, then, does not relate to homosexual practices of a casual nature, but asks whether homosexual partnerships—lifelong and loving—are a Christian option. Our concern is to subject prevailing attitudes (which range from total revulsion to equally uncritical endorsement) to biblical scrutiny. Is our sexual "preference" purely a matter of personal "taste"? Or has God revealed his will regarding a norm? In particular, can the Bible be shown to sanction homosexual partnerships, or at least not to condemn them? What, in fact, does the Bible condemn?

The Biblical Prohibitions

The late Derrick Sherwin Bailey was the first Christian theologian to reevaluate the traditional understanding of the biblical prohibitions. His famous book, of which all subsequent writers on this topic have had to take careful account, namely *Homosexuality and the Western Christian Tradition*, was published in 1955. Although many have not been persuaded by his attempted reconstruction, in particular his reinterpretation of the sin of Sodom, there are other writers, less cautious in scholarly standards than he, who regard his argument as merely preliminary and build on his foundations a much more permissive position. It is essential to consider this debate.

There are four main biblical passages which refer (or appear to refer) to the homosexual question negatively: (1) the story of Sodom (Genesis 19:1–13), with which it is natural to associate the very similar story of Gibeah (Judges 19); (2) the Levitical texts (Leviticus 18:22 and 20:13) which explicitly prohibit lying "with a man as one lies with a woman"; (3) the apostle Paul's portrayal of decadent pagan society in his day (Romans 1:18–32); and (4) two Pauline lists of sinners, each of which includes a reference to homosexual practices of some kind (1 Corinthians 6:9–10 and 1 Timothy 1:8–11).

The Stories of Sodom and Gibeah

The Genesis narrative makes it clear that "the men of Sodom were wicked and were sinning greatly against the LORD" (13:13), and that "the outcry against Sodom and Gomorrah" was "so great and their sin so grievous" that God determined to investigate it (18:20–21), and in the end "overthrew those cities and the entire plain, including all those living in the cities" (19:25) by an act of judgment which was entirely consistent with the justice of "the Judge of all the earth" (18:25). There is no controversy about this background to the biblical story. The question is: what was the sin of the people of Sodom (and Gomorrah) which merited their obliteration?

192

The traditional Christian view has been that they were guilty of homosexual practices, which they attempted (unsuccessfully) to inflict on the two angels whom Lot was entertaining in his home. Hence the word "sodomy." But Sherwin Bailey challenged this interpretation on two main grounds. First, it is a gratuitous assumption (he argued) that the demand of the men of Sodom, "Bring them out to us, so that we may know them" meant "so that we can have sex with them" (NIV). For the Hebrew word for "know" (*yada'*) occurs 943 times in the Old Testament, of which only 10 occurrences refer to physical intercourse, and even then only to heterosexual intercourse. It would therefore be better to translate the phrase "so that we may get acquainted with them." We can then understand the men's violence as due to their anger that Lot had exceeded his rights as a resident alien, for he had welcomed two strangers into his home "whose intentions might be hostile and whose credentials—had not been examined."[6] In this case the sin of Sodom was to invade the privacy of Lot's home and flout the ancient rules of hospitality. Lot begged them to desist because, he said, the two men "have come under the protection of my roof" (19:8).

Bailey's second argument was that the rest of the Old Testament nowhere suggests that the nature of Sodom's offense was homosexual. Instead, Isaiah implies that it was hypocrisy and social injustice; Jeremiah adultery, deceit and general wickedness; and Ezekiel arrogance, greed and indifference to the poor (Isaiah 1:10–16; Jeremiah 23:14; Ezekiel 16:49–50; cf. the references to pride in Ecclesiasticus 16:8 and to inhospitableness in Wisdom 19:8). Then Jesus himself (though Bailey does not mention this) on three separate occasions alluded to the inhabitants of Sodom and Gomorrah, declaring that it would be "more bearable" for them on the day of judgment than for those who reject his gospel (Matthew 10:15; 11:24; Luke 10:12). Yet in all these references there is not even a whiff or rumor of homosexual malpractice! It is only when we reach the Palestinian pseudepigraphical writings of the second century B.C. that Sodom's sin is identified as unnatural sexual behavior.[7] And this finds a clear echo in the Letter of Jude, in which it is said that "Sodom and Gomorrah and the surrounding towns gave themselves up to sexual immorality and perversion" (v. 7), and in the works of Philo and Josephus, Jewish writers who were shocked by the homosexual practices of Greek society.

Sherwin Bailey handled the Gibeah story in the same way, for they are closely parallel. Another resident alien (this time an anonymous "old man") invites two strangers (not angels but a Levite and his concubine) into his home. Evil men surround the house and make the same demand as the Sodomites, that the visitor be brought out "so that we may know him." The owner of the house first begs them not to be so "vile" to his "guest," and then offers his daughter and the concubine to them instead. The sin of the men of Gibeah, it is again suggested, was not their proposal of homosexual intercourse but their violation of the laws of hospitality.

Although Bailey must have known that his reconstruction of both stories was at most tentative, he yet made the exaggerated claim that "there is not the least reason to believe, as a matter of either historical fact or of revealed truth, that the city of Sodom and its neighbours were destroyed because of their homosexual practices."[8] Instead, the Christian tradition about "sodomy" was derived from late, apocryphal Jewish sources.

But Sherwin Bailey's case is not convincing for a number of reasons: (1) The adjectives "wicked," "vile" and "disgraceful" (Genesis 19:7; Judges 19:23) do not seem appropriate to describe a breach of hospitality; (2) the offer of women instead "does look as if there is some sexual connotation to the episode";[9] (3) although the verb *yada'* is used only ten times of sexual intercourse, Bailey omits to mention that six of these occurrences are in Genesis and one in the Sodom story itself (about Lot's daughters, who had not "known" a man, 19:8); (4) for those of us who take the New Testament documents seriously, Jude's unequivocal reference to the "sexual immorality and perversion" of Sodom and Gomorrah (v. 7) cannot be dismissed as merely an error copied from Jewish pseudepigrapha. To be sure, homosexual behavior was not Sodom's only sin; but according to Scripture it was certainly one of its sins, which brought down upon it the fearful judgment of God.

The Leviticus Texts

Both texts in Leviticus belong to the "Holiness Code" which is the heart of the book and which challenges the people of God to follow his laws and not copy the practices either of Egypt (where they used to live) or of Canaan (to which he was bringing them). These practices included sexual relations within the prohibited degrees, a variety of sexual deviations, child sacrifice, idolatry and social injustice of different kinds. It is in this context that we must read the following two texts:

Do not lie with a man as one lies with a woman; that is detestable (Leviticus 18:22).

If a man lies with a man as one lies with a woman, both of them have done what is detestable. They must be put to death; their blood will be on their own heads (Leviticus 20:13).

"It is hardly open to doubt," wrote Bailey, "that both the laws in Leviticus relate to ordinary homosexual acts between men, and not to ritual or other acts performed in the name of religion."[10] Others, however, affirm the very point which Bailey denies. They point out that the two texts are embedded in a context preoccupied largely with ritual cleanness, and Peter Coleman adds that the word translated "detestable" or "abomination" in both verses is associated with idolatry. "In English the word expresses disgust or disapproval, but in the Bible its predominant meaning is concerned with religious truth rather than morality or aesthetics."[11] Are these prohibitions merely religious taboos, then? Are they connected with that other prohibition, "No Israelite man or woman is to become a shrine prostitute" (Deuteronomy 23:17)? For certainly the Canaanitish fertility cult did include ritual prostitution, and therefore provided both male and female "sacred prostitutes" (even if there is no clear evidence that either engaged in homosexual intercourse). The evil kings of Israel and Judah were constantly introducing them into the religion of Yahweh, and the righteous kings were constantly expelling them (see, e.g., 1 Kings 14:22–24; 15:12; 22:46 and 2 Kings 23:7). The homosexual lobby argues therefore that the Levitical texts prohibit religious practices which have long since ceased, and have no relevance to same-sex partnerships today. The burden of proof is with them, however. The plain, natural interpretation of these two verses is that they prohibit homosexual intercourse of every kind. And the requirement of the death penalty (long since abrogated, of course) indicates the extreme seriousness with which homosexual practices were viewed.

Paul's Teaching in Romans 1

Because of this, God gave them over to shameful lusts. Even their women exchanged natural relations for unnatural ones (v. 26). In the same way the men also abandoned natural relations with women and were inflamed with lust for one another. Men committed indecent acts with other men, and received in themselves the due penalty for their perversion (v. 27).

All are agreed that the apostle is describing idolatrous pagans in the Greco-Roman world of his day. They had a certain knowledge of God through the created universe (vv. 19–20) and their own moral sense (v. 32), yet they suppressed the truth they knew in order to practice wickedness. Instead of giving to God the honor due to him, they turned to idols, confusing the Creator with his creatures. In judgment upon them, "God gave them over" to their depraved mind and their decadent practices (vv. 24, 26, 28), including "unnatural" sex. It seems at first sight to be a definite condemnation of homosexual behavior. But two arguments are advanced on the other side: (1) although Paul knew nothing of the modern distinction between "inverts" (who have a homosexual disposition) and "perverts" (who, though heterosexually inclined, indulge in homosexual practices), nevertheless it is the latter he is condemning, not the former. This must be so, it is urged, because they are described as having "abandoned" natural relations with women, whereas no exclusively homosexual male would ever have had them. (2) Paul is evidently portraying the reckless, shameless, profligate, promiscuous behavior of people whom God has judicially "given up"; what relevance has this to committed, loving homosexual partnerships? These two arguments can be rebutted, however, especially by the apostle's reference to "nature," that is, the created order, as I hope to show later.

The Other Pauline Texts

Do you not know that the wicked will not inherit the kingdom of God? Do not be deceived: Neither the sexually immoral nor idolaters nor adulterers nor male prostitutes (*malakoi*) nor homosexual offenders (*arsenokoitai*) nor thieves nor the greedy nor drunkards nor slanderers nor swindlers will inherit the kingdom of God (1 Corinthians 6:9–10).

We also know that law is made not for the righteous but for lawbreakers and rebels, the ungodly and sinful, the unholy and irreligious; for those who kill their fathers or mothers, for murderers, for adulterers and perverts (*arsenokoitai*), for slave traders and liars and perjurers—and for whatever else is contrary to the sound doctrine that conforms to the glorious gospel of the blessed God . . . (1 Timothy 1:9–11).

Here are two ugly lists of sins which Paul affirms to be incompatible in the first place with the Kingdom of God and in the second with either the law or the gospel. It will be observed that one group of offenders are called *malakoi* and the other (in both lists) *arsenokoitai*. What do these words mean? To begin with, it is extremely unfortunate that in the original Revised Standard Version translation of 1 Corinthians 6:9 they were combined and translated "homosexuals." Sherwin Bailey was right to protest, since the use of the word "inevitably suggests that the genuine invert, even though he be a man of irreproachable morals, is automatically branded as unrighteous and excluded from the Kingdom of God."[12] Fortunately, the revisers heeded the protest, and the second edition (1973), though still combining the words, rendered them "sexual perverts." The point is that all ten categories listed in 1 Corinthians 6:9–10 (with the possible exception of "the greedy") denote people who have offended by their actions—for example, idolaters, adulterers and thieves.

The two Greek words *malakoi* and *arsenokoitai* should not be combined, however, since they "have precise meanings. The first is literally 'soft to the touch' and metaphorically, among the Greeks, meant males (not necessarily boys) who played the passive role in homosexual intercourse. The second means literally 'male in a bed,' and the Greeks used this expression to describe the one who took the active role."[13] The Jerusalem Bible follows James Moffatt in using the ugly words "catamites and sodomites," while among his conclusions Peter Coleman suggests that "probably Paul had commercial paederasty in mind between older men and post-pubertal boys, the most common pattern of homosexual behaviour in the classical world."[14] If this is so, then once again it can be (and has been) argued that the Pauline condemnations are not relevant to homosexual adults who are both consenting and committed to one another. This is not, however, the conclusion which Peter Coleman himself draws. His summary is as follows: "Taken together, St Paul's writings repudiate homosexual behaviour as a vice of the Gentiles in Romans, as a bar to the Kingdom in Corinthians, and as an offence to be repudiated by the moral law in 1 Timothy."[15]

Reviewing these biblical references to homosexual behavior, which I have grouped, we have to agree that there are only four of them. Must we then conclude that the topic is marginal to the main thrust of the Bible? Must we further concede that they constitute a rather flimsy basis on which to take a firm stand against a homosexual lifestyle? Are those protagonists right who claim that the biblical prohibitions are "highly specific"[16]—against violations of hospitality (Sodom and Gibeah), against cultic taboos (Leviticus), against shameless orgies (Romans) and against male prostitution or the corruption of the young (1 Corinthians and 1 Timothy), and that none of these passages alludes to, let alone condemns, a loving partnership between genuine homosexual inverts? This is the conclusion reached, for example, by Letha Scanzoni and Virginia Mollenkott in their book *Is The Homosexual My Neighbour?* They write:

> The Bible clearly condemns certain kinds of homosexual practice (. . . gang rape, idolatry and lustful promiscuity). However, it appears to be silent in certain other aspects of homosexuality—both the "homosexual orientation" and "a committed love-relationship analogous to heterosexual monogamy."[17]

But no, plausible as it may sound, we cannot handle the biblical material in this way. The Christian rejection of homosexual practices does not rest on "a few isolated and obscure proof texts" (as is sometimes said), whose traditional explanation (it is further claimed) can be overthrown. And it is disturbing that those who write on this subject, and include in their treatment a section on the biblical teaching, all seem to deal with it in this way. For example, "Consideration of the Christian attitude to homosexual practices," wrote Sherwin Bailey, "inevitably begins with the story of the destruction of Sodom and Gomorrah."[18] But this beginning is not at all "inevitable." In fact, it is positively mistaken. For the negative prohibitions of homosexual practices in Scripture make sense only in the light of its positive teaching in Genesis 1 and 2 about human sexuality and heterosexual marriage. Yet Sherwin Bailey's book contains no allusion to these chapters at all. And even Peter Coleman, whose *Christian Attitudes to Homosexuality* is probably the most comprehensive biblical, historical and moral survey which has yet been published, mentions them only in a passing reference to 1 Corinthians 6 where Paul quotes Genesis 2:24. Yet without the wholesome positive teaching of the Bible on sex and marriage, our perspective on the homosexual question is bound to be skewed.

Sexuality and Marriage in the Bible

The essential place to begin our investigation, it seems to me, is the institution of marriage in Genesis 2, although we have already looked at it in chapters 5 and 6. Since members of the Lesbian and Gay Christian Movement deliberately draw a parallel between heterosexual marriages and homosexual partnerships, it is necessary to ask whether this parallel can be justified.

We have seen that in his providence God has given us two distinct accounts of Creation. The first (Genesis 1) is general and affirms the equality of the sexes, since both share in the image of God and the stewardship of the earth. The second (Genesis 2) is particular and affirms the complementarity of the sexes, which constitutes the basis for heterosexual marriage. In this second account of Creation three fundamental truths emerge.

First, the human need for companionship. "It is not good for the man to be alone" (v. 18). True, this assertion was later qualified when the apostle Paul (surely echoing Genesis) wrote: "It is good for a man not to marry" (1 Corinthians 7:1). That is to say, although marriage is the good institution of God, the call to singleness is also the good vocation of some. Nevertheless, as a general rule, "It is not good for the man to be alone." For God has created us social beings. Since he is love and has made us in his own likeness, he has given us a capacity to love and be loved. He intends us to live in community, not in solitude. In particular, God continued, "I will make a helper suitable for him." Moreover, this "helper" or companion, whom God pronounced "suitable for him," was also to be his sexual partner, with whom he was to become "one flesh," so that they might thereby both consummate their love and procreate their children.

Secondly, Genesis 2 reveals the divine provision to meet this human need. Having affirmed Adam's need for a partner, the search for a suitable one began. God first paraded the birds and beasts before him, and Adam proceeded to "name" them, to symbolize his taking them into his service. But (v. 20) "for Adam no suitable helper was found," who could live "alongside" or "opposite" him, who could be his complement, his counterpart, his companion, let alone his mate. So a special creation was necessary.

The debate about how literally we are intended to understand what follows (the divine surgery under a divine anaesthetic) must not prevent us from grasping the point. Something happened during Adam's deep sleep. A special work of divine creation took place. The sexes became differentiated. Out of the undifferentiated humanity of Adam, male and female emerged. And Adam awoke from his deep sleep to behold before him a reflection of himself, a complement to himself, indeed a very part of himself. Next, having created the woman out of the man, God himself brought her to him, much as today the bride's father gives the bride away. And Adam broke spontaneously into history's first love poem, saying that now at last there stood before him a creature of such beauty in herself and similarity to him that she appeared to be (as indeed she was) "made for him":

> This is now bone of my bones
> and flesh of my flesh;
> She shall be called "woman,"
> for she was taken out of man.

There can be no doubting the emphasis of this story. According to Genesis 1 Eve, like Adam, was created in the image of God. But as to the manner of her creation, according to Genesis 2, she was made neither out of nothing (like the universe), nor out of "the dust of the ground" (like Adam, v. 7), but out of Adam.

The third great truth of Genesis 2 concerns the resulting institution of marriage. Adam's love poem is recorded in verse 23. The "therefore" or "for this reason" of verse 24 is the narrator's deduction: "For this reason a man will leave his father and mother and be united to his wife, and they will become one flesh."

Even the inattentive reader will be struck by the three references to "flesh": "this is . . . flesh of my flesh . . . they will become one flesh." We may be certain that this is deliberate, not accidental. It teaches that heterosexual intercourse in marriage is more than a union; it is a kind of reunion. It is not a union of alien persons who do not belong to one another and cannot appropriately become one flesh. On the contrary, it is the union of two persons who originally were one, were then separated from each other, and now in the sexual encounter of marriage come together again.

It is surely this which explains the profound mystery of heterosexual intimacy, which poets and philosophers have celebrated in every culture. Heterosexual intercourse is much more than a union of bodies; it is a blending of complementary personalities through which, in the midst of prevailing alienation, the rich created oneness of human being is experienced again. And the complementarity of male and female sexual organs is only a symbol at the physical level of a much deeper spiritual complementarity.

In order to become one flesh, however, and experience this sacred mystery, certain preliminaries are necessary, which are constituent parts of marriage. "Therefore"

> "a man" (the singular indicates that marriage is an exclusive union between two individuals)
> "shall leave his father and mother" (a public social occasion is in view)
> "and cleave to his wife" (marriage is a loving, cleaving commitment or covenant, which is heterosexual and permanent)
> "and they will become one flesh" (for marriage must be consummated in sexual intercourse, which is a sign and seal of the marriage covenant, and over which no shadow of shame or embarrassment had yet been cast)

> verses 24–25

It is of the utmost importance to note that Jesus himself later endorsed this Old Testament definition of marriage. In doing so, he both introduced it with words from Genesis 1:27 (that the Creator "made them male and female") and concluded it with his own comment ("so they are no longer two, but one. Therefore, what God has joined together, let man not separate"—Matthew 19:6). He thus made three statements about God the Creator's activity. First, God "made" them male and female. Secondly, God "said" that a man must leave his parents and cleave to his wife. Thirdly, he "joined" them together in such a way that no human being might put them apart. Here then are three truths which Jesus affirmed: (1) heterosexual gender is a divine creation; (2) heterosexual marriage is a divine institution; and (3) heterosexual fidelity is the divine intention. A homosexual liaison is a breach of all three of these divine purposes.

It is in this context of the Creation narratives of Genesis 1 and 2 that I need to respond to Michael Vasey's sincere but misguided attempt, in his 1995 book *Strangers and Friends,* to combine evangelical faith with homosexual advocacy. In regard to his historical thesis, that there was "widespread acceptance of homosexual desire and behavior among Christians until about the thirteenth century,"[19] he is dependent on the writings of John Boswell.[20] The scholarly assessment of Boswell's work by his fellow historians, however, has ranged "from the sharply critical to the dismissive to the devastating."[21] Dr. David Wright of Edinburgh University ends his article on homosexuality in *The Encyclopedia of Early Christianity* with these words: "The conclusion must be that, for all its interest and stimulus, Boswell's book provides at the end of the day not one firm piece of evidence that the teaching mind of the early church countenanced homosexual activity."[22]

200

Michael Vasey's handling of the biblical material is even less plausible. He virtually dismisses any appeal to the implications of Genesis 2:24 on the ground that "it imposes on scripture the domestic ideals of the nuclear family,"[23] isolated, self-contained and self-centered. He evinces a surprising degree of hostility to marriage and the family, caricaturing them as destructive "idols" of modern society.[24] Jesus did not marry, he reminds us, and implies by this that he disapproved of marriage, for "it is precisely the passage in which Jesus quotes Genesis 2:24 that commends the renunciation of marriage."[25] Indeed, he suggests, there is a fundamental conflict between marriage and the gospel in the teaching of Jesus and his apostles. "For them the family was part of the present world order which was characterized by rebellion against God."[26] Hence "withdrawal from the social institutions and responsibilities of marriage and the family was a step into Christian freedom," so that people need not "continue as slaves within the present transient order."[27] In such an analysis the way is opened for homosexual partnerships as another, even a better, option.

But Michael Vasey has twisted the biblical material to suit his purpose. Neither Jesus' own singleness, nor his teaching that singleness is a divine vocation for some (Matthew 19:11–12), may be taken as evidence that he opposed marriage and family, for they belong to the created order. Nor is the family envisaged in Genesis 1 and 2 "nuclear" in a negative or selfish sense. To be sure, Jesus did inaugurate a new order, refer to his new community as his family (Mark 3:34), and warn that if an unavoidable conflict arises between our loyalty to him and our loyalty to our natural family, then our loyalty to him takes precedence (Matthew 10:37; Luke 14:26). But Jesus and his apostles also insisted that Christians have a continuing obligation to their natural family, including reciprocal duties between parents and children, and between husbands and wives (e.g., Mark 7:9–13; Ephesians 5:22–6:4). The new creation restores and redeems the old; it does not reject or replace it. As for idols, every good gift of God can become an idol, including marriage and family; but in themselves neither is idolatrous or enslaving. A homosexual partnership, however, is essentially incompatible with marriage as the God-ordained context for one-flesh intimacy.

Thus, Scripture defines the marriage God instituted in terms of heterosexual monogamy. It is the union of one man with one woman, which must be publicly acknowledged (the leaving of parents), permanently sealed (he will "cleave to his wife") and physically consummated ("one flesh"). And Scripture envisages no other kind of marriage or sexual intercourse, for God provided no alternative.

Christians should not therefore single out homosexual intercourse for special condemnation. The fact is that every kind of sexual relationship and activity which deviates from God's revealed intention is ipso facto displeasing to him and under his judgment. This includes polygamy and polyandry (which infringe the "one man–one woman" principle), cohabitation and clandestine unions (since these have involved no decisive public leaving of parents), casual encounters and temporary liaisons, adultery and many divorces (which conflict with "cleaving" and with Jesus' prohibition, "let man not separate") and homosexual partnerships (which violate the statement that "a man" shall be joined to "his wife."

In sum, the only "one flesh" experience which God intends and Scripture contemplates is the sexual union of a man with his wife, whom he recognizes as "flesh of his flesh." As George Carey, Archbishop of Canterbury, said in an address at Virginia Theological Seminary on 10 February 1997, "I do not find any justification, from the Bible or from the entire Christian tradition, for sexual activity outside marriage."

Contemporary Arguments Considered

Homosexual Christians are not, however, satisfied with this biblical teaching about human sexuality and the institution of heterosexual marriage. They bring forward a number of objections to it, in order to defend the legitimacy of homosexual partnerships.

The Argument about Scripture and Culture

Traditionally, it has been assumed that the Bible condemns all homosexual acts. But are the biblical writers reliable guides in this matter? Were their horizons not bounded by their own experience and culture? The cultural argument usually takes one of two forms.

First, the biblical authors were addressing themselves to questions relevant to their own circumstances, and these were very different from ours. In the Sodom and Gibeah stories they were preoccupied either with conventions of hospitality in the ancient Near East which are now obsolete or (if the sin was sexual at all) with the extremely unusual phenomenon of homosexual gang rape. In the Levitical laws the concern was with antiquated fertility rituals, while Paul was addressing himself to the particular sexual preferences of Greek pederasts. It is all so antiquarian. The biblical authors' imprisonment in their own cultures renders their teaching on this topic irrelevant.

The second and complementary culture problem is that the biblical writers were not addressing themselves to our questions. Thus, the problem of Scripture is not only with its teaching but also with its silence. Paul (let alone the Old Testament authors) knew nothing of post-Freudian psychology. They had never heard of "the homosexual condition"; they knew only about certain practices. The difference between "inversion" and "perversion" would have been incomprehensible to them. The very notion that two men or two women could fall in love with each other and develop a deeply loving, stable relationship comparable to marriage simply never entered their heads.

If the only biblical teaching on this topic were to be found in the prohibition texts, it might be difficult to answer these objections. But once those texts are seen in relation to the divine institution of marriage, we are in possession of a principle of divine revelation which is universally applicable. It was applicable to the cultural situations of both the ancient Near East and the first-century Greco-Roman world, and it is equally applicable to modern sexual questions of which the ancients were quite ignorant. The reason for the biblical prohibitions is the same reason why modern loving homosexual partnerships must also be condemned, namely that they are incompatible with God's created order. And since that order (heterosexual monogamy) was established by Creation, not culture, its validity is both permanent and universal. There can be no "liberation" from God's created norms; true liberation is found only in accepting them.

This argumentation is the opposite of the "biblical literalism" of which the gay lobby tend to accuse us. It is rather to look beneath the surface of the biblical prohibitions to the essential positives of divine revelation on sexuality and marriage. It is significant that those who are advocating same-sex partnerships usually omit Genesis 1 and 2 from their discussion, even though Jesus our Lord himself endorsed their teaching.

The Argument about Creation and Nature

People sometimes make this kind of statement: "I'm gay because God made me that way. So gay must be good. I cannot believe that God would create people homosexual and then deny them the right to sexual self-expression. I intend, therefore, to affirm, and indeed celebrate, what I am by creation." Or again, "You may say that homosexual practice is against nature and normality; but it's not against my nature, nor is it in the slightest degree abnormal for me." Norman Pittenger was quite outspoken in his use of this argument a couple of decades ago. A homosexual person, he wrote, is "not an 'abnormal' person with 'unnatural' desires and habits." On the contrary, "a heterosexually oriented person acts 'naturally' when he acts heterosexually, while a homosexually oriented person acts equally 'naturally' when he acts in accordance with his basic, inbuilt homosexual desire and drive."[28]

Others argue that homosexual behavior is "natural" (a) because in many primitive societies it is fairly acceptable, (b) because in some advanced civilizations (ancient Greece, for example) it was even idealized and (c) because it is said to be quite widespread in animals. Yet, according to Thomas E. Schmidt, the research consensus is that "no evidence has as yet emerged to suggest that any non-human primate . . . would rate a 6 (exclusively homosexual) on the Kinsey scale . . ."[29]

In any case these arguments express an extremely subjective view of what is "natural" and "normal." We should not accept Norman Pittenger's statement that there are "no eternal standards of normality or naturalness."[30] Nor can we agree that animal behavior sets standards for human behavior! For God has established a norm for sex and marriage by creation. This was already recognized in the Old Testament era. Thus, sexual relations with an animal were forbidden, because "that is a perversion" (Leviticus 18:23), in other words a violation or confusion of nature, which indicates an "embryonic sense of natural law."[31] The same verdict is passed on Sodom by the second century B.C. Testament of Naphtali: "As the sun and the stars do not change their order, so the tribe of Naphtali are to obey God rather than the disorderliness of idolatry. Recognizing in all created things the Lord who made them, they are not to become as Sodom which changed the order of nature . . ."[32]

The same concept was clearly in Paul's mind in Romans 1. When he wrote of women who had "exchanged natural relations for unnatural ones," and of men who had "abandoned natural relations," he meant by "nature" (*physis*) the natural order of things which God has established (as in Romans 2:14, 27 and 11:24). What Paul was condemning, therefore, was not the perverted behavior of heterosexual people who were acting against their nature, as John Boswell argued,[33] but any human behavior that is against "Nature," that is, against God's created order. Richard B. Hays has written a thorough rebuttal of John Boswell's exegesis of Romans 1. He provides ample contemporary evidence that the opposition of "natural" (*kata physin*) and "unnatural" (*para physin*) was "very frequently used . . . as a way of distinguishing between heterosexual and homosexual behaviour."[34]

British commentators confirm his conclusion. As C. K. Barrett puts it: "In the obscene pleasures to which he [Paul] refers is to be seen precisely that perversion of the created order which may be expected when men put the creation in place of the Creator."[35] Similarly, Charles Cranfield writes that by "natural" and "unnatural" "Paul clearly means 'in accordance with the intention of the Creator' and 'contrary to the intention of the Creator,' respectively." Again, "the decisive factor in Paul's use of it [*physis*, "nature"] is his biblical doctrine of creation. It denotes that order which is manifest in God's creation and which men have no excuse for failing to recognize and respect."[36]

An appeal to the created order should also be our response to another argument which is being developed by a few people today, especially in the Church of England. They point out that the early Church distinguished between primary and secondary issues, insisting on agreement about the former but allowing freedom to disagree about the latter. The two examples of Christian liberty which they usually quote are circumcision and idol-meats. They then draw a parallel with homosexual practice, suggesting that it is a second-order issue in which we can give one another freedom. But actually the early Church was more subtle than they allow in its argumentation. The Jerusalem Council (Acts 15) decreed that circumcision was definitely not necessary for salvation (a first-order question), but allowed its continuance as a matter of policy or culture (second-order). The Council also decided that, although of course idolatry was forbidden (first-order), eating idol-meats was not necessarily idolatrous, so that Christians with a strong, educated conscience might eat them (second-order). Thus the second-order issues, in which Christian liberty was allowed, were neither theological nor moral but cultural. But this is not the case with homosexual practice.

A second parallel is sometimes drawn. When the debate over women's ordination was at its height, General Synod agreed that the Church should not be obliged to choose between the two positions (for and against), declaring one to be right and the other wrong, but should rather preserve unity by recognizing both to have integrity. In consequence, we are living with "the two integrities." Why, it is asked, should we not equally acknowledge "two integrities" in relation to same-sex partnerships, and not force people to choose? The answer should be clear. Even if women's ordination is a second-order issue (which many would deny), homosexual partnerships are not. Gender in relation to marriage is a much more fundamental matter than gender in relation to ministry. For marriage has been recognized as a heterosexual union from the beginning of God's Creation and institution; it is basic to human society as God intended it, and its biblical basis is incontrovertible. Dr. Wolfhart Pannenberg, professor of theology at Munich University, is outspoken on this subject. Having declared that "the biblical assessments of homosexual practice are unambiguous in their rejection," he concludes that a Church which were to recognize homosexual unions as equivalent to marriage "would cease to be the one, holy, catholic and apostolic church."[37]

The Argument about Quality of Relationships

The Lesbian and Gay Christian Movement borrows from Scripture the truth that love is the greatest thing in the world (which it is) and from the "new morality" or "situation ethics" of the 1960s the notion that love is an adequate criterion by which to judge every relationship (which it is not).

Yet this view is gaining ground today. One of the first official documents to embrace it was the *Friends' Report Towards a Quaker View of Sex* (1963). It included the statements "One should no more deplore 'homosexuality' than lefthandedness"[38] and "Surely it is the nature and quality of a relationship that matters."[39] Similarly in 1979, the Methodist Church's Division of Social Responsibility, in its report *A Christian Understanding of Human Sexuality*, argued that "homosexual activities" are "not intrinsically wrong," since "the quality of any homosexual relationship is . . . to be assessed by the same basic criteria which have been applied to heterosexual relationships. For homosexual men and women, permanent relationships characterized by love can be an appropriate Christian way of expressing their sexuality."[40] The same year (1979) an Anglican working party issued the report *Homosexual Relationships: A Contribution to Discussion*. It was more cautious, judicious and ambivalent than the Quaker and Methodist reports. Its authors did not feel able to repudiate centuries of Christian tradition, yet they "did not think it possible to deny" that in some circumstances individuals may "justifiably choose" a homosexual relationship in their search for companionship and sexual love "similar" to those found in marriage.[41]

In his *Time for Consent* Norman Pittenger lists what he sees to be the six characteristics of a truly loving relationship. They are (1) commitment (the free self-giving of each to the other), (2) mutuality in giving and receiving (a sharing in which each finds his or her self in the other), (3) tenderness (no coercion or cruelty), (4) faithfulness (the intention of a lifelong relationship), (5) hopefulness (each serving the other's maturity), and (6) desire for union.[42]

If then a homosexual relationship, whether between two men or two women, is characterized by these qualities of love, surely (the argument runs) it must be affirmed as good and not rejected as evil. For it rescues people from loneliness, selfishness and promiscuity. It can be just as rich and responsible, as liberating and fulfilling, as a heterosexual marriage.

More recently, in the spring of 1997, in a lecture delivered at St. Martin-in-the-Fields in London, Bishop John Austin Baker gave his own version of this argument. Formerly Bishop of Salisbury, chairman of the Church of England's Doctrine Commission and chairman of the drafting group which produced the moderate report *Issues in Human Sexuality* (1991), he astonished the Church by his apparent about-face. The goal of Christian discipleship, he rightly affirmed, is "Christlikeness," that is, "a creative living out of the values, priorities and attitudes that marked his humanity," especially of love. Now sex in marriage can be "a true making of love," and "erotic love can and often does have the same beneficial effects in the life of same-sex couples."

There are three reasons, however, why this claim for the quality of same-sex love is flawed. First, the concept of lifelong, quasi-marital fidelity in homosexual partnerships is largely a myth, a theoretical ideal which is contradicted by the facts. The truth is that gay relationships are characterized more by promiscuity than by fidelity. A number of researches have been made. "One of the most carefully researched studies of the most stable homosexual pairs," writes Dr. Jeffrey Satinover, namely *The Male Couple*, "was researched and written by two authors who are themselves a homosexual couple. . . ." They found that "of the 156 couples studied, only seven had maintained sexual fidelity; of the hundred couples that had been together for more than five years, none had been able to maintain sexual fidelity." They added that "the expectation for outside sexual activity was the rule for male couples and the exception for heterosexuals."[43] The result of these research studies led Thomas Schmidt to conclude: "Promiscuity among homosexual men is not a mere stereotype, and it is not merely the majority experience—it is virtually the only experience. . . . In short, there is practically no comparison possible to heterosexual marriage in terms of either fidelity or longevity. Tragically, lifelong faithfulness is almost nonexistent in the homosexual experience."[44] There seems to be something inherently unstable about homosexual partnerships. The quality of relationships argument does not hold water.

Secondly, it is difficult to maintain that homosexual partnerships are just as much an expression of love as heterosexual marriages in the light of the known damage and danger involved in usual gay sexual practices. Dr. Satinover has the courage to give us "the brute facts about the adverse consequences of homosexuality," based on the most recent medical studies. He writes of infectious hepatitis which increases the risk of liver cancer, of frequently fatal rectal cancer, and of a 25–30-year decrease in life expectancy.[45] Thomas Schmidt is even more explicit, describing seven nonviral and four viral infections which are transmitted by oral and anal sex. It is true that some diseases can also be transmitted by similar activity between heterosexual people, but "these health problems are rampant in the homosexual population because they are easily spread by promiscuity and by most of the practices favoured by homosexuals." And these diseases are apart from AIDS, to which we will come shortly. Thomas Schmidt justly calls this chapter "The Price of Love."[46] If these physical dangers attend common gay sexual activities, can authentic lovers engage in them?

But, thirdly, the biblical Christian cannot accept the basic premise on which this case rests, namely that love is the only absolute, that besides it all moral law has been abolished and that whatever seems to be compatible with love is ipso facto good, irrespective of all other considerations. This cannot be so. For love needs law to guide it. In emphasizing love for God and neighbor as the two great commandments, Jesus and his apostles did not discard all other commandments. On the contrary, Jesus said, "If you love Me, you will keep My commandments," and Paul wrote, "Love is the fulfillment [not the abrogation] of the law" (John 14:15 NASB; Romans 13:8–10).

So then, although the loving quality of a relationship is an essential, it is not by itself a sufficient criterion to authenticate it. For example, if love were the only test of authenticity, there would be nothing against polygamy, for a polygamist could certainly enjoy a relationship with several wives which reflects all Dr. Pittenger's six characteristics. Or let me give you a better illustration, drawn from my own pastoral experience. On several different occasions a married man has told me that he has fallen in love with another woman. When I have gently remonstrated with him, he has responded in words like these: "Yes, I agree, I already have a wife and family. But this new relationship is the real thing. We were made for each other. Our love for each other has a quality and depth we have never known before. It must be right." But no, I have had to say to him, it is not right. No man is justified in breaking his marriage covenant with his wife on the ground that the quality of his love for another woman is richer. Quality of love is not the only yardstick by which to measure what is good or right.

Similarly, we should not deny that homosexual relationships can be loving (although a priori they cannot attain the same richness as the heterosexual complementarity which God has ordained). As the 1994 Ramsey Colloquium put it, "Even a distorted love retains traces of love's grandeur."[47] But the love-quality of gay relationships is not sufficient to justify them. Indeed, I have to add that they are incompatible with true love because they are incompatible with God's law. Love is concerned for the highest welfare of the beloved. And our highest human welfare is found in obedience to God's law and purpose, not in revolt against them.

Some leaders of the Lesbian and Gay Christian Movement appear to be following the logic of their own position, for they are saying that even monogamy could be abandoned in the interests of "love." Malcolm Macourt, for example, has written that the Gay Liberationist's vision is of "a wide variety of life patterns," each of which is "held in equal esteem in society." Among them he lists the following alternatives: monogamy and multiple partnerships; partnerships for life and partnerships for a period of mutual growth; same-sex partners and opposite sex partners; living in community and living in small family units.[48] There seem to be no limits to what some people seek to justify in the name of love.

The Argument about Justice and Rights

If some argue for homosexual partnerships on the basis of the love involved, others do so on the basis of justice. Desmond Tutu, for example, formerly Archbishop of Cape Town and universally admired for his courageous stand against apartheid and for racial equality, has several times said that for him the homosexual question is a simple matter of justice. Others agree. The justice argument runs like this: "Just as we may not discriminate between persons on account of their gender, color, ethnicity or class, so we may not discriminate between persons on account of their sexual preference. For the God of the Bible is the God of justice, who is described as loving justice and hating injustice. Therefore the quest for justice must be a paramount obligation of the people of God. Now that slaves, women and blacks have been liberated, gay liberation is long overdue. What civil rights activists were in the 1950s and '60s, gay rights activists are today. We should support them in their cause and join them in their struggle."

The vocabulary of oppression, liberation, rights and justice, however, needs careful definition. "Gay liberation" presupposes an oppression from which homosexual people need to be set free, and "gay rights" imply that homosexual people are suffering a wrong which should be righted. But what is this oppression, this wrong, this injustice? If it is that they are being despised and rejected by sections of society on account of their sexual inclination, are in fact victims of homophobia, then indeed they have a grievance which must be redressed. For God opposes such discrimination and requires us to love and respect all human beings without distinction. If, on the other hand, the "wrong" or "injustice" complained of is society's refusal to recognize homosexual partnerships as a legitimate alternative to heterosexual marriages, then talk of "justice" is inappropriate, since human beings may not claim as a "right" what God has not given them.

The analogy between slaves, blacks, women and gays is inexact and misleading. In each case we need to clarify the Creator's original intention. Thus, in spite of misguided attempts to justify slavery and racism from Scripture, both are fundamentally incompatible with the created equality of human beings. Similarly, the Bible honors womanhood by affirming that men and women share equally in the image of God and the stewardship of the environment, and its teaching on masculine "headship" or responsibility may not be interpreted as contradicting this equality (see chapter 5). But sexual intercourse belongs, according to the plain teaching of Scripture, to heterosexual marriage alone. Therefore homosexual intercourse cannot be regarded as a permissible equivalent, let alone a divine right. True gay liberation (like all authentic liberation) is not freedom from God's revealed purpose in order to construct our own morality; it is rather freedom from our self-willed rebellion in order to love and obey him.

The Argument about Acceptance and the Gospel

"Surely," some people are saying, "it is the duty of heterosexual Christians to accept homosexual Christians. Paul told us to accept—indeed welcome—one another. If God has welcomed somebody, who are we to pass judgment on him (Romans 14:1–4; 15:7)?" Norman Pittenger goes further and declares that those who reject homosexual people "have utterly failed to understand the Christian gospel." We do not receive the grace of God because we are good and confess our sins, he continues; it is the other way round. "It's always God's grace which comes first . . . his forgiveness awakens our repentance."[49] He even quotes the hymn "Just as I am, without one plea," and adds: "The whole point of the Christian gospel is that God loves and accepts us just as we are."[50]

This is a very confused statement of the gospel, however. God does indeed accept us "just as we are," and we do not have to make ourselves good first, indeed we cannot. But his "acceptance" means that he fully and freely forgives all who repent and believe, not that he condones our continuance in sin. Again, it is true that we must accept one another, but only as fellow-penitents and fellow-pilgrims, not as fellow-sinners who are resolved to persist in our sinning. Michael Vasey makes much of the fact that Jesus was called (and was) "the friend of sinners." And indeed his offer of friendship to sinners like us is truly wonderful. But he welcomes us in order to redeem and transform us, not to leave us alone in our sins. No acceptance, either by God or by the Church, is promised to us if we harden our hearts against God's Word and will. Only judgment.

The AIDS Epidemic

Is AIDS, then, the judgment of God on practicing homosexual men? This is what some evangelical Christians have confidently declared, and is the reason why I have included a section on AIDS in this particular chapter. Before we are in a position to decide, however, we need to know the basic facts.

AIDS (the Acquired Immune Deficiency Syndrome) was identified and described for the first time in 1981 in the United States. It is spread through HIV (the Human Immuno-deficiency Virus), which may then lie dormant and unsuspected in its human host for ten years or even longer. But eventually it will in most cases manifest itself by attacking and damaging the body's immune and nervous systems, and so making it defenseless against certain fatal diseases. The origin of this human virus is unknown, although the accepted wisdom is that it developed as a spontaneous mutation of a virus which had long infected African monkeys.

Many myths surround AIDS (specially in relation to its transmission and its extent), which need to be dispelled.

First, AIDS is not an easily caught infectious disease. The virus is transmitted only in body fluids, particularly in semen and blood. The commonest ways of getting it are through sexual intercourse with an infected partner and through an injection either of contaminated blood or with an unsterilized needle (the sharing of needles by drug addicts is a very dangerous practice). A child in the womb is also greatly at risk if the pregnant mother is HIV positive.

Secondly, AIDS is not a specifically "gay plague." It was given that inaccurate designation in the early 1980s because it first appeared in the male homosexual communities of San Francisco and New York. But the virus is transmitted by heterosexual as well as homosexual intercourse (overwhelmingly so in Africa, where homosexual behavior is almost unknown), and AIDS sufferers include many women and babies as well as men. It is promiscuous sexual behavior which spreads the disease most rapidly; whether this takes place with same-sex or opposite-sex partners is largely irrelevant. "The greater the numbers, the greater the risk," writes Dr. Patrick Dixon, founder of ACET (AIDS Care Education and Training), whose well-researched and compassionate book *The Truth about AIDS* I recommend.[51]

Thirdly, AIDS is not a peculiarly western phenomenon. It seemed in the early eighties to be so, because American and European hospitals, possessing the necessary resources, were the first to diagnose it. But it is increasingly a worldwide disease. In East and Central Africa it has already reached epidemic proportions.

Fourthly, AIDS is not a problem which is going to be quickly solved. It is an incurable disease, with neither preventative vaccine nor therapeutic drug in sight. The drug known as AZT can prolong an AIDS victim's life by about a year, and alleviate suffering, but it has unpleasant side effects and is a treatment, not a cure. Meanwhile, the statistics are growing at an alarming rate. The American Psychiatric Association Press reports that "30% of all 20-year-old gay men will be HIV positive or dead of AIDS by the time they are age 30."[52] In 1996 alone there were an estimated 3.1 million new HIV infections around the world. In sub-Saharan Africa there are 14 million people living with HIV/AIDS. In parts of East Africa over 10 percent of women attending antenatal clinics are HIV infected, with some clinics reporting numbers over 40 percent. Almost 1 million children in Kenya, Rwanda, Uganda and Zambia have been orphaned as a result of AIDS, with approximately 8 percent of these children infected themselves. AIDS is also spreading with incredible ferocity in some parts of India: with up to 10 percent of truck drivers infected, it is moving beyond the urban centers and into the countryside. The 10,000 estimated cases of HIV infection in China in 1993 increased to 100,000 in 1995. But the most appalling figure of all was given by a 1997 joint UN and WHO report. Confessing that the scale of the global epidemic had been "grossly underestimated," they reckoned that the total number of people living with HIV/AIDS was then more than 30 million and would reach 40 million by A.D. 2000.[53]

Fifthly, AIDS cannot be avoided merely by the use of a condom, which is known to be an unreliable contraceptive. Dr. Dixon sums the matter up succinctly: "Condoms do not make sex safe; they simply make it safer. Safe sex is sex between two partners who are not infected! This means a lifelong, faithful partnership between two people who were virgins and who now remain faithful to each other for life."[54] Or, to quote the United States Catholic Conference, "Abstinence outside of marriage and fidelity within marriage, as well as the avoidance of intravenous drug abuse, are the only morally correct and medically sure ways to prevent the spread of AIDS."[55]

A threefold Christian response to these sobering facts and figures would seem to be appropriate.

First, theological. Reverting to the question of whether AIDS is a divine judgment on practicing homosexual men, I think we have to answer, "Yes and no." "No" because Jesus warned us not to interpret calamities as God's specific judgments upon evil people (Luke 13:1–5). "No" also because AIDS victims include many women, especially faithful married women who have been infected by their unfaithful husbands, with a substantial minority of innocent hemophiliacs and children. But "yes" in the sense that Paul meant when he wrote: "Do not deceive yourselves; no one makes a fool of God. A person will reap exactly what he plants" (Galatians 6:7 GNB). The fact that we reap what we sow, or that evil actions bring evil consequences, seems to have been written by God into the ordering of his moral world. Christians cannot regard it as an accident, for example, that promiscuity exposes people to venereal diseases, that heavy smoking can lead to lung cancer, excessive alcohol to liver disorders, and overeating (directly or indirectly) to heart conditions. Moreover, this cause-and-effect mechanism is viewed in Scripture as one of the ways in which God's "wrath," that is, his just judgment on evil, is revealed (Romans 1:18–32). Before the day of judgment arrives, Jesus taught, a process of judgment is already taking place (John 3:18–21; 5:24–29). AIDS may rightly be seen, then, as "part of God's judgment on society." "It is calling the bluff of the permissive society that there is any such thing as sexual liberation in promiscuity."[56]

Our second Christian response must be pastoral. We do not deny that many people have contracted AIDS as a result of their own sexual promiscuity. But this provides us with no possible justification for shunning or neglecting them, any more than we would those who damage themselves through drunken driving or other forms of recklessness. As the American Roman Catholic bishops have put it, "Stories of persons with AIDS must not become occasions for stereotyping or prejudice, for anger or recrimination, for rejection or isolation, for injustice or condemnation." Instead, "they provide us with an opportunity to walk with those who are suffering, to be compassionate towards those whom we might otherwise fear, to bring strength and courage both to those who face the prospect of dying as well as to their loved ones."[57] "Don't judge me," an American AIDS patient called Jerome said. "I'm living under my own judgment. What I need is for you to walk with me."[58] Local churches need specially to reach out to AIDS sufferers in their own fellowship and in their wider community. The Terrence Higgins Trust, named after the first person in Britain who is known to have died of AIDS (in 1982), teaches high standards of counseling and care, especially through the "buddy" service of volunteers which it has pioneered.[59] At the same time, we may be thankful that both the origins of the hospice movement and its extension from terminal cancer patients to AIDS victims, have been due largely to Christian initiatives.[60]

Our third response must be educational. It is true that some people scorn this as a hopelessly inadequate reaction to the AIDS crisis and propose instead the compulsory isolation of all virus carriers. But the Christian conscience shrinks from such a ruthless measure, even if it could be democratically accepted and successfully imposed. Mandatory regular screening is also advocated by some, and the arguments for and against were well developed by Dr. David Cook in his 1989 London Lectures entitled "Just Health."[61] But Christians are likely to prefer a thoroughgoing educational program as the most human and Christian way to combat ignorance, prejudice, fear and promiscuous behavior, and so turn back the AIDS tide. Certainly the current complacency and indifference, which are helping to spread the disease, can be overcome only by the relentless force of the facts. Dr. Patrick Dixon, in his "Ten Point Plan for the Government," urges that they "get an army of health educators on the road," to visit and address all the country's schools and colleges, factories and shops, clubs and pubs. In such a preventive education program the churches should have a major role. Is it not the failure of the churches to teach and exemplify God's standards of sexual morality which, more than anything else, is to blame for the current crisis?[62] We must not fail again, but rather challenge society to sexual self-control and faithfulness, and point to Jesus as the source of forgiveness and power. Several Christian groups have been set up to alert the churches to their responsibilities, to provide educational resources and to encourage support groups.[63]

Above all, "the AIDS crisis challenges us profoundly to be the Church in deed and in truth: to be the Church as a healing community." Indeed, because of our tendency to self-righteousness, "the healing community itself will need to be healed by the forgiveness of Christ."[64]

Faith, Hope and Love

If homosexual practice must be regarded, in the light of the whole biblical revelation, not as a variant within the wide range of accepted normality, but as a deviation from God's norm; and if we should therefore call homosexually inclined people to abstain from homosexual practices and partnerships, what advice and help can we give to encourage them to respond to this call? I would like to take Paul's triad of faith, hope and love, and apply it to homosexually inclined people.

The Christian Call to Faith

Faith is our human response to divine revelation; it is believing God's Word.

First, faith accepts God's standards. The only alternative to heterosexual marriage is singleness and sexual abstinence. I think I know the implications of this. Nothing has helped me to understand the pain of homosexual celibacy more than Alex Davidson's moving book *The Returns of Love*. He writes of "this incessant tension between law and lust," "this monster that lurks in the depths," this "burning torment."[65]

The secular world says: "Sex is essential to human fulfillment. To expect homosexual people to abstain from homosexual practice is to condemn them to frustration and to drive them to neurosis, despair and even suicide. It's outrageous to ask them to deny themselves what to them is a normal and natural mode of sexual expression. It's 'inhuman and inhumane.'[66] Indeed, it's positively cruel."

But no, the teaching of the Word of God is different. Sexual experience is not essential to human fulfillment. To be sure, it is a good gift of God. But it is not given to all, and it is not indispensable to humanness. People were saying in Paul's day that it was. Their slogan was, Food for the stomach and the stomach for food; sex for the body and the body for sex (see 1 Corinthians 6:13). But this is a lie of the devil. Jesus Christ was single, yet perfect in his humanity. So it is possible to be single and human at the same time! Besides, God's commands are good and not grievous. The yoke of Christ brings rest, not turmoil; conflict comes only to those who resist it.

At the very center of Christian discipleship is our participation in the death and resurrection of Jesus Christ. "The Saint Andrew's Day Statement" on the homosexuality debate (1995), commissioned by the Church of England Evangelical Council, emphasized this. We are "called to follow in the way of the cross." For "we all are summoned to various forms of self-denial. The struggle against disordered desires, or the misdirection of innocent desire, is part of every Christian's life, consciously undertaken in baptism." But after struggle comes victory, out of death resurrection.[67]

So ultimately it is a crisis of faith: whom shall we believe? God or the world? Shall we submit to the lordship of Jesus, or succumb to the pressures of prevailing culture? The true "orientation" of Christians is not what we are by constitution (hormones), but what we are by choice (heart, mind and will).

Secondly, faith accepts God's grace. Abstinence is not only good, if God calls us to celibacy; it is also possible. Many deny it, however. "You know the imperious strength of our sex drive," they say. "To ask us to control ourselves is just not on." It is "so near to an impossibility," writes Norman Pittenger, "that it's hardly worth talking about."[68]

Really? What then are we to make of Paul's statement following his warning to the Corinthians that male prostitutes and homosexual offenders will not inherit God's Kingdom? "And that is what some of you were," he cries. "But you were washed, you were sanctified, you were justified in the name of the Lord Jesus Christ and by the Spirit of our God" (1 Corinthians 6:11). And what shall we say to the millions of heterosexual people who are single? To be sure, all unmarried people experience the pain of struggle and loneliness. But how can we call ourselves Christians and declare that chastity is impossible? It is made harder by the sexual obsession of contemporary society. And we make it harder for ourselves if we listen to the world's plausible arguments, or lapse into self-pity, or feed our imagination with pornographic material and so inhabit a fantasy world in which Christ is not Lord, or ignore his command about plucking out our eyes and cutting off our hands and feet, that is, being ruthless with the avenues of temptation. But, whatever our "thorn in the flesh" may be, Christ comes to us as he came to Paul and says: "My grace is sufficient for you, for my power is made perfect in weakness" (2 Corinthians 12:9). To deny this is to portray Christians as the helpless victims of the world, the flesh and the devil, to demean them into being less than human, and to contradict the gospel of God's grace.

The Christian Call to Hope

I have said nothing so far about "healing" for homosexual people, understood not now as self-mastery but as the reversal of their sexual bias. Our expectation of this possibility will depend largely on our understanding of the etiology of the homosexual condition, and no final agreement on this has yet been reached. Many studies have been conducted, but they have failed to establish a single cause, whether inherited or learned. So scholars have tended to turn to theories of multiple causation, combining a biological predisposition (genetic and hormonal) with cultural and moral influences, childhood environment and experience and repeatedly reinforced personal choices. Dr. Jeffrey Satinover concludes his investigation with an appeal to common sense: "One's character traits are in part innate, but are subject to modification by experience and choice."[69] So, if homosexuality is at least partly learned, can it be unlearned?

Just as opinions differ on the causes of homosexuality, so they also differ on the possibilities and the means of "cure." This issue divides people into three categories—those who consider healing unnecessary, and those who consider it possible or impossible.

First, we have to recognize that many homosexual people categorically reject the language of "cure" and "healing." They see no need, and they have no wish, to change. Their position has been summed up in three convictions. Biologically, their condition is innate (being inherited), psychologically it is irreversible, and sociologically it is normal.[70] They regard it as a great victory that in 1973 the trustees of the American Psychiatric Association removed homosexuality from its official list of mental illnesses. Michael Vasey declares that this decision was not the result of some "liberal" conspiracy.[71] But that is exactly what it was. Seventy years of psychiatric opinion were overthrown not by science (for no fresh evidence was produced) but by politics.[72] At least the Roman Catholic Church was neither impressed nor convinced. The American bishops in their 1986 "Pastoral Letter" continued to describe homosexuality as "intrinsically disordered" (paragraph 3).

Secondly, there are those who regard "healing," understood as the reversal of sexual orientation, as impossible. "No known method of treatment or punishment," writes D. J. West, "offers hope of making any substantial reduction in the vast army of adults practising homosexuality"; it would be "more realistic to find room for them in society." He pleads for "tolerance," though not for "encouragement," of homosexual behavior.[73]

Are not these views, however, the despairing opinions of the secular mind? They challenge us to articulate the third position, which is to believe that at least some degree of change is possible. Christians know that the homosexual condition, being a deviation from God's norm, is not a sign of created order but of fallen disorder. How, then, can we acquiesce in it or declare it incurable? We cannot. The only question is when and how we are to expect the divine deliverance and restoration to take place. The fact is that, though Christian claims of homosexual "healings" are made, either through regeneration or through a subsequent work of the Holy Spirit, it is not easy to substantiate them.[74]

Martin Hallett, who before his conversion was active in the gay scene, has written a very honest account of his experience of what he calls "Christ's way out of homosexuality." He is candid about his continuing vulnerability, his need for safeguards, his yearning for love and his occasional bouts of emotional turmoil. I am glad he entitled his autobiographical sketch *I Am Learning to Love* in the present tense, and subtitled it *A Personal Journey to Wholeness in Christ*. His final paragraph begins: "I have learnt; I am learning; I will learn to love God, other people and myself. This healing process will only be complete when I am with Jesus."[75]

True Freedom Trust has published a pamphlet entitled "Testimonies." In it homosexual Christian men and women bear witness to what Christ has done for them. They have found a new identity in him, and have a new sense of personal fulfillment as children of God. They have been delivered from guilt, shame and fear by God's forgiving acceptance and have been set free from thraldom to their former homosexual lifestyle by the indwelling power of the Holy Spirit. But they have not been delivered from their homosexual inclination, and therefore some inner pain continues alongside their new joy and peace. Here are two examples: "My prayers were not answered in the way I had hoped for, but the Lord greatly blessed me in giving me two Christian friends who lovingly accepted me for what I was." "After I was prayed over with the laying on of hands a spirit of perversion left me. I praise God for the deliverance I found that afternoon. . . . I can testify to over three years of freedom from homosexual activity. But I have not changed into a heterosexual in that time."

Similar testimonies are given by ex-gay ministries in the United States. Over two hundred of them belong to the coalition called Exodus International.[76] Tim Stafford in the 18 August 1989 edition of *Christianity Today* describes his investigation into several of them. His conclusion was one of "cautious optimism." What ex-gays were claiming was "not a quick 180-degree reversal of their sexual desires" but rather "a gradual reversal in their spiritual understanding of themselves as men and women in relationship to God." And this new self-understanding was "helping them to relearn distorted patterns of thinking and relating. They presented themselves as people in process . . ."

Is there really, then, no hope of a substantial change of inclination? Dr. Elizabeth Moberly believes there is. She has been led by her research to the view that "a homosexual orientation does not depend on a genetic predisposition, hormonal imbalance, or abnormal learning process, but on difficulties in the parent-child relationships, especially in the earlier years of life." The "underlying principle," she continues, is "that the homosexual—whether man or woman—has suffered from some deficit in the relationship with the parent of the same sex; and that there is a corresponding drive to make good this deficit through the medium of same-sex or 'homosexual' relationships."[77] The deficit and the drive go together. The reparative drive for same-sex love is not itself pathological, but "quite the opposite—it is the attempt to resolve and heal the pathology." "The homosexual condition does not involve abnormal needs, but normal needs that have, abnormally, been left unmet in the ordinary process of growth." Homosexuality "is essentially a state of incomplete development" or of unmet needs.[78] So the proper solution is "the meeting of same-sex needs without sexual activity," for to eroticize growth deficits is to confuse emotional needs with physiological desires.[79] How, then, can these needs be met? The needs are legitimate, but what are the legitimate means of meeting them? Dr. Moberly's answer is that "substitute relationships for parental care are in God's redemptive plan, just as parental relationships are in his creative plan."[80] What is needed is deep, loving, lasting, same-sex but non-sexual relationships, especially in the Church. "Love," she concludes, "both in prayer and in relationships, is the basic therapy. . . . Love is the basic problem, the great need, and the only true solution. If we are willing to seek and to mediate the healing and redeeming love of Christ, then healing for the homosexual will become a great and glorious reality."[81]

Even then, however, complete healing of body, mind and spirit will not take place in this life. Some degree of deficit or disorder remains in each of us. But not for ever! For the Christian's horizons are not bound by this world. Jesus Christ is coming again; our bodies are going to be redeemed; sin, pain and death are going to be abolished; and both we and the universe are going to be transformed. Then we shall be finally liberated from everything which defiles or distorts our personality. And this Christian assurance helps us to bear whatever our present pain may be. For pain there is, in the midst of peace. "We know that the whole creation has been groaning as in the pains of childbirth right up to the present time. Not only so, but we ourselves, who have the firstfruits of the Spirit, groan inwardly as we wait eagerly for our adoption as sons, the redemption of our bodies" (Romans 8:22–23). Thus our groans express the birthpangs of the new age. We are convinced that "our present sufferings are not worth comparing with the glory that will be revealed in us" (Romans 8:18). This confident hope sustains us.

Alex Davidson derives comfort in the midst of his homosexuality from his Christian hope. "Isn't it one of the most wretched things about this condition," he writes, "that when you look ahead, the same impossible road seems to continue indefinitely? You're driven to rebellion when you think of there being no point in it and to despair when you think of there being no limit to it. That's why I find a comfort, when I feel desperate, or rebellious, or both, to remind myself of God's promise that one day it will be finished . . ."[82]

The Christian Call to Love

At present we are living "in between times," between the grace which we grasp by faith and the glory which we anticipate in hope. Between them lies love.

Yet love is just what the Church has generally failed to show to homosexual people. Jim Cotter complains bitterly about being treated as "objects of scorn and insult, of fear, prejudice and oppression."[83] Norman Pittenger describes the "vituperative" correspondence he has received, in which homosexuals are dismissed even by professing Christians as "filthy creatures," "disgusting perverts," "damnable sinners" and the like.[84] Pierre Berton, a social commentator, writes that "a very good case can be made out that the homosexual is the modern equivalent of the leper."[85] Rictor Norton is yet more shrill: "The church's record regarding homosexuals is an atrocity from beginning to end: it is not for us to seek forgiveness, but for the church to make atonement."[86]

The attitude of personal antipathy towards homosexuals is nowadays termed "homophobia."[87] It is a mixture of irrational fear, hostility and even revulsion. It overlooks the fact that the majority of homosexual people are probably not responsible for their condition (though they are, of course, for their conduct). Since they are not deliberate perverts, they deserve our understanding and compassion (though many find this patronizing), not our rejection. No wonder Richard Lovelace calls for "a double repentance," namely "that gay Christians renounce the active lifestyle" and that "straight Christians renounce homophobia."[88] Dr. David Atkinson is right to add: "We are not at liberty to urge the Christian homosexual to celibacy and to a spreading of his relationships, unless support for the former and opportunities for the latter are available in genuine love."[89] I rather think that the very existence of the Lesbian and Gay Christian Movement is a vote of censure on the Church.

At the heart of the homosexual condition is a deep loneliness, the natural human hunger for mutual love, a search for identity and a longing for completeness. If homosexual people cannot find these things in the local "church family," we have no business to go on using that expression. The alternative is not between the warm physical relationship of homosexual intercourse and the pain of isolation in the cold. There is a third option, namely a Christian environment of love, understanding, acceptance and support. I do not think there is any need to encourage homosexual people to disclose their sexual inclinations to everybody; this is neither necessary nor helpful. But they do need at least one confidant to whom they can unburden themselves, who will not despise or reject them, but will support them with friendship and prayer; probably some professional, private and confidential pastoral counsel; possibly in addition the support of a professionally supervised therapy group; and (like all single people) many warm and affectionate friendships with people of both sexes. Same-sex friendships, like those in the Bible between Ruth and Naomi, David and Jonathan, and Paul and Timothy, are to be encouraged. There is no hint that any of these was homosexual in the erotic sense, yet they were evidently affectionate and (at least in the case of David and Jonathan) even demonstrative (e.g., 1 Samuel 18:1–4; 20:41 and 2 Samuel 1:26). Of course sensible safeguards will be important. But in African and Asian cultures it is common to see two men walking down the street hand in hand, without embarrassment. It is sad that our western culture inhibits the development of rich same-sex friendships by engendering the fear of being ridiculed or rejected as a "queer."

The best contribution of Michael Vasey's book *Strangers and Friends*, in my view, is his emphasis on friendship. "Friendship is not a minor theme of the Christian faith," he writes, "but is integral to its vision of life."[90] He sees society as "a network of friendships held together by bonds of affection." He also points out that Scripture does "not limit the notion of covenant to the institution of marriage."[91] As David and Jonathan made a covenant with each other (1 Samuel 18:3), we too may have special covenanted friendships.

These and other relationships, both same-sex and opposite-sex, need to be developed within the family of God which, though universal, has its local manifestations. He intends each local church to be a warm, accepting and supportive community. By "accepting" I do not mean "acquiescing"; similarly, by a rejection of "homophobia" I do not mean a rejection of a proper Christian disapproval of homosexual behavior. No, true love is not incompatible with the maintenance of moral standards. On the contrary, it insists on them, for the good of everybody. There is, therefore, a place for church discipline in the case of members who refuse to repent and willfully persist in homosexual relationships. But it must be exercised in a spirit of humility and gentleness (Galatians 6:1–2); we must be careful not to discriminate between men and women, or between homosexual and heterosexual offenses; and necessary discipline in the case of a public scandal is not to be confused with a witch-hunt.

Perplexing and painful as the homosexual Christian's dilemma is, Jesus Christ offers him or her (indeed, all of us) faith, hope and love—the faith to accept both his standards and his grace to maintain them, the hope to look beyond present suffering to future glory, and the love to care for and support one another. "But the greatest of these is love" (1 Corinthians 13:13).

9

A Call for
Christian Leadership

There is a serious dearth of leaders in the contemporary world. Massive problems confront us, some of which we have looked at in this book. Globally, there are still the terrifying size of nuclear arsenals, the widespread violations of human rights, the environmental and energy crises, and North-South economic inequality. Socially, there are the tragedy of long-term unemployment, the continuance of conflict in industrial relations, and the outbreaks of racial violence. Morally, Christians are disturbed by the forces which are undermining the stability of marriage and the family, the challenges to sexual mores and sexual roles, and the scandal of what is virtually abortion on demand. Spiritually, I might add, there are the spread of materialism and the corresponding loss of any sense of transcendent reality. Many people are warning us that the world is heading for disaster; few are offering us advice on how to avert it. Technical know-how abounds, but wisdom is in short supply. People feel confused, bewildered, alienated. To borrow the metaphors of Jesus, we seem to be like "sheep without a shepherd," while our leaders often appear to be "blind leaders of the blind."

There are many kinds and degrees of leadership. Leadership is not restricted to a small minority of world statesmen, or to the national top brass. In every society it takes a variety of forms. Clergy are leaders in the local church and community. Parents are leaders in their home and family. So are teachers in school and lecturers in college. Senior executives in business and industry, judges, doctors, politicians, social workers and union officials all have leadership responsibilities in their respective spheres. So do the opinion-formers who work in the media—authors and playwrights, journalists, sound and vision broadcasters, artists and producers. And student leaders, especially since the 1960s, have been exercising influence beyond their years and their experience. There is a great need in all these and other situations for more clearsighted, courageous and dedicated leaders.

Such leaders are both born and bred. As Bennie E. Goodwin, a black American educator, has written: "Although potential leaders are born, effective leaders are made."[1] In Shakespeare's famous lines, "Be not afraid of greatness! Some are born great, some achieve greatness, and some have greatness thrust upon them."[2] Books on management refer to "BNLs" (born natural leaders"), men and women endowed with strong intellect, character and personality. And we would want to add with Oswald Sanders that Christian leadership is "a blending of natural and spiritual qualities,"[3] or of natural talents and spiritual gifts. Nevertheless, God's gifts have to be cultivated, and leadership potential has to be developed.

What, then, are the marks of leadership in general, and of Christian leadership in particular? How can we give up sitting around, waiting for somebody else to take the initiative, and take one ourselves? What is needed to blaze a trail which others will follow?

Although many different analyses of leadership have been made, I want to suggest that it has five essential ingredients.

Vision

"Where there is no vision, the people perish" is a proverb from the King James Version of the Bible, which has passed into common usage. And although it is almost certainly a mistranslation of the Hebrew, it is nonetheless a true statement.[4] Indeed, it has been a characteristic of the post-Pentecost era that "your young men will see visions" and "your old men will dream dreams" (Acts 2:17). Monsignor Ronald Knox of Oxford concluded his critical though somewhat wistful book *Enthusiasm* with these words:

> Men will not live without vision; that moral we do well to carry away with us from contemplating, in so many strange forms, the record of the visionaries. If we are content with the humdrum, the second-best, the hand-over-hand, it will not be forgiven us.[5]

Dreams and visions, dreamers and visionaries, sound somewhat unpractical, however, and remote from the harsh realities of life on earth. So more prosaic words tend to be used. Management experts tell us we must set both long-term and short-term goals. Politicians publish election manifestos. Military personnel lay down a campaign strategy. But whether you call it a "goal," a "manifesto" or a "strategy," it is a vision that you are talking about.

So what is vision? It is an act of seeing, of course, an imaginative perception of things, combining insight and foresight. But more particularly, in the sense in which I am using the word, it is compounded of a deep dissatisfaction with what is and a clear grasp of what could be. It begins with indignation over the status quo, and it grows into the earnest quest for an alternative. Both are quite clear in the public ministry of Jesus. He was indignant over disease and death, and the hunger of the people, for he perceived these things as alien to the purpose of God. Hence his compassion for their victims. Indignation and compassion form a powerful combination. They are indispensable to vision, and therefore to leadership.

It will be remembered that Bobby Kennedy was assassinated in 1968 at the age of forty-two. In an appreciation of him which appeared ten years later, David S. Broder wrote that "his distinguishing quality was his capacity for what can only be called moral outrage. 'That is unacceptable,' he said of many conditions that most of us accepted as inevitable. . . . Poverty, illiteracy, malnutrition, prejudice, crookedness, conniving—all such accepted evils were a personal affront to him."[6] Apathy is the acceptance of the unacceptable; leadership begins with a decisive refusal to do so. As George F. Will wrote in December 1981, after the declaration of martial law in Poland, "What is outrageous is the absence of outrage." There is a great need today for more righteous indignation, anger, outrage over those evils which are an offense to God. How can we tolerate what he finds intolerable?

But anger is sterile if it does not provoke us to positive action to remedy what has aroused our anger. "One must oppose those things that one believes to be wrong," writes Robert Greenleaf, "but one cannot lead from a predominantly negative posture."[7] Before Robert McNamara retired in 1981 as President of the World Bank after thirteen years, he addressed its annual meeting for the last time, and in his speech he quoted George Bernard Shaw: "You see things as they are and ask 'Why?' But I dream things that never were, and ask 'Why not?' "

History abounds in examples, both biblical and secular. Moses was appalled by the cruel oppression of his fellow Israelites in Egypt, remembered God's covenant with Abraham, Isaac and Jacob, and was sustained throughout his long life by the vision of the "Promised Land." Nehemiah heard in his Persian exile that the wall of the Holy City was in ruins, and its inhabitants in great distress. The news overwhelmed him, until God put into his heart what he could and should do. "Come, let us rebuild the wall of Jerusalem," he said. And the people replied, "Let us start rebuilding" (Nehemiah 2:12, 17, 18).

Moving on to New Testament times, the early Christians were well aware of the might of Rome and the hostility of the Jews. But Jesus had told them to be his witness "to the ends of the earth," and the vision he gave them transformed them. Saul of Tarsus had been brought up to accept as inevitable and unbridgeable the chasm between Jews and Gentiles. But

Jesus commissioned him to take the gospel to the Gentile world, and he was "not disobedient to the vision from heaven." Indeed the vision of a single, new, reconciled humanity so captured his heart and mind, that he labored, suffered and died in its cause (see, e.g., Acts 26:16–20; Ephesians 2:11–3:13 for Paul's vision).

In our own generation Presidents of the United States have had noble visions of a "New Deal" and of a "Great Society," and the fact that their expectations did not altogether materialize is no criticism of their vision. Martin Luther King, incensed by the injustices of segregation, had a dream of dignity for blacks in a free, multiracial America; he both lived and died that his dream might come true.

There can be little doubt that the phenomenal early success of Communists (within fifty years from the Russian Revolution of 1917 they had won over a third of the world) was due to the vision of a better society which they were able to inspire in their followers. This, at least, was the considered opinion of Douglas Hyde who in March 1948 resigned both from the British Communist Party (after twenty years' membership) and from being News Editor of the *Daily Worker*, and became a Roman Catholic. The subtitle he gave to his book *Dedication and Leadership* was *Learning from the Communists*, and he wrote it to answer the question "Why are Communists so dedicated and successful as leaders, whilst others so often are not?" Here is how he put it: "If you ask me what is the distinguishing mark of the Communist, what is it that Communists most outstandingly have in common . . . I would say that beyond any shadow of doubt it is their idealism . . ."[8] They dream, he continued, of a new society in which (quoting from Liu Shao-chi) there will be "no oppressed and exploited people, no darkness, ignorance, backwardness" and "no such irrational things as mutual deception, mutual antagonism, mutual slaughter and war."[9] Marx wrote in his *Theses on Feuerbach* (1888): "The philosophers have only in various ways interpreted the world: the point, however, is to change it." That slogan "change the world," comments Douglas Hyde, "has proved to be one of the most dynamic of the past 120 years . . . Marx concluded his *Communist Manifesto* with the words: 'You have a world to win.'"[10] This vision fired the imagination and zeal of young idealistic Communists. Because of it, Hyde wrote about the first half of this century, "the recruit is made to feel that there is a great battle going on all over the world," and "that this includes his own country, his own town, his own neighbourhood, the block of flats in which he lives, the factory or office where he works."[11] "One reason why the Communist is prepared to make his exceptional sacrifices," Douglas Hyde argued, "is that he believes he is taking part in a crusade."[12]

But Jesus Christ is a far greater and more glorious leader than Karl Marx could ever be, and the Christian good news is a much more radical and liberating message than the *Communist Manifesto*. The world can be won for

224

Christ by evangelism, and made more pleasing to Christ by social action. Why then does this prospect not set our hearts on fire? Where are the Christian people today who see the status quo, who do not like what they see (because there are things in it which are unacceptable to God), who therefore refuse to come to terms with it, who dream dreams of an alternative society which would be more acceptable to God, and who determine to do something about it? "Nothing much happens without a dream. And for something great to happen, there must be a great dream. Behind every great achievement is a dreamer of great dreams."[13]

We see with our mind's eye the 2 billion people who may never even have heard of Jesus, and the further 2 billion who have heard but have had no valid opportunity to respond to the gospel;[14] the poor, the hungry and the disadvantaged; people crushed by political, economic or racial oppression; the millions of babies aborted and incinerated; and the so-called "balance" of nuclear terror. We see these things; do we not care? We see what is; do we not see what could be? Things could be different. The unevangelized could be reached with the good news of Jesus; the hungry could be fed, the oppressed liberated, the alienated brought home. We need a vision of the purpose and power of God.

David Bleakley writes about such visionaries, "the people with a 'hunch' alternative, those who believe that it is possible to build a better world." He calls them "Pathfinders," who are "lovers of our planet, who feel a responsibility for God's creation, and wish to give true meaning to the lives of all his people." Indeed, he is confident, as I am, that such "Pathfinders represent a growing ground-swell of change in our society and in societies elsewhere."[15]

Industry

The world has always been scornful of dreamers. "Here comes that dreamer!" Joseph's older brothers said to one another. "Come now, let's kill him. . . . Then we'll see what comes of his dreams" (Genesis 37:19–20). The dreams of the night tend to evaporate in the cold light of the morning.

So dreamers have to become in turn thinkers, planners and workers, and that demands industry or hard labor. Men of vision need to become men of action. It was Thomas Carlyle, the nineteenth-century Scottish writer, who said of Frederick the Great that genius means first of all "the transcendent capacity of taking trouble," and it was Thomas Alva Edison, the inventor of electrical devices, who defined genius as "1 percent inspiration and 99 percent perspiration." All great leaders, not least great artists, find this to be true. Behind their apparently effortless performance there lies the most rigorous and painstaking self-discipline. A good example is the world-renowned pianist, Paderewski. He spent hours in practice every day. It was not unknown for him to repeat a bar or phrase fifty times to perfect it. Queen Victoria once said to him, after she had heard him play, "Mr Paderewski, you are a genius." "That may be, Ma'am," he replied, "but before I was a genius, I was a drudge."[16]

This addition of industry to vision is an evident hallmark of history's great leaders. It was not enough for Moses to dream of the land flowing with milk and honey; he had to organize the Israelite rabble into at least the semblance of a nation and lead them through the dangers and hardships of the desert before they could take possession of the Promised Land. Similarly, Nehemiah was inspired by his vision of the rebuilt Holy City, but first he had to gather materials to reconstruct the wall and weapons to defend it. Winston Churchill loathed the Nazi tyranny and dreamed of Europe's liberation. But he was under no illusions about the cost of the enterprise. On 13 May 1940, in his first speech to the House of Commons as Prime Minister, he warned members that he had "nothing to offer but blood, toil, tears and sweat," and "many long months of struggle and suffering."

Moreover the same combination of vision and industry is needed in our more ordinary individual lives. William Morris, who became Lord Nuffield the public benefactor, began his career repairing bicycles. What was the secret of his success? It was "creative imagination wedded to indomitable industry."[17] Thus dream and reality, passion and practicalities must go together. Without the dream the campaign loses its direction and its fire; but without hard work and practical projects the dream vanishes into thin air.

Perseverance

Thomas Sutcliffe Mort was an early nineteenth-century settler in Sydney, Australia, after whom the "Mort Docks" are named. He was determined to solve the problem of refrigeration, so that meat could be exported from Australia to Britain, and he gave himself three years in which to do it. But it took him twenty-six. He lived long enough to see the first shipment of refrigerated meat leave Sydney but died before learning whether it had reached its destination safely. The house he built in Edgecliffe is now Bishopscourt, the residence of the Anglican Archbishop of Sydney. Painted twenty times round the cornice of the study ceiling are the words "To persevere is to succeed," and engraved in stone outside the front door is the Mort family motto (a play on their Huguenot name) *"Fidèle à la Mort."*

Perseverance is certainly an indispensable quality of leadership. It is one thing to dream dreams and see visions. It is another to convert a dream into a plan of action. It is yet a third to persevere with it when opposition comes. For opposition is bound to arise. As soon as the campaign gets under way, the forces of reaction muster, entrenched privilege digs itself in more deeply, commercial interests feel threatened and raise the alarm, the cynical sneer at the folly of "do-gooders," and apathy becomes transmuted into hostility.

But a true work of God thrives on opposition. Its silver is refined and its steel hardened. Of course those without the vision, who are merely being carried along by the momentum of the campaign, will soon capitulate. So it is that the protesting youth of one decade become the conservative establishment of the next. Young rebels lapse into middle-class, middle-aged, middle-of-the-road mediocrity. Even revolutionaries, once the revolution is over, tend to lose their ideals. But not the real leader. He has the resilience to take setbacks in his stride, the tenacity to overcome fatigue and discouragement, and the wisdom (in a favorite phrase of John Mott's) to "turn stumbling-blocks into stepping stones."[18] For the real leader adds to vision and industry the grace of perseverance.

In the Old Testament Moses is again the outstanding example. On about a dozen distinct occasions the people "murmured" against him, and he had the beginnings of a mutiny on his hands. When Pharaoh's army was threatening them, when the water ran out or was too bitter to drink, when there was no meat to eat, when the scouts brought back a bad report of the strength of the Canaanite fortifications, when small minds became jealous of his position—these were some of the occasions on which the people complained of his leadership and challenged his authority. A lesser man would have given up and abandoned them to their own pettiness. But not Moses. He never forgot that these were God's people by God's covenant, who by God's promise would inherit the land.

In the New Testament the man who came to the end of his life with his ideals intact and his standards uncompromised was the apostle Paul. He too faced bitter and violent opposition. He had to endure severe physical afflictions, for on several occasions he was beaten, stoned and imprisoned. He suffered mentally too, for his footsteps were dogged by false prophets who contradicted his teaching and slandered his name. He also experienced great loneliness. Towards the end of his life he wrote "everyone in the province of Asia has deserted me" and "at my first defense . . . everyone deserted me" (2 Timothy 1:15; 4:16). Yet he never lost his vision of God's new, redeemed society, and he never gave up proclaiming it. In his underground dungeon, from which there was to be no escape but death, he could write: "I have fought the good fight, I have finished the race, I have kept the faith" (2 Timothy 4:7). He persevered to the end.

In recent centuries perhaps nobody has exemplified perseverance more than William Wilberforce. Sir Reginald Coupland wrote of him that, in order to break the apathy of parliament, a would-be social reformer "must possess, in the first place, the virtues of a fanatic without his vices. He must be palpably single-minded and unself-seeking. He must be strong enough to face opposition and ridicule, staunch enough to endure obstruction and delay."[19] These qualities Wilberforce possessed in abundance.

It was in 1787 that he first decided to put down a motion in the House of Commons about the slave trade. This nefarious traffic had been going on for three centuries, and the West Indian slave-owners were determined to oppose abolition to the end. Besides, Wilberforce was not a very pre-possessing man. He was little and ugly, with poor eyesight and an upturned nose. When Boswell heard him speak, he pronounced him "a perfect shrimp," but then had to concede that "presently the shrimp swelled into a whale."[20] In 1789 in the House Wilberforce said of the slave trade: "So enormous, so dreadful, so irremediable did its wickedness appear that my own mind was completely made up for Abolition. . . . Let the consequences be what they would, I from this time determined that I would never rest until I had effected its Abolition."[21] So Abolition Bills (which related to the trade) and Foreign Slave Bills (which would prohibit the involvement of British ships in it) were debated in the Commons in 1789, 1791, 1792, 1794, 1796 (by which time Abolition had become "the grand object of my parliamentary existence"), 1798 and 1799. Yet they all failed. The Foreign Slave Bill was not passed until 1806 and the Abolition of the Slave Trade Bill until 1807. This part of the campaign had taken eighteen years.

Next, soon after the conclusion of the Napoleonic wars, Wilberforce began to direct his energies to the abolition of slavery itself and the emancipation of the slaves. In 1823 the Anti-Slavery Society was formed. Twice that year and twice the following year Wilberforce pleaded the slaves' cause in the House of Commons. But in 1825 ill health compelled him to resign as a Member and to continue his campaign from outside. In 1831 he sent a message to the Anti-Slavery Society, in which he said: "Our motto must continue to be perseverance. And ultimately I trust the Almighty will crown our efforts with success."[22] He did. In July 1833 the Abolition of Slavery Bill was passed in both Houses of Parliament, even though it included the undertaking to pay £20,000,000 in compensation to the slave-owners. "Thank God," wrote Wilberforce, "that I have lived to witness a day in which England is willing to give £20,000,000 sterling for the abolition of slavery."[23] Three days later he died. He was buried in Westminster Abbey, in national recognition of his forty-five years of persevering struggle on behalf of African slaves.

Mind you, perseverance is not a synonym for pigheadedness. True leaders are not impervious to criticism. On the contrary, they listen to it and weigh it, and may modify their program accordingly. But they do not waver in their basic conviction of what God has called them to do. Whatever the opposition aroused or the sacrifice entailed, they persevere.

Service

A note of caution needs to be added at this point. "Leadership" is a concept shared by the Church and the world. We must not assume, however, that Christian and non-Christian understandings of it are identical. Nor should we adopt models of secular management without first subjecting them to critical Christian scrutiny. For Jesus introduced into the world an altogether new style of leadership. He expressed the difference between the old and the new in these terms:

> You know that those who are regarded as rulers of the Gentiles lord it over them, and their high officials exercise authority over them. Not so with you. Instead, whoever wants to become great among you must be your servant, and whoever wants to be first must be slave of all. For even the Son of Man did not come to be served, but to serve, and to give his life as a ransom for many.
>
> Mark 10:42–45

Among the followers of Jesus, therefore, leadership is not a synonym for lordship. Our calling is to be servants not bosses, slaves not masters. True, a certain authority attaches to all leaders, and leadership would be impossible without it. The apostles were given authority by Jesus, and exercised it in both teaching and disciplining the Church. Even Christian pastors today, although they are not apostles and do not possess apostolic authority, are to be "respected" because of their position "over" the congregation (1 Thessalonians 5:12–13), and even "obeyed" (Hebrews 13:17). Yet the emphasis of Jesus was not on the authority of a ruler-leader but on the humility of a servant-leader. The authority by which the Christian leader leads is not power but love, not force but example, not coercion but reasoned persuasion. Leaders have power, but power is safe only in the hands of those who humble themselves to serve.

What is the reason for Jesus' stress on the leader's service? Partly, no doubt, because the chief occupational hazard of leadership is pride. The Pharisaic model would not do in the new community which Jesus was building. The Pharisees loved deferential titles like "Father," "Teacher," "Rabbi," but this was both an offense against God to whom these titles properly belong and disruptive of the Christian brotherhood (Matthew 23:1–12).

Jesus' main reason for emphasizing the servant role of the leader, however, was surely that the service of others is a tacit recognition of their value. I have been troubled recently to observe that the "service" model of leadership is being borrowed by the world and commended for the wrong reasons. Robert K. Greenleaf, for example, a specialist in the field of management research and education, wrote in 1977 a long book called *Servant Leadership*, to which he gave the intriguing subtitle *A Journey into the Nature of Legitimate Power and Greatness*. He tells us that the concept of "the servant as leader" came to him from the reading of Hermann Hesse's *Journey to the East*, in which Leo, the menial servant of a group of travelers, turns out in the end to have been their leader. The "moral principle" which Mr. Greenleaf draws from this is that "the great leader is seen as the servant first." Or, expressed more fully: "The only authority deserving one's allegiance is that which is freely and knowingly granted by the led to the leader in response to, and in proportion to, the clearly evident servant stature of the leader. Those who choose to follow this principle . . . will freely respond only to individuals who are chosen as leaders because they are proven and trusted as servants."[24] I do not deny the truth of this, that leaders have first to win their spurs by service. But the danger of the principle as thus stated is that it regards service as being only a means to another end (namely qualifying one as a leader), and is therefore commended only because of its pragmatic usefulness. This is not what Jesus taught, however. To him service was an end in itself. T. W. Manson expressed the difference beautifully when he wrote: "In the Kingdom of God service is not a stepping-stone to nobility: it is nobility, the only kind of nobility that is recognised."[25]

Why then did Jesus equate greatness with service? Must not our answer relate to the intrinsic worth of human beings, which was the presupposition underlying his own ministry of self-giving love, and which is an essential element of the Christian perspective? If human beings are Godlike beings, then they must be served not exploited, respected not manipulated. As Oswald Sanders has expressed it, "True greatness, true leadership, is achieved not by reducing men to one's service but in giving oneself in selfless service to them."[26] Herein also lies the peril of seeing leadership in terms of projects and programs. Leadership will inevitably involve the development of these, but people take precedence over projects. And people must be neither "manipulated" nor even "managed." Though the latter is less demeaning to human beings than the former, yet both words are derived from *manus*, meaning "a hand," and both express a "handling" of people as if they were commodities rather than persons.

So Christian leaders serve, indeed serve not their own interests but rather the interests of others (Philippians 2:4). This simple principle should deliver the leader from excessive individualism, extreme isolation and self-centered empire-building. For those who serve others serve best in a team. Leadership teams are more healthy than solo leadership, for several reasons. First, team members supplement one another, building on one another's strengths and compensating for one another's weaknesses. No leader has all the gifts, so no leader should keep all the reins of leadership in his or her own hands. Secondly, team members encourage one another, identifying each other's gifts and motivating each other to develop and use them. As Max Warren used to say, "Christian leadership has nothing whatever to do with self-assertion, but everything to do with encouraging other people to assert themselves."[27] Thirdly, team members are accountable to one another. Shared work means shared responsibility. Then we listen to one another and learn from one another. Both the human family and the divine family (the Body of Christ) are contexts of solidarity in which any incipient illusions of grandeur are rapidly dispelled. "The way of a fool seems right to him, but a wise man listens to advice" (Proverbs 12:15).

In all this Christian emphasis on service, the disciple is only seeking to follow and reflect his teacher. For though he was Lord of all, Jesus became the servant of all. Putting on the apron of servitude, he got down on his knees to wash the apostles' feet. Now he tells us to do as he did, to clothe ourselves with humility, and in love to serve one another (John 13:12–17; 1 Peter 5:5; Galatians 5:13). No leadership is authentically Christ-like which is not marked by the spirit of humble and joyful service.

Discipline

Every vision has a tendency to fade. Every visionary is prone to discouragement. Hard work begun with zest can easily degenerate into drudgery. Suffering and loneliness take their toll. The leader feels unappreciated and gets tired. The Christian ideal of humble service sounds fine in theory but seems impractical. So leaders may catch themselves soliloquizing: "It is quicker to ride roughshod over other people; you get things done that way. And if the end is good, does it really matter what means we employ to attain it? Even a little prudent compromise can sometimes be justified, can't it?"

It is evident, then, that leaders are made of flesh and blood, not plaster or marble or stained glass. Indeed, as Peter Drucker has written, "Strong people always have strong weaknesses too."[28] Even the great leaders of the biblical story had fatal flaws. They too were fallen and fallible and frail. Righteous Noah got drunk. Faithful Abraham was despicable enough to risk his wife's chastity for the sake of his own safety. Moses lost his temper. David broke all five commandments of the second table of the law, committing adultery, murder, theft, false witness and covetousness, in that single episode of moral rebellion over Bathsheba. Jeremiah's lonely courage was marred by self-pity. John the Baptist, whom Jesus described as the greatest man who had ever lived, was overcome by doubt. And Peter's boastful impetuosity was doubtless a cloak for his deep personal insecurity. If those heroes of Scripture failed, what hope is there for us?

The final mark of Christian leaders is discipline, not only self-discipline in general (in the mastery of their passions, their time and their energies), but in particular the discipline with which they wait on God. They know their weakness. They know the greatness of their task and the strength of the opposition. But they also know the inexhaustible riches of God's grace.

Many biblical examples could be given. Moses sought God, and "the LORD would speak to Moses face to face, as a man speaks with his friend." David looked to God as his shepherd, his light and salvation, his rock, the stronghold of his life, and in times of deep distress "found strength in the LORD his God." The apostle Paul, burdened with a physical or psychological infirmity which he called his "thorn in my flesh," heard Jesus say to him, "My grace is sufficient for you," and learned that only when he was weak was he strong.

But our supreme exemplar is our Lord Jesus himself. It is often said that he was always available to people. This is not true. He was not. There were times when he sent the crowds away. He refused to allow the urgent to displace the important. Regularly he withdrew from the pressures and the glare of his public ministry, in order to seek his Father in solitude and replenish his reserves of strength. Then, when it came to the end, he and his apostles faced the final test together. How is it, I have often asked myself, that they forsook him and fled, while he went to the cross with such serenity? Is not the answer that he prayed while they slept? (For Moses see Exodus 33:11 and Deuteronomy 34:10; for David, Psalm 23:1; 27:1 and 1 Samuel 30:6; for Paul, 2 Corinthians 12:7–10; and for Jesus, Mark 4:36; 6:45–46; 14:32–42 and 50.)

It is only God who "gives strength to the weary and increases the power of the weak." For "even youths grow tired and weary, and young men stumble and fall." But those who "hope in the Lord," and wait patiently for him, "will renew their strength. They will soar on wings like eagles; they will run and not grow weary, they will walk and not be faint" (Isaiah 40:29–31). It is only those who discipline themselves to seek God's face who keep their vision bright. It is only those who live before Christ's cross whose inner fires are constantly rekindled and never go out. Those leaders who think they are strong in their own strength are the most pathetically weak of all people; only those who know and acknowledge their weakness can become strong with the strength of Christ.

I have tried to analyze the concept of Christian leadership. It appears to consist of five main ingredients—clear vision, hard work, dogged perseverance, humble service and iron discipline.

In conclusion, it seems to me that we need to repent of two particularly horrid sins. The first is pessimism, which is dishonoring to God and incompatible with Christian faith. To be sure, we do not forget the fallenness, indeed the depravity, of human beings. We are well aware of the pervasiveness of evil. We are not so foolish as to imagine that society will ever become perfect before Christ comes and establishes the fullness of his rule.[29] Nevertheless, we also believe in the power of God—in the power of God's gospel to change society. We need to renounce both naive optimism and cynical pessimism, and replace them with the sober but confident realism of the Bible.

The second sin of which we need to repent is mediocrity, and the acceptance of it. I find myself wanting to say, especially to young people: "Don't be content with the mediocre! Don't settle for anything less than your full God-given potential! Be ambitious and adventurous for God! God has made you a unique person by your genetic endowment, upbringing and education. He has himself created you and gifted you, and he does not want his work to be wasted. He means you to be fulfilled, not frustrated. His purpose is that everything you have and are should be stretched in his service and in the service of others."

This means that God has a leadership role of some degree and kind for each of us. We need, then, to seek his will with all our hearts, to cry to him to give us a vision of what he is calling us to do with our lives, and to pray for grace to be faithful (not necessarily successful) in obedience to the heavenly vision.

Only then can we hope to hear from Christ those most coveted of all words, "Well done, good and faithful servant!"

Notes

Chapter 1: *Work and Unemployment*

1. James A. C. Brown, *The Social Psychology of Industry* (Penguin, 1954), 186.

2. H. L. Mencken, quoted by David Weir in *Men and Work in Modern Britain* (Fontana, 1973), 75.

3. Quoted from Dorothy Sayers's "Creed or Chaos?" in Ted W. Engstrom and Alec Mackenzie, *Managing Your Time* (Zondervan, 1967), 21–23.

4. Pope John Paul II, *Laborem Exercens*, Encyclical Letter on "Human Work" (Catholic Truth Society, 1981), 4.

5. Ibid., 13.

6. Ibid., 12.

7. Ibid., 33.

8. Henri Blocher, *In the Beginning: The Opening Chapters of Genesis* (Inter-Varsity Press, 1984), 57.

9. E. F. Schumacher, *Good Work* (Abacus, 1980), 27.

10. Ibid., 119–20.

11. Ibid., 121.

12. Report in the *Guardian Weekly*, 14 February 1970.

13. From Henri de Man, *Joy in Work* (1929), quoted in Sherwood E. Wirt, *The Social Conscience of the Evangelical* (Scripture Union, 1968), 38.

14. Schumacher, *Good Work*, 3–4.

15. Ibid., 122.

16. The story is told by Basil Willey in *Religion Today* (A & C Black, 1969), 74.

17. From one of thirteen interviews in David Field and Elspeth Stephenson, *Just the Job* (Inter-Varsity Press, 1978), 93–94.

18. Miroslav Volf, *Work in the Spirit* (Oxford University Press, 1991), 92.

19. Ibid., 114.

20. Quoted in F. A. Iremonger, *William Temple* (Oxford University Press, 1948), 440. See also chapter 1, "The Unemployment Experience," in Michael Moynagh, *Making Unemployment Work* (Lion, 1985), and Ann Warren, *Living with Unemployment* (Hodder & Stoughton, 1986).

21. These figures were taken from the European Union Web site at <www.europa.int.eu>.

22. TUC press release, 6 June 1997.

23. *Unemployment and the Future of Work* (CCBI, 1997), 33.

24. Ibid., 30.

25. Ibid., 11, 174.

26. George Goyder, *The Just Enterprise* (Andre Deutsch, 1987), 93.

235

27. David Bleakley, *Work: The Shadow and the Substance, a Reappraisal of Life and Labour* (SCM, 1983), 56. See also *In Place of Work . . . The Sufficient Society: A Study of Technology from the Point of View of People* (SCM, 1981), 3.

28. Peter Elsom and David Porter, *Four Million Reasons to Care: How Your Church Can Help the Unemployed* (MARC Europe and CAWTU, 1985), is a mine of information and practical suggestions on how local churches can get into action.

29. Church in Action with the Unemployed published a book entitled *Action on Unemployment*, which describes one hundred church projects for and with the unemployed.

30. Marshall McLuhan, *Understanding Media* (1964; Abacus, 1973), 381.

31. John Palmer, *Trading Places: The Future of the European Community* (Radius, 1988), 133–71.

32. Moynagh, *Making Unemployment Work*, 89–93.

33. James Robertson, *Future Work: Jobs, Self-Employment and Leisure after the Industrial Age* (Gower/Maurice Temple Smith, 1985), 1.

34. Ibid., 14–15.

35. Ibid., x, 130–31.

36. *Unemployment and the Future of Work*, 8, 171.

37. Ibid., 79.

38. Sir Fred Catherwood, *Jobs and Justice, Homes and Hope: Analysing the State of the Nation* (Hodder & Stoughton, 1997), xiv.

39. Ibid., 75, 85.

40. *Unemployment and the Future of Work*, 101.

41. Two further books that deal helpfully with many practical and pastoral issues relating to work and unemployment are Mark Greene's *Thank God It's Monday* (Scripture Union, 1994), and David Westcott's *Work Well, Live Well: Rediscovering a Biblical View of Work* (Marshall Pickering, 1994).

Chapter 2: *Industrial Relations*

1. John V. Taylor, *Enough Is Enough* (SCM, 1975), 102. For the central importance of relationships, see Michael Schluter and David Lee, *The R Factor* (Hodder & Stoughton, 1993).

2. Catherwood, *Jobs and Justice, Homes and Hope*, 77–79.

3. Will Hutton, *The State We're In* (1995; rev. ed., Vintage, 1996), 132–68.

4. From a news report in *Christianity Today* in 1979, a tape-recorded conference address, and especially R. C. Sproul's *Stronger than Steel: The Wayne Alderson Story* (Harper & Row, 1980).

5. Richard Hyman and Ian Brough, *Social Values and Industrial Relations: A Study of Fairness and Inequality* (Blackwell, 1975).

6. Ibid., 11.

7. TUC press release, 16 September 1996.

8. TUC press release, 20 December 1996.

9. Schumacher, *Good Work*, 79.

10. William Temple, *Christianity and the Social Order* (Penguin, 1942), 87.

11. Ibid., 61.

12. Erving Goffman, *Asylums: Essays on the Social Situation of Mental Patients and Other Inmates* (Anchor Books, Doubleday, 1961).

13. Ibid., xiii.

14. Ibid., 6.

15. Ibid., 7.

16. Ibid., 9.

17. Ibid., 43.

18. See my *I Believe in Preaching* (Hodder & Stoughton, 1981), 174–78.

19. From Charles Colson's lecture entitled "The Rehabilitation of Prisoners," published in *Crime and the Responsible Community* (Hodder & Stoughton, 1980), 156.

20. The Nuremberg Code (1947); reproduced in A. S. Duncan, G. R. Dunstan and R. B. Welbourn, eds., *Dictionary of Medical Ethics* (DLT, 1981), 130–32.

21. Declaration of Helsinki (1964; revised 1975) in Duncan et al., *Dictionary of Medical Ethics*, 132–35.

22. Alexander Solzhenitsyn, *Cancer Ward* (1968; Penguin, 1971).

23. Ibid., 240.

24. Ibid., 85–86.

25. Ibid., 320.

26. Temple, *Christianity and the Social Order*, 96.

27. Ibid.

28. Quoted in Bleakley, *In Place of Work . . . The Sufficient Society*, 16, 17.

29. Temple, *Christianity and the Social Order*, 87.

30. Ibid., 99.

31. The Donovan Report (1968) was produced by the fifth Royal Commission on Trade Unions and Employers' Associations, which was set up by the Labour government and sat between 1965 and 1968.

32. P. J. Armstrong, J. F. B. Goodman and J. D. Hyman, *Ideology and Shop-Floor Industrial Relations* (Croom Helm, 1981).

33. The principle of "codetermination," first developed in the 1930s, was put into practice in West Germany after World War I. In essence it advocated (1) a "works council," which represented the workers, (2) a "supervisory board" (two-thirds of whose members being owners and one-third workers' representatives), which appointed (3) the executive board, which ran the company. West Germany's post-war economic progress and good record of labor relations are thought by many to be at least partly due to this arrangement. See H. F. R. Catherwood, *A Better Way: The Case for a Christian Social Order* (Inter-Varsity Press, 1975), 121.

34. Sir Fred Catherwood, *At the Cutting Edge* (Hodder & Stoughton, 1996), 130–32.

35. For facts and figures about Europe, see Timothy Bainbridge with Anthony Teasdale, *The Penguin Companion to European Union* (Penguin, 1995).

36. Bishop Robin Woods of Worcester, letter to *The Times*, 16 February 1997.

37. See "Employee Share Schemes," published in 1979 by the Wider Share Ownership Council, Juxon House, St. Paul's Courtyard, London EC4M 8EH. The booklet also explains the profit-sharing provisions of the 1978 Finance Act. Other businesses which early adopted dividend limitation and profit-sharing were ICI, Courtaulds and Rowntrees.

38. Thomas J. Peters and Robert H. Waterman, *In Search of Excellence: Lessons from America's Best-Run Companies* (Harper & Row, 1982).

39. Ibid., 39.

40. Richard Tanner Pascale and Anthony G. Athos, *The Art of Japanese Management* (Simon & Schuster, 1981; Penguin, 1982), 50.

41. Ibid., 122.

42. George Goyder, *The Responsible Company* (Blackwell, 1961), ix.

43. Ibid., 109–11.

44. Ibid., 118, 126.

45. Goyder, *The Just Enterprise*, xi.

46. Ibid., 5.

47. Ibid., 79.

48. Ibid., 82.

49. The Christian Association of Business Executives, 12 Palace Street, London SW1E 5JA.

50. Goyder, *The Just Enterprise*, 16.

Chapter 3: *The Multiracial Dream*

1. Martin Luther King's "I Have a Dream" speech is recorded in Coretta Scott King's *My Life with Martin Luther King, Jr* (Hodder & Stoughton, 1969), 249.

2. From an address by Roy Jenkins, Home Secretary, May 1966 to a meeting of Voluntary Liaison Committees.

3. David Brion Davies, *The Problem of Slavery in Western Cultures* (Cornell University Press, 1966), 31.

4. Edward Long, *The History of Jamaica* (Lowndes, London, 1774), 351–56.

5. J. H. Guenebault, *The Natural History of the Negro Race,* English trans. (Charleston, South Carolina: Dowling, 1837), 1–19. See also the references to this book in Wilson Armistead, *A Tribute for the Negro* (Manchester, 1848), e.g., p. 36.

6. Stanley M. Elkins, *Slavery: A Problem in American Institutional and Intellectual Life* (1959; 2nd ed., University of Chicago Press, 1968), 82.

7. Ibid., 84.

8. Ibid., 113.

9. Ibid., especially chapter III, "Slavery and Personality."

10. Armistead, *A Tribute for the Negro,* 5.

11. M. F. Ashley Montagu, *Man's Most Dangerous Myth: The Fallacy of Race* (1942; 5th ed. revised and enlarged, Oxford University Press, 1974), 101.

12. Ibid., 67.

13. Ibid., 416.

14. Ibid., 3.

15. Columbus Salley and Ronald Behm, *What Color Is Your God? Black Consciousness and the Christian Faith,* first published 1970 under the title *Your God Is Too White* (Inter-Varsity Press, rev. ed. 1981).

16. Montagu, *Man's Most Dangerous Myth,* 420.

17. Adolf Hitler, *Mein Kampf,* trans. James Murphy (1925; Hutchinson, 1940), 150.

18. Ibid., 284.

19. Richard Gutteridge, *Open Thy Mouth for the Dumb: The German Evangelical Church and the Jews 1870–1950* (Blackwell, 1976), 69.

20. Ibid., 48.

21. Quoted in Montagu, *Man's Most Dangerous Myth,* 50.

22. Quoted in John W. de Gruchy, *The Church Struggle in South Africa* (Eerdmans, 1979), 30–31. For recent assessments of Christian attitudes to racism in South Africa, see Zolile Mbali, *The Churches and Racism: A Black South African Perspective* (SCM, 1987), and Michael Cassidy, *The Passing Summer: A South African Pilgrimage in the Politics of Love* (Hodder & Stoughton, 1989).

23. "Human Relations and the South African Scene in the Light of Scripture," a 1974 report of the Dutch Reformed Church (Dutch Reformed Publishers, 1976), 14, 32, 71.

24. Hitler, *Mein Kampf,* 248.

25. Professor Dr. A. B. Dupreez, *Inside the South African Crucible* (HAUM, Kapstaad-Pretoria, 1959), 63.

26. Montagu, *Man's Most Dangerous Myth,* 10.

27. Ibid., 190–93.

28. Ibid., 202.

29. Ibid., 204–34.

30. Cassidy, *The Passing Summer,* 154.

31. Margery Perham, *The Colonial Reckoning: The 1961 Reith Lectures* (Collins, 1961), 39.

32. Jeremy Murray-Brown, *Kenyatta* (Allen & Unwin, 1972), 306.

33. Mzee Jomo Kenyatta, *Suffering without Bitterness* (East African Publishing House, 1968), 166. For similar African reactions to French colonial rule, see Frantz Fanon, *Black Skin, White Masks* (1952).

34. Paul Scott, *The Jewel in the Crown* (1966; Granada, 1973), 260.

35. Arnold Toynbee, *A Study of History*, vol. 1, p. 213, quoted by Archbishop Cyril Garbett in *World Problems of Today* (Hodder & Stoughton, 1955), 135.

36. See Anne Owers, *Sheep and Goats: British Nationality Law and Its Effects*, and *Families Divided: Immigration Control and Family Life* (CIO, 1984).

37. See also "The Churches' Charter for Racial Justice in Europe" (1996).

38. Martin Walker, *The National Front* (Collins, 1977), 34.

39. Ibid., 78–84.

40. Ibid., 185.

41. Lord Scarman, *The Scarman Report: The Brixton Disorders 10–12 April 1981* (Penguin, 1981), 77–78.

42. Ibid., 209.

43. Ibid., 196.

44. David Haslam, *Race for the Millennium: A Challenge to Church and Society* (Church House Publishing, 1996).

45. David J. Smith, *Racial Disadvantage in Britain* (Penguin, 1977), 109–10.

46. David Sheppard, *Bias to the Poor* (Hodder & Stoughton, 1983), 69.

47. *Unemployment and the Future of Work*, 106.

48. TUC news release, April 1997.

49. See Haslam, *Race for the Millennium*, 121–22, and *Unemployment and the Future of Work*, 116–17.

50. Malcolm X, *The Autobiography of Malcolm X* (Grove Press, 1964), 175, 275.

51. Ibid., 179, 272.

52. Haslam, *Race for the Millennium*, 167.

53. Ibid., 175.

54. Montagu, *Man's Most Dangerous Myth*, 74.

55. Ibid., 307.

56. Quoted in Walker, *The National Front*, 47.

57. The Lausanne Covenant, para. 10, "Evangelism and Culture," in John Stott, ed., *Making Christ Known: Historic Mission Documents from the Lausanne Movement 1974–1989* (Paternoster, 1996; Eerdmans, 1997), 39–42.

58. J. C. G. Klotze, *Principle and Practice in Race Relations according to Scripture* (SCA Publications, Stellenbosch, 1962), 55.

59. O. R. Johnston, *Nationhood: Towards a Christian Perspective* (Latimer Studies, no. 7, 1980), 14.

60. The Pasadena Statement on the Homogeneous Unit Principle, in Stott, *Making Christ Known*, 64. For a black Christian's experience of living in Britain, see Philip Mohabir, *Building Bridges* (Hodder & Stoughton, 1988). Also recommended is the "Study Pack for Christians in a Multi-Racial Society," entitled *New Humanity* and produced by Evangelical Christians for Racial Justice, 29 Trinity Road, Aston, Birmingham B6 6AJ.

Chapter 4: *Poverty, Wealth and Simplicity*

1. From an article by Malcolm Muggeridge which first appeared in *The Observer* on 26 June 1966 and was subsequently published in *Jesus Rediscovered* (Collins Fontana, 1969), 57.

2. U.S. Census Bureau press release, 26 September 1996.

3. Social Security Statistics 1996 (HMSO, 1996), 17.

4. *Faith in the City: A Call for Action by Church and Nation* (Church House Publishing, 1985), 359.

5. "Evangelization at Present and in the Future of Latin America," *Conclusions of the Third General Conference of Latin American Bishops,* Puebla, 1980 (St. Paul Publications, 1980), 107, para. 494.

6. *UN Human Development Report 1997,* executive summary, taken from Web site <www.undp.org>.

7. *UN Human Development Report 1996* (Oxford University Press, 1996), 148–49.

8. Michael Todaro, ed., *Economic Development* (Longman, 1997), 46.

9. *The World Bank Annual Report 1989,* 27.

10. UNDP press release, 12 June 1997, from *Human Development Report 1997* launch.

11. Bishop David Sheppard's Richard Dimbleby Lecture, "The Poverty That Imprisons the Spirit," was published in *The Listener* (19 April 1984). See also Paul Harrison, *Inside the Inner City* (Penguin, 1983).

12. See, e.g., Albert Gelin, *The Poor of Yahweh* (1964; English trans., Liturgical Press, Minnesota); Julio de Santa Ana, *Good News to the Poor* (WCC, 1977), and Julio de Santa Ana, ed., *Towards a Church of the Poor* (Orbis, 1979); Conrad Boerma, *Rich Man, Poor Man and the Bible* (1978; SCM, 1979); Atholl Gill, *Christians and the Poor* (Zadok Centre Series, Canberra, no. 9, undated); "Christian Witness to the Urban Poor" (Lausanne Occasional Paper no. 22, 1980), a group report from the Consultation on World Evangelization at Pattaya, Thailand, which incorporates as an appendix Jim Punton's analysis of the nine Hebrew words for the poor; *Your Kingdom Come,* the report of the World Conference on Mission and Evangelism, held in Melbourne in 1980; Vinay Samuel and Chris Sugden, *Evangelism and the Poor* (Partnership in Mission, Asia, Bangalore, rev. ed., 1983); Redmond Mullin, *The Wealth of Christians* (Paternoster, 1983); and Peter Lee, *Poor Man, Rich Man: The Priorities of Jesus and the Agenda of the Church* (Hodder & Stoughton, 1986).

13. Raymond Fung's speech, "Good News to the Poor," is published in *Your Kingdom Come* (WCC, 1980), 83–92.

14. Sheppard, *Bias to the Poor,* 16.

15. Ibid., 225.

16. "Evangelization . . . of Latin America," 178, para. 1134.

17. Ibid., 179, paras. 1141–42.

18. Ibid., 180, para. 1154.

19. *Your Kingdom Come,* 171.

20. This was Professor Kosuke Koyama's expression at Melbourne (*Your Kingdom Come,* 161).

21. Robert Holman, *Poverty: Explanations of Social Deprivation* (Martin Robertson, 1978).

22. Ibid., 134.

23. Ibid., 188.

24. Martin Hengel, *Property and Riches in the Early Church: Aspects of a Social History of the Early Church* (1973; English trans., SCM and Fortress, 1974), 26–27.

25. Ibid., 32–33.

26. Cathy Pharaoh, ed., *Dimensions of the Voluntary Sector* (CAF, 1997), 60.

27. Quoted by Bishop Otto Dibelius in his autobiography, *In the Service of the Lord* (Holt, Rinehart & Winston, 1964), 31.

28. Taylor, *Enough Is Enough,* 81–82.

29. See "The Lausanne Covenant—An Exposition and Commentary," in Stott, ed., *Making Christ Known.*

30. "An Evangelical Commitment to Simple Lifestyle," in Stott, *Making Christ Known,* 139–53. See also the papers prepared for the International Conference on Simple Lifestyle, in Ronald J. Sider, ed., *Lifestyle in the Eighties* (Paternoster, 1982), 16, 35–36.

31. Andrew Hartropp, ed., *Families in Debt: The Nature, Causes and Effects of Debt Problems, and Policy Proposals for Their Alleviation* (Jubilee Centre Publications, 1987). See also Roy

McCloughry and Andrew Hartropp, *Debt* (Grove Ethical Studies, no. 71, 1988); Michael Schluter and David Lee, *Credit and Debit: Sorting It Out* (Marshalls, 1989), and the study pack on debt produced by The Institute for Contemporary Christianity for use by church groups (St. Peter's Church, Vere Street, London W1M 9HP).

Chapter 5: *Women, Men and God*

1. Plato, *Timaeus*, Loeb Classical Library, trans. R. G. Bury (Heinemann, 1929), 249, para. 91a.

2. Aristotle, *The Generation of Animals*, II, iii, Loeb Classical Library, trans. A. L. Peck (Heinemann, 1943), 175.

3. Josephus, *Against Apion, or On the Antiquity of the Jews*, book II, Loeb Classical Library, trans. H. St. J. Thackeray (Heinemann, 1926), 373, para. 201.

4. William Barclay, *Ephesians: Daily Study Bible* (St. Andrews Press), 199ff.

5. Tertullian, *On the Apparel of Women*, book 1, chapter 1. *The Ante-Nicene Fathers*, vol. IV (Eerdmans, reprinted 1982), 14.

6. Claiming that the twentieth century "has brought greater change to women's lives than any other period in human history," Helen Wilkinson and Melanie Howard summarize what they call "the long march to equality" (*Tomorrow's Women* [Demos, 1997], 14–49). They then paint five different portraits of tomorrow's women, who represent a variety of feminisms (pp. 50–158). They are uncertain, however, whether the future will be an extrapolation from current trends or will slow down and even halt "the forward march of women" (pp. 159–70).

7. Germaine Greer, *The Female Eunuch* (Paladin, 1971), 12, 18, 22. In her more recent book *Sex and Destiny: The Politics of Human Fertility* (Secker & Warburg, 1984), while retaining her power to startle and shock by her unconventional opinions, Germaine Greer is much more positive towards the human family. Indeed, she almost romanticizes the parent-child relationships which are traditional in Asia and Africa, in contrast to the tendency of the western nuclear family which (in her view) despises and neglects children.

8. Ibid., 59–60.

9. See Greer, *Sex and Destiny*, and note 7 above.

10. Janet Radcliffe Richards, *The Sceptical Feminist: A Philosophical Enquiry* (1980; Penguin, 1982), 11.

11. Ibid., 13–14, 16.

12. Elaine Storkey, *What's Right with Feminism* (SPCK/Third Way Books, 1985).

13. A recommended symposium which opens up the issues fairly is Shirley Lees, ed., *The Role of Women* (Inter-Varsity Press, 1984), in which eight prominent Christians debate with one another. Its American equivalent is Bonnidell Clouse and Robert G. Clouse, *Women in Ministry: Four Views* (InterVarsity Press, 1989).

14. *An Inclusive Language Lectionary: Readings for Year A* (Cooperative Publications Association, 1983). The quotations are from the preface and the introduction. See also Graham Leonard, Iain Mackenzie and Peter Toon, *Let God Be God* (Darton, Longman & Todd, 1989). The Church of England General Synod's Liturgical Commission produced a judicious report in 1988 entitled *Making Women Visible*, subtitled *The Use of Inclusive Language with the Alternative Service Book*. They did not recommend any changes in the biblical and traditional ways of referring to God. In relation to "the use of male terms to include both genders" (e.g., "man," "men," "mankind"), they avoided the two extremes of those wishing to eliminate them all as inherently offensive to the dignity of women and those wishing to retain them all as deeply embedded in culture and literature. The Commission has recommended a sensitive and flexible way forward, accepting many of the theological arguments of the former group and some of the linguistic arguments of the latter (see especially paras. 81–83).

15. Mahatma Gandhi, *Gandhi: An Autobiography* (1949; Jonathan Cape, 1966), 155.

16. The Koran, trans. N. J. Dawood (Penguin, 1956), 360ff.

17. Raymond de Coccola, *Ayorama* (1955; Ontario: Paper Jacks, 1973), 212.

18. John Wenham argues cogently in *Easter Enigma* (Paternoster, 1984) that "Mary of Bethany" was in fact Mary Magdalene (pp. 22–33).

19. John Howard Yoder, *The Politics of Jesus* (Eerdmans, 1972), 177, footnote 23.

20. Betty Friedan, *The Feminine Mystique* (Pelican, 1963), 68. In her subsequent book, *The Second Stage* (1981; Abacus, 1983), Betty Friedan declares the first stage of the feminist battle to be over. Women have been liberated from feminine role stereotypes into equality with men. The second stage will transcend the male-female polarization and involve a restructuring of society, especially of the family. The feminine mystique has been overcome; now the feminist mystique must be renounced, which denied the need for the nurturing environment of the family.

21. Leslie F. Church, ed., *Matthew Henry's Commentary* (1708; Marshall Morgan & Scott, 1960), 7.

22. Richards, *The Sceptical Feminist*, 65.

23. George F. Gilder, *Sexual Suicide* (1973; Bantam, 1975), v.

24. Ibid., 46.

25. Ibid., 246.

26. Ibid., 63.

27. Deborah Tanner, *You Just Don't Understand: Women and Men in Conversation* (William Morrow, 1990; Vintage, 1991).

28. Ibid., 42.

29. John Gray, *Men Are from Mars, Women Are from Venus* (HarperCollins, 1992), 16–18.

30. Ibid., 15.

31. Ibid., 31.

32. Ibid., 43.

33. Ibid., 10, 286.

34. David Pawson, *Leadership Is Male: A Challenge to Christian Feminism* (Highland Books, 1988), 17, 18, 57, 58.

35. Paul K. Jewett, *Man as Male and Female* (Eerdmans, 1975), 86. A somewhat similar uncertainty about how to interpret the Pauline texts is to be found in the Second Report of the House of Bishops of the General Synod of the Church of England, entitled *The Ordination of Women to the Priesthood* (GS829, 1988), especially its chapter 3, "Priesthood, Headship and the Exercise of Authority."

36. Jewett, *Man as Male and Female*, 86.

37. Ibid., 112.

38. Ibid., 134.

39. Ibid., 138.

40. Gretchen Gaebelein Hull, *Equal to Serve: Women and Men in the Church and Home* (Revell, 1987), 65.

41. Ibid., 229.

42. Ibid., 210.

43. Ibid., 73–74.

44. Ibid., 55–56, 128, 210, 240, 244.

45. See Donald W. Dayton, *Discovering an Evangelical Heritage* (Harper & Row, 1976). In his chapter entitled "The Evangelical Roots of Feminism" (pp. 85–98), Dr. Dayton traces the roots of the American feminist movement to the revivals of Charles G. Finney, whose Oberlin College "became the first co-educational college in the world" (p. 88).

46. James B. Hurley, *Man and Woman in Biblical Perspective: A Study in Role Relationships and Authority* (Inter-Varsity Press, 1981), 206–14.

47. James B. Hurley gives us a thorough treatment of "veils." He points out that the Old Testament contains no law about wearing a veil and that the Hebrew and Greco-Roman cus-

tom was for women to be normally unveiled. In both cultures too it was usual for women to put their hair up: loose or hanging hair was a sign either of mourning or of separation from the community (e.g., because of leprosy, Nazirite vows or being suspected of adultery). Dr. Hurley argues, therefore, that the "covering" and "uncovering" Paul mentions refers to the putting up and letting down of the hair. The NIV margin also adopts this interpretation (ibid., 45–47, 66–68, 162–71, 178–79, 254–71).

48. See my appreciative critique of this book in *The Message of 1 Timothy and Titus* (Inter-Varsity Press, 1996), 76–77.

49. Richard and Catherine Kroeger, "Pandemonium and Silence in Corinth," *The Reformed Journal* 28, no. 6 (June 1978).

50. Richard and Catherine Kroeger, "May Women Teach? Heresy in the Pastoral Epistles," *The Reformed Journal* 30, no. 10 (October 1980). See also Catherine Clark Kroeger, "1 Timothy 2:12—A Classicist's View," in Alvera Mickelson, ed., *Women, Authority and the Bible* (1986; Marshalls, 1987), 225–44.

51. Mickelson, ed., *Women, Authority and the Bible*, 229–32. See also C. C. Kroeger, "Ancient Heresies and a Strange Greek Verb," *The Reformed Journal* 29, no. 3 (March 1979).

52. Wayne Grudem, "Does *Kephale* (Head) Mean 'Source' or 'Authority Over' in Greek Literature? A Survey of 2,336 Examples," first published in 1977, reprinted in *Trinity Journal*, no. 6 (1985).

53. See, e.g., Berkeley and Alvera Mickelson, "What Does *Kephale* Mean in the New Testament?" in *Women, Authority and the Bible*, 97–110, and especially Philip Barton Payne in his response to their paper, ibid., 118–32. See also Gilbert Bilezikian, *Beyond Sex Roles* (Baker, 1985), and C. C. Kroeger, "The Classical Concept of Head as 'Source,'" appendix III of Hull, *Equal to Serve*, although in these works neither author betrays any knowledge of Dr. Grudem's survey. Dr. Bilezikian directly challenged Dr. Grudem's thesis, however, at a meeting of the Evangelical Theological Society in Atlanta in November 1986. See also Dr. Grudem's paper, "The Meaning of *Kephale* ('Head'): A Response to Recent Studies," published as appendix I in John Piper and Wayne Grudem, *Recovering Biblical Manhood and Womanhood* (Crossway Books, 1991), 425–68.

54. *Christianity Today* (16 January 1987).

55. Stephen B. Clark opts for this word in his magisterial survey *Man and Woman in Christ: An Examination of the Roles of Men and Women in the Light of Scripture and the Social Sciences* (Servant Books, 1980), 23–45. Despite his distinctions between "coercive," "mercenary" and "voluntary" subordination, I remain uncomfortable with the word and have written further about "authority" and "submission" (1 Timothy 2:11–15) in *The Message of 1 Timothy and Titus*, 73–88.

56. For a fuller exposition of Ephesians 5:21–33 and of its implications for marriage, see *The Message of Ephesians* in the *Bible Speaks Today* series (Inter-Varsity Press, 1979), 213–36.

57. Piper and Grudem, *Recovering Biblical Manhood and Womanhood*, 36–45.

58. Roy McCloughry, *Men and Masculinity: From Power to Love* (Hodder & Stoughton, 1992), 249, 130, 260.

59. Margaret Mead, *Male and Female* (1949; Penguin, 1962), e.g., 41, 71, 86 and 192ff. Consider also the very ancient Chinese teaching about the equilibrium between Yin (the feminine or passive principle) and Yang (the masculine or active). Stephen B. Clark summarizes the findings of psychology and anthropology on the differences between the sexes (*Man and Woman in Christ*, 371–465).

60. Richards, *The Sceptical Feminist*, 192.

61. Ibid., 175.

62. Mead, *Male and Female*, 88.

63. Letha Scanzoni and Nancy Hardesty, *All We're Meant to Be: A Biblical Approach to Women's Liberation* (Word, 1974), 12, 206.

64. See, e.g., C. E. B. Cranfield, *Commentary on Romans*, vol. 2 (T & T Clark, 1979), 788.

65. See my fuller exposition of these crucial verses in *The Message of 1 Timothy and Titus*, 73–88.

66. For a thorough defense of the Catholic doctrine of priesthood, see Manfred Hauke, *Women in the Priesthood? A Systematic Analysis in the Light of the Order of Creation and Redemption* (first published in German in 1986; English trans., Ignatius, 1988).

67. Quoted in Mickelsen, ed., *Women, Authority and the Bible*, 299.

Chapter 6: *Marriage and Divorce*

1. See O. Raymond Johnston's 1978 London Lectures in Contemporary Christianity, published under the title *Who Needs the Family?* (Hodder & Stoughton, 1979).

2. Jack Dominian, *Marriage, Faith and Love* (Darton, Longman & Todd, 1981), 49–83. See also his earlier book, *Christian Marriage* (Darton, Longman & Todd, 1965).

3. See Judson J. Swihart and Steven L. Brigham, *Helping Children of Divorce* (InterVarsity Press, 1982).

4. "1996 Statistical Abstract of the USA," by the Census Bureau. Taken from the Web site of the Census Bureau: <www.census.gov>.

5. Census Bureau press release, 13 March 1996.

6. *Social Trends 1997* (HMSO, 1997), 46.

7. *Something to Celebrate: Valuing Families in Church and Society*, the report of a working party of the Church of England Board for Social Responsibility (Church House, 1995), 35.

8. Figures from *Social Trends 1996* (HMSO, 1996), 34, and *Social Trends 1997*, 47.

9. George and Nena O'Neill, *Open Marriage: A New Lifestyle for Couples* (New York: Evans, 1972). This book is referred to and quoted in Gilder, *Sexual Suicide*, 47ff.

10. John H. Adam and Nancy Williamson Adam, *Divorce: How and When to Let Go* (Prentice-Hall, 1979).

11. For a lyrical meditation on married love, and its call to self-giving, see Mike Mason, *The Mystery of Marriage* (Triangle, SPCK, 1997). He writes: "Love is an earthquake that relocates the centre of the universe" (p. 26).

12. John Williams, *For Every Cause? A Biblical Study of Divorce* (Paternoster, 1981), 12.

13. Jack Dominian, *Marital Breakdown* (Penguin, 1968), 42.

14. *Something to Celebrate*, 109.

15. Ibid., 117.

16. Ibid., 34.

17. Ibid., 114.

18. Ibid., 115–16.

19. London, 30 November 1995.

20. The details may also be found in the tract "Gittin in the Babylonian Talmud." See also Ecclesiasticus 25:26.

21. William L. Lane, *The Gospel of Mark* in the *New International Commentary Series* (Eerdmans and Marshall Morgan & Scott, 1974), 353.

22. Hurley, *Man and Woman in Biblical Perspective*, 22–28.

23. Gordon Wenham, "The Biblical View of Marriage and Divorce," three articles published in *Third Way* 1, nos. 20–22 (October and November 1977).

24. It is true that in Mark 10:3ff. Jesus is recorded as having used the verb "command," but there he seems to have been referring either to the Mosaic legislation in general or in particular to the issuing of the divorce certificate.

25. C. E. B. Cranfield, *The Gospel According to Mark*, Cambridge Greek Testament Commentary (Cambridge University Press, 1959), 319–20.

26. John Murray, *Divorce* (Committee on Christian Education, Orthodox Presbyterian Church, 1953), 21. It is only fair to add that the moderate position developed in these pages, although based on careful exegesis, has not been acceptable to all. Some understand Jesus as

having been more lenient than I have suggested, and others as more strict. The more lenient view was expressed by Ken Crispin, an Australian lawyer, in *Divorce: The Forgivable Sin?* (1988). Incensed by "callous and irresponsible" church leaders, he interpreted *porneia* so broadly as to include every kind of misconduct which undermines a marriage. The stricter position was presented by William A. Heth and Gordon J. Wenham in *Jesus and Divorce* (1984). They argued from Scripture and Church history that Jesus placed an absolute ban on divorce and remarriage. Andrew Cornes in *Divorce and Remarriage* (1993) takes a similarly strict position. He concedes that Jesus permitted divorce in the case of a serious sexual offense, and that Paul permitted a Christian to acquiesce if his/her non-Christian partner insists on leaving. But, he urges, Jesus did not permit a remarriage to the divorcee. This is "not because he is divorced but because he is still married. It is because God yoked him and his original partner together. It is because in God's eyes they became, in marriage, no longer two but one" (pp. 307–8). Although I am not myself convinced about the total ban on remarriage, Andrew Cornes combines biblical scholarship and pastoral experience, courage and compassion. His book will provoke some furious rethinking; it is indispensable reading for those anxious to develop a Christian mind on these topics.

27. Murray, *Divorce*, 65.

28. RSV and NIV translate "how do you know . . . whether you will save your wife/husband?," understanding the question to express doubt, even resignation. It may well be, however, that the apostle is rather expressing hope. The GNB renders the verse: "how can you be sure . . . that you will not save your wife/husband?" The NEB is even stronger: "think of it: as a wife you may be your husband's salvation . . ." As F. F. Bruce comments, "a mixed marriage had thus missionary potentialities" (New Century Bible, 1971, p. 70). So the Christian partner must do his/her utmost to preserve the marriage.

29. In *The Teaching of the New Testament on Divorce* (William & Norgate, 1921), R. H. Charles argued that, since in 1 Corinthians 7:39 the opposite of "bound" is "free to marry," therefore in verse 9 "the right of remarriage is here conceded to the believing husband or wife who is deserted by an unbelieving partner" (p. 58).

30. David Atkinson, *To Have and to Hold: The Marriage Covenant and the Discipline of Divorce* (Collins, 1979), 28.

31. *Marriage, Divorce and the Church* (SPCK, 1971).

32. *Marriage and the Church's Task* (CIO, 1978).

33. Alan Storkey, *Marriage and Its Modern Crisis* (Hodder & Stoughton, 1996), 197.

34. Atkinson, *To Have and to Hold*, 70.

35. Ibid., 71.

36. Ibid., 75–76.

37. Ibid., 91.

38. Ibid., 151.

39. Ibid., 152.

40. Ibid., 154.

41. I especially recommend a book by Bishop Michael and Mrs. Myrtle Baughen, *Your Marriage* (Hodder & Stoughton, 1994); U.S. edition entitled *Christian Marriage* (Baker Book House).

42. Dominian, *Marital Breakdown*, 61.

43. See Lynn R. Buzzard and Laurence Eck, *Tell It to the Church: Reconciling Out of Court* (David C. Cook, 1982). The Christian Legal Society's address is 4208 Evergreen Ln., Suite 222, Annandale, VA 22003. See also *Reconciliation and Conciliation in the Context of Divorce* (The Order of Christian Unity, 1982) and "Marriage Breakdown and Conciliation," Board for Social Responsibility, Newsletter no. 111 (December 1982).

44. Oliver O'Donovan, "Marriage and Permanence," *Grove Booklet on Ethics*, no. 26 (Grove Books, 1978), 20.

45. Ibid., 21.

Chapter 7: *Abortion and Euthanasia*

1. Desmond Doig, *Mother Teresa: Her People and Her Work* (Collins, 1976), 162.

2. Francis A. Schaeffer and C. Everett Koop, *Whatever Happened to the Human Race?* (Revell, 1979; rev. British ed. by Marshall Morgan & Scott, 1980). See particularly chapter 1, "The Abortion of the Human Race," pp. 2–27, and chapter 4, "The Basis for Human Dignity," pp. 68–99.

3. The Japanese abortion statistics are given by C. Everett Koop in his *The Right to Live, the Right to Die* (Tyndale House and Coverdale House [UK], 1976), 46.

4. *Report of the Committee on the Working of the Abortion Act 1967*, vol. 1 (HMSO Cmnd, 5579, April 1974), 11.

5. The Registrar General's Statistical Review of England and Wales for the years 1968–73; Supplement on "Abortion" (HMSO). The more recent statistics were supplied in 1996 by the Society for the Protection of Unborn Children.

6. A full description and discussion of the *Roe v. Wade* case may be found in Harold O. J. Brown, *Death before Birth* (Thomas Nelson, 1977), 73–96.

7. These figures are taken from (1) *Statistical Abstract of the United States: 1982–83* (U.S. Bureau of the Census, 1982), 68, (2) "Intercessors for America Newsletter," vol. 10, no. 2 (February 1983), and (3) the Family Research Council, Washington, D.C.

8. Quoted from Daniel Callahan's *Abortion: Law, Choice and Morality*, 298, in Lewis B. Smedes, *Mere Morality* (Eerdmans, 1983), 267, footnote 21.

9. See, e.g., Richard Winter, *Choose Life: A Christian Perspective on Abortion and Embryo Experimentation* (Marshall Pickering, 1988), 8.

10. John Powell, SJ, *Abortion: The Silent Holocaust* (Allen, Tex.: Argus Communications, 1981), e.g., pp. 20–39.

11. For ancient perspectives and practices, see Michael J. Gorman, *Abortion and the Early Church: Christian, Jewish and Pagan Attitudes in the Graeco-Roman World* (Inter-Varsity Press, 1982).

12. One of the most thorough treatments of this topic is *Abortion: A Christian Understanding and Response* (Baker, 1987). It is an American symposium, edited by James K. Hoffmeier. Fifteen of its contributors are members of the faculty of Wheaton College. See also Nigel M. de S. Cameron, *Is Life Really Sacred?* (Kingsway, 1990).

13. Quoted from *Abortion Law Reformed* (1971) in R. F. R. Gardner, *Abortion: The Personal Dilemma* (Paternoster Press, 1972), 62.

14. Gardner, *Abortion: The Personal Dilemma*, 126.

15. Quoted by John T. Noonan in *The Morality of Abortion* (Harvard University Press, 1970), 45.

16. Quoted in Koop, *The Right to Live, the Right to Die*, 43–44.

17. Ronald Dworkin, *Life's Dominion* (HarperCollins, 1993), 28.

18. Ibid., 13.

19. Ibid., 39.

20. Ibid., 11, 21.

21. Ibid., 90.

22. John M. Frame discusses this passage fully, including the meaning of the Hebrew words used, in his chapter in Richard L. Ganz, *Thou Shalt Not Kill: The Christian Case against Abortion* (Arlington House, 1978), 50–57.

23. Lennart Nilsson, *A Child Is Born* (Faber, 1965).

24. For Oliver O'Donovan's position, see his "The Christian and the Unborn Child," *Grove Booklet on Ethics*, no. 1 (Grove Books, 1973), and his 1983 London Lectures in Contemporary Christianity, *Begotten or Made? Human Procreation and Medical Technique* (Oxford University Press, 1984). See also Paul Fowler, *Abortion: Toward an Evangelical Consensus* (Multnomah, 1987).

Notes

25. Donald MacKay wrote up his position in an essay entitled "The Beginnings of Personal Life," which was published in the Christian Medical Fellowship's magazine *In the Service of Medicine* 2, no. 30 (1984), 9–13. See also his 1977 *London Lectures in Contemporary Christianity, Human Science and Human Dignity* (Hodder & Stoughton, 1979), especially pp. 64–65 and 98–102. The two positions represented by Professors O'Donovan and MacKay were given further expression in the Church of England Board for Social Responsibility report *Personal Origins* (CIO, 1985). The minority emphasized the continuity of the individual from the moment of fusion, while the majority stressed consciousness as necessary for personhood, and a certain brain structure as necessary for consciousness. Then in 1987 Professor Gareth Jones contributed a full discussion of "personhood" in relation to the fetus in his *Manufacturing Humans: The Challenge of the New Reproductive Technologies* (Inter-Varsity Press), chapter 5, pp. 125–67.

26. Tertullian's *Apology*, chapter ix. Michael J. Gorman gives a popular but thorough account of the unanimous pro-life, antiabortion stance of the first five centuries of Christianity in his *Abortion and the Early Church*. His references to Tertullian are on pp. 54–58.

27. Paul Ramsey, *Fabricated Man: The Ethics of Genetic Control* (Yale University Press, 1970), 11.

28. Smedes, *Mere Morality*, 129.

29. Quoted in the Church of Scotland's Board of Social Responsibility 1985 report to the General Assembly. See Professor Torrance's booklet "Test-Tube Babies" (Scottish Academic Press, 1984).

30. *Report of the Committee of Enquiry into Human Fertilization and Embryology*, chaired by Dame Mary Warnock (HMSO, 1984), 1.1.

31. A recent alternative to IVF is GIFT (Gamete Intra Fallopian Transfer). In this case ovum and sperm, after being mixed, are immediately transferred to the end of the fallopian tube, where conception takes place as normal. Many consider GIFT preferable to IVF. Technically, it is simpler and cheaper. Ethically, it precludes the production of "spare" embryos for research.

32. *Report . . . into Human Fertilization and Embryology*, para. 11.9.

33. O'Donovan, *Begotten or Made?* 1–2, 65.

34. Richard Higginson, *Whose Baby? The Ethics of In Vitro Fertilization* (Marshall Morgan & Scott, 1985), x.

35. *Instruction on Respect for Human Life in Its Origin and on the Dignity of Procreation*, written by the Congregation for the Doctrine of the Faith (Catholic Truth Society, 1987), 26.

36. Paul Ramsey, the distinguished American ethicist, also wrote about God's intention that sexual intercourse be simultaneously an act of love and procreation. See his *Fabricated Man*. Richard Higginson helpfully compares and contrasts Roman Catholic and Protestant positions in his *Whose Baby?* 19–40.

37. *Report . . . into Human Fertilization and Embryology*, para. 11.17.

38. Ibid., 90–91.

39. *Instruction on Respect for Human Life*, 17.

40. Ibid., 16.

41. From Professor G. R. Dunstan's contribution to the article on "Abortion" in Duncan, Dunstan and Welbourn, eds., *Dictionary of Medical Ethics*.

42. The expression used by Mr. Justice McNaughten in the *Rex v. Bourne* case of 1938.

43. Glanville Williams, *The Sanctity of Life and the Criminal Law* (Faber, 1958), 212.

44. Ibid., 31.

45. Quoted from Rostan's book *Humanly Possible*, at the beginning of Koop, *The Right to Live, the Right to Die*.

46. Quoted by Norman St. John Stevas in *The Right to Life* (Hodder & Stoughton, 1963), 20.

47. Gardner, *Abortion: The Personal Dilemma*, 225–26.

48. The addresses of these organizations are as follows: "Birthright," 777 Coxwell Avenue, Toronto, Ontario, Canada M4C 3C6. Alternatives to Abortion International, 2606 1/2 West

8th Street, Los Angeles, CA 90057. LIFE, 7 The Parade, Leamington Spa, Warwickshire, England. SPUC, 7 Tufton Street, London, England SW1. CARE Trust, 53 Romney Street, London, England SW1P 3RF. CARENET, 109 Carpenter Dr., Suite 100, Sterling, VA 20164.

49. Quoted in Gardner, *Abortion: The Personal Dilemma*, 276. See also Louise Summerhill, *The Story of Birthright: The Alternative to Abortion* (Kenosha: Prow Books, 1973).

50. *Abortion: An Ethical Dilemma*, a report of the Board for Social Responsibility (CIO, 1965), 57.

51. Gardner, *Abortion: The Personal Dilemma*, 248–62.

52. Peter Singer, *Rethinking Life and Death: The Collapse of Our Traditional Ethics* (1994; Oxford University Press, 1995), 176, 180–83.

53. Ibid., 220.

54. Ibid., 217.

55. Ibid., 214.

56. Ibid., 213.

57. Ibid., 237.

58. See Nigel Cameron, *The New Medicine: Life and Death after Hippocrates* (Crossway, 1991).

59. See, e.g., her contribution "Euthanasia: The Hospice Alternative," in Nigel M. de S. Cameron, ed., *Death without Dignity* (Rutherford House Books, 1990).

60. Dworkin, *Life's Dominion*, 239.

61. From the encyclical *Evangelium Vitae*, March 1995.

Chapter 8: *Same-Sex Partnerships?*

1. See A. C. Kinsey's *Sexual Behavior in the Human Male* (1948) and *Sexual Behavior in the Human Female* (1953).

2. From an article entitled "God, Sex and You," in *Eternity* magazine (August 1972).

3. J. N. D. Anderson, *Morality, Law and Grace* (Tyndale Press, 1972), 73.

4. Malcolm Macourt, ed., *Towards a Theology of Gay Liberation* (SCM Press, 1977), 3. The quotation comes from Mr. Macourt's own introduction to the book.

5. See Bishop John S. Spong, *Living in Sin? A Bishop Rethinks Human Sexuality* (Harper & Row, 1988).

6. Derrick Sherwin Bailey, *Homosexuality and the Western Christian Tradition* (Longmans, Green, 1955), 4.

7. Sherwin Bailey gives references in the Book of Jubilees and the Testaments of the Twelve Patriarchs, ibid., 11–20. There is an even fuller evaluation of the writings of the intertestamental period in Peter Coleman's *Christian Attitudes to Homosexuality* (SPCK, 1980), 58–85.

8. Bailey, *Homosexuality and the Western Christian Tradition*, 27.

9. See James D. Martin in Macourt, ed., *Towards a Theology of Gay Liberation* (SCM, 1977), 53.

10. Bailey, *Homosexuality and the Western Christian Tradition*, 30.

11. Coleman, *Christian Attitudes to Homosexuality*, 49.

12. Bailey, *Homosexuality and the Western Christian Tradition*, 39.

13. Coleman, *Christian Attitudes to Homosexuality*, 95–96.

14. Ibid., 277.

15. Ibid., 101.

16. Rictor Norton, in Macourt, ed., *Towards a Theology of Gay Liberation*, 58.

17. Letha Scanzoni and Virginia R. Mollenkott, *Is the Homosexual My Neighbour?* (Harper & Row and SCM, 1978), 111.

18. Bailey, *Homosexuality and the Western Christian Tradition*, 1.

19. Michael Vasey, *Strangers and Friends* (Hodder & Stoughton, 1995), 46, 82–83.

20. See John Boswell, *Christianity, Social Tolerance and Homosexuality* (University of Chicago Press, 1980), and *Same-Sex Unions in Pre-Modern Europe* (Villard Books, 1994).

Notes

21. Richard John Neuhaus, "The Case against John Boswell," excerpted in Julie Belding and Bruce Nicholls, eds., *A Reason for Hope: Christian Perspectives on Homosexuality and Healing* (Auckland, New Zealand: The Human Relationships Foundation, 1996), 14.

22. Everett Ferguson, ed., *The Encyclopedia of Early Christianity* (Garland, 1990).

23. Vasey, *Strangers and Friends*, 116.

24. Ibid., 176–77.

25. Ibid., 117 (Vasey is referring to Matthew 19:11–12).

26. Ibid., 33.

27. Ibid., 34.

28. Norman Pittenger, *Time for Consent*, 3d ed. (SCM, 1976), 7, 73.

29. Thomas E. Schmidt, *Straight and Narrow? Compassion and Clarity in the Homosexuality Debate* (Inter-Varsity Press, 1995), 134–35.

30. Pittenger, *Time for Consent*, 7.

31. Coleman, *Christian Attitudes to Homosexuality*, 50.

32. Chapter 3.3–5, quoted in Coleman, *Christian Attitudes to Homosexuality*, 71.

33. Boswell, *Christianity, Social Tolerance and Homosexuality*, 107ff.

34. Richard B. Hays, "A Response to John Boswell's Exegesis of Romans 1," *Journal of Religious Ethics* (spring 1986), 192. See also his *The Moral Vision of the New Testament* (T & T Clark, 1996), 383–89.

35. C. K. Barrett, *Commentary on the Epistle to the Romans* (A & C Black, 1962), 39.

36. C. E. B. Cranfield, *Commentary on Romans* in the *International Critical Commentary*, vol. 1 (T & T Clark, 1975), 126. He attributes the same meaning to *physis* in his comment on 1 Corinthians 11:14. What NIV translates "the very nature of things" Professor Cranfield renders "the very way God has made us."

37. *Christianity Today* (11 November 1996).

38. *The Friends' Report Towards a Quaker View of Sex* (1963), 21.

39. Ibid., 36.

40. Methodist Church's Division of Social Responsibility, *A Christian Understanding of Human Sexuality* (1979), chapter 9.

41. *Homosexual Relationships: A Contribution to Discussion* (1979), chapter 5.

42. Pittenger, *Time for Consent*, 31–33.

43. Jeffrey Satinover, *Homosexuality and the Politics of Truth* (Baker, 1996), 55. He is quoting from D. McWhirter and A. Mattison, *The Male Couple: How Relationships Develop* (Prentice-Hall, 1984).

44. Schmidt, *Straight and Narrow?* 108.

45. Satinover, *Homosexuality and the Politics of Truth*, 51. See the whole of his chapter 3.

46. Schmidt, *Straight and Narrow?* 122. See the whole of his chapter 6.

47. "The Homosexual Movement: A Response by the Ramsey Colloquium," first published in *First Things* (March 1994).

48. Macourt, ed., *Towards a Theology of Gay Liberation*, 25.

49. Pittenger, *Time for Consent*, 2.

50. Ibid., 94.

51. Patrick Dixon, *The Truth about AIDS* (Kingsway, 1987), 78.

52. Quoted in Satinover, *Homosexuality and the Politics of Truth*, 17. See also p. 57.

53. Statistics on AIDS taken from the UNAIDS Web site at <www.unaids.org>. This is a good source for up-to-date information on AIDS around the world.

54. Dixon, *The Truth about AIDS*, 113. See also p. 88 and the whole chapter entitled "Condoms are Unsafe," 110–22.

55. *The Many Faces of AIDS: A Gospel Response* (United States Catholic Conference, 1987), 18.

56. Roy McCloughry and Carol Bebawi, *AIDS: A Christian Response* (Grove Ethical Studies, no. 64, 1987), 4, 18. See the theological discussion "Is AIDS the Judgment of God?" 12–19.

57. *The Many Faces of AIDS*, 6.

58. Quoted in *Christianity Today* (7 August 1987), 17.

59. The Terrence Higgins Trust, BM/AIDS, London WC1N 3XX.

60. For example, The London Lighthouse (a 26-bed AIDS hospice), 178 Lancaster Road, London W11 1QU, and the internationally known 32-suite AIDS ward at the Mildmay Mission Hospital, Hackney Road, London E2 7NA. Both hospices also arrange home care. ACACIA (AIDS Care, Compassion in Action) cares for about 75 people with HIV/AIDS in their own homes in Manchester.

61. These lectures were never published.

62. So Gavin Reid rightly argues in his *Beyond AIDS: The Real Crisis and the Only Hope* (Kingsway, 1987).

63. For example, Christian Action on AIDS was established in 1986 (PO Box 76, Hereford, HR1 1JX). Also ACET (AIDS Care Education and Training), with an aim of developing a nationwide network of hospices, home care volunteers and church support groups. Its address is PO Box 3693, London SW15 2BQ.

64. *AIDS*, a report by the Church of England Board for Social Responsibility (GS 795, 1987), 29.

65. Alex Davidson, *The Returns of Love* (Inter-Varsity Press, 1970), 12, 16, 49.

66. Norman Pittenger, in Macourt, ed., *Towards a Theology of Gay Liberation*, 87.

67. The Saint Andrew's Day Statement (published 30 November 1995) begins with three theological "Principles" relating to the Incarnate Lord (in whom we come to know both God and ourselves), the Holy Spirit (who enables us to interpret the times) and God the Father (who restores the broken creation in Christ). The Statement's second half consists of three "Applications" relating to such questions as our human identity, empirical observations, the reaffirmation of the good news of salvation, and the hope of final fulfillment in Christ. Two years later *The Way Forward?* was published, with the subtitle *Christian Voices on Homosexuality and the Church*. This symposium, edited by Tim Bradshaw, consists of thirteen responses to the Saint Andrew's Day Statement, from a wide range of different viewpoints. One appreciates the call to patient and serious theological reflection. But it is inaccurate to write of "dialogue" and "diatribe" as if they were the only options. Some of us have been listening and reflecting for thirty or forty years! How long must the process continue before we are allowed to reach a conclusion? In spite of claims to the contrary, no fresh evidence has been produced which could overthrow the clear witness of Scripture and the longstanding tradition of the Church. The Saint Andrew's Day Statement says that the Church recognizes two vocations (marriage and singleness), and adds that "there is no place for the Church to confer legitimacy upon alternatives to these." Further, the authors of the Statement do not consider that "the considerable burden of proof to support a major change in the Church's teaching and practice has been met" by the contributors to the book (p. 3). Yet the book makes a more uncertain sound than the Statement. So by all means let there be serious theological reflection, but then let the Church make up its mind.

68. Pittenger, *Time for Consent*, 7. Contrast *The Courage to Be Chaste: An Uncompromising Call to the Biblical Standard of Chastity* (Paulist Press, 1986). Written by Benedict J. Groeschel, a Capuchin friar, the book contains much practical advice.

69. Satinover, *Homosexuality and the Politics of Truth*, 117.

70. Ibid., 18, 19, 71.

71. Vasey, *Strangers and Friends*, 103.

72. See Satinover, *Homosexuality and the Politics of Truth*, 31–40.

73. D. J. West, *Homosexuality* (1955; 2nd ed. Pelican, 1960; 3rd ed. Duckworth, 1968), 266, 273.

74. Nelson Gonzalez's article "Exploding Ex-Gay Myths," in *Regeneration Quarterly* 1, no. 3 (summer 1995), challenged the aims and claims of the ex-gay movement. In 1991 Charles Socarides founded the National Association for Research and Therapy of Homosexuality (NARTH), which investigates the possibilities for "healing."

75. Martin Hallett, *I Am Learning to Love: A Personal Journey to Wholeness in Christ* (Marshall Morgan & Scott, 1987), 155. Martin Hallett's organization is called True Freedom Trust (PO Box 3, Upton Wirral, Merseyside, L49 6NY). It offers an interdenominational teaching and counseling ministry on homosexuality and related problems.

76. Exodus International, PO Box 2121, San Rafael, CA 94912.

77. Elizabeth R. Moberly, *Homosexuality: A New Christian Ethic* (James Clarke, 1983), 2. See also Lance Pierson, *No-Gay Areas: Pastoral Care of Homosexual Christians* (Grove Pastoral Studies, no. 38, 1989), which helpfully applies Elizabeth Moberly's teaching.

78. Moberly, *Homosexuality: A New Christian Ethic*, 28.

79. Ibid., 18–20.

80. Ibid., 35–36.

81. Ibid., 52.

82. Davidson, *The Returns of Love*, 51.

83. Macourt, ed., *Towards a Theology of Gay Liberation*, 63.

84. Pittenger, *Time for Consent*, 2.

85. Quoted from Letha Scanzoni and Virginia Mollenkott, *The Comfortable Pew* (1965).

86. Macourt, ed., *Towards a Theology of Gay Liberation*, 45.

87. The word seems to have been used first by George Weinberg in *Society and the Healthy Homosexual* (Doubleday, 1973).

88. Richard R. Lovelace, *Homosexuality and the Church* (Revell, 1978), 129, and cf. p. 125.

89. David J. Atkinson, *Homosexuals in the Christian Fellowship* (Latimer House, 1979), 118. See also Dr. Atkinson's more extensive treatment in his *Pastoral Ethics in Practice* (Monarch, 1989). Dr. Roger Moss concentrates on pastoral questions in his *Christians and Homosexuality* (Paternoster, 1977).

90. Vasey, *Strangers and Friends*, 122.

91. Ibid., 233.

Chapter 9: *A Call for Christian Leadership*

1. Bennie E. Goodwin II, *The Effective Leader: A Basic Guide to Christian Leadership* (Inter-Varsity Press, 1971), 8.

2. William Shakespeare, *Twelfth Night*, II, iv, 158.

3. J. Oswald Sanders, *Spiritual Leadership* (Marshall Morgan & Scott, 1967; Lakeland, 1981), 20.

4. Proverbs 29:18. The NIV rendering is, "Where there is no revelation, the people cast off restraint."

5. Ronald A. Knox, *Enthusiasm: A Chapter in the History of Religion* (Oxford University Press, 1950), 591.

6. From the *Washington Post*, republished in *The Guardian Weekly*, June 1978.

7. Robert K. Greenleaf, *Servant Leadership: A Journey into the Nature of Legitimate Power and Greatness* (Paulist Press, 1977), 236.

8. Douglas Hyde, *Dedication and Leadership: Learning from the Communists* (University of Notre Dame Press, 1966), 15–16.

9. Ibid., 121.

10. Ibid., 30–31.

11. Ibid., 52.

12. Ibid., 59.

13. Greenleaf, *Servant Leadership*, 16.

14. See The Manila Manifesto, 1989, para. 11, in Stott, ed., *Making Christ Known*, 245–46.

15. Bleakley, *Work: The Shadow and the Substance*, 85.

16. Quoted by William Barclay in his *Spiritual Autobiography, or Testament of Faith* (Mowbray and Eerdmans, 1975), 112.

17. From a review by Canon R. W. Howard of James Leasor, *Wheels to Fortune: The Life and Times of Lord Nuffield* (1955).

18. Basil Matthews, *John R. Mott: World Citizen* (SCM, 1934), 357.

19. Reginald Coupland, *Wilberforce* (Collins, 1923; 2nd ed. 1945), 77.

20. John C. Pollock, *Wilberforce* (Lion, 1977), 27. (Sir Reginald Coupland recounts the same incident in different words, ibid., 9.)

21. Ibid., 56.

22. Ibid., 304.

23. Ibid., 308.

24. Greenleaf, *Servant Leadership*, 7–10.

25. T. W. Manson, *The Church's Ministry* (Hodder & Stoughton, 1948), 27.

26. Sanders, *Spiritual Leadership*, 13.

27. M. A. C. Warren, *Crowded Canvas* (Hodder & Stoughton, 1974), 44.

28. Peter F. Drucker, *The Effective Executive* (Harper & Row, 1966), 72.

29. See The Lausanne Covenant, para. 15, in Stott, ed., *Making Christ Known*, 49–53.

Dr. John R. W. Stott has an international ministry as an evangelist, preacher, scholar, and author of many books. For many years he served All Souls Church in London. He is president of the Institute for Contemporary Christianity.